Terrorist Criminal Enterprises

Terrorist Criminal Enterprises

Financing Terrorism through Organized Crime

KIMBERLEY L. THACHUK AND
ROLLIE LAL, EDITORS

Foreword by
Christopher A. Kojm

Praeger Security International

BLOOMSBURY ACADEMIC
NEW YORK · LONDON · OXFORD · NEW DELHI · SYDNEY

BLOOMSBURY ACADEMIC
Bloomsbury Publishing Inc
1385 Broadway, New York, NY 10018, USA
50 Bedford Square, London, WC1B 3DP, UK
29 Earlsfort Terrace, Dublin 2, Ireland

BLOOMSBURY, BLOOMSBURY ACADEMIC and the Diana logo
are trademarks of Bloomsbury Publishing Plc

First published in the United States of America by ABC-CLIO 2018
Paperback edition published by Bloomsbury Academic 2024

Copyright © Bloomsbury Publishing Inc, 2024

For legal purposes the Acknowledgments on p. xi constitute
an extension of this copyright page.

Cover design by Silverander Communications
Cover photos: Flowers set in a window shattered by a bullet at the Carillon cafe in Paris, France,
November 15, 2015. (AP Photo/Jerome Delay); Pakistani female police commandos
attend a training session in Nowshera, near Peshawar, Pakistan, February 11, 2015.
(AP Photo/Mohammad Sajjad)

Library of Congress Cataloging-in-Publication Data
Names: Thachuk, Kimberley L., 1962– editor. | Lal, Rollie, editor.
Title: Terrorist criminal enterprises: financing terrorism through organized
crime / Kimberley L. Thachuk and Rollie Lal, editors; foreword by Christopher A. Kojm.
Description: Santa Barbara, California: Praeger, [2018] |
Series: Praeger Security International | Includes bibliographical references and index.
Identifiers: LCCN 2018005888 (print) | LCCN 2018006684 (ebook) |
ISBN 9781440860683 (eBook) | ISBN 9781440860676 (alk. paper)
Subjects: LCSH: Terrorism—Finance. | Organized crime.
Classification: LCC HV6431 (ebook) |
LCC HV6431.T5267 2018 (print) | DDC 363.325—dc23
LC record available at https://lccn.loc.gov/2018005888

ISBN: HB: 978-1-4408-6067-6
PB: 979-8-7651-1901-3
ePDF: 978-1-4408-6068-3
eBook: 979-8-2161-5461-7

Series: Praeger Security International

To find out more about our authors and books visit www.bloomsbury.com
and sign up for our newsletters.

Contents

Foreword

Since 9/11, there has been a vast outpouring of research and scholarship on terrorist organizations. Al-Qaida, Da'esh, and many, many terrorist groups have received detailed scrutiny. The U.S. government, among others, has been generous in funding work on terrorist groups' origins, internal organization, and plans and operations.

The academic and policy world also produce significant work on transnational criminal organizations. Originally, much of the focus was on drug cartels and narcotics trafficking. The scope of work has expanded over time. There is superb work today on criminal organizations engaged in human trafficking, weapons trafficking, credit card fraud and cybercrime, and many other forms of illegal revenue generation.

Where the academic and policy communities need to devote more attention and effort is on the link between terrorist and criminal activity. The world of terrorism analysis has long focused—understandably—on preventing terrorist acts. Criminal activity by these same organizations traditionally has been viewed as incidental and, at most, instrumental on behalf of terrorist goals.

The world of criminal enterprise analysis, on the other hand, has traditionally taken the view that crime organizations want to run operations and maximize profit. They want to stay away from activities that bring unwanted attention from governments and law enforcement. In other words, criminal enterprises want to bribe government officials, not overthrow governments.

This edited collection, *Terrorist Criminal Enterprises*, makes a welcome and significant contribution because it addresses both worlds. It demonstrates, across many terrorist organizations, that there is a complete fusion of terrorist and criminal activity. There is not a "nexus" between the two worlds; they are one and the same. Editors Kimberley L. Thachuk and Rollie Lal provide compelling examples of how criminal activity is inseparable from every aspect of terrorist organizations and their behavior.

For policy makers, there are many implications of the fusion of these two worlds.

First, our current organizational structures and mental frameworks are inadequate to understanding the problem before us. We cannot understand the phenomenon of terrorist criminal enterprises when analysis takes place in separate Counterterrorism Centers and Crime and Narcotics Centers. We hinder our ability both to conceptualize policy and implement it when there is a Bureau of Counterterrorism on one hand and a Bureau of International Narcotics and Law Enforcement on the other. The Justice Department, too, has its National Security and Criminal Divisions. We need to address the stovepiping of organizations and the mental rigidities that follow from the structures within which people live and work.

The Intelligence Community, the Federal Bureau of Investigation (FBI), Congress, and the entire Executive Branch worked hard to break down the "walls" between intelligence and law enforcement after 9/11. A similar effort is needed today to share information and understanding across the bounded horizons of those in government who work on the problems of terrorism and criminal enterprises.

Second, and related to the first, we can develop new tools to address the problem of terrorism when we see it through the lens of terrorist criminal enterprises. We can move beyond military and intelligence tactics and embrace a wide array of legal actions to take down terrorist groups. Al Capone wasn't arrested for gangland killings; he went to jail because he cheated on his taxes. In the same manner, criminal charges for extortion, drug trafficking, money laundering, and other crimes can decimate the leadership of terrorist organizations.

As Prof. Lal points out in her excellent concluding chapter, "Radicalization in itself is not a basis for legal action in most countries." It is far better to stop suspect individuals based on their documented criminal activity, rather than wait until they have committed a terrorist act. Moreover, governments around the world have well-established legal procedures and norms to address crime; political or religious views are of no interest to the courts, only the pattern of documented criminal activity.

Third, a focus on terrorist criminal enterprises provides policy makers a powerful ideological and public diplomacy tool to counter terrorist messaging. An ideological or political agenda that appeals to some may soon appeal to none, when an organization's pervasive criminal activities and corruption are brought to light.

As Kimberley L. Thachuk and Rollie Lal note, terrorist organizations change over time. When new members see lavish lifestyles based on criminal profits as the daily reality of the organization, past commitments to political or religious goals become simply a convenient ideological façade. Exposure of this sordid reality and hypocrisy can be an important means of turning public opinion against terrorist groups, thereby undermining their ability to function.

Fourth, this volume underscores the central importance of preventing terrorist groups from controlling territory. Chapter after chapter—on Da'esh in Syria and Iraq, on Boko Haram and al-Shabaab in Africa, the FARC in Colombia, the Haqqani Network in Afghanistan—show that such organizations reap tremendous profits from their exploitation of resources, trade, and the people in the territory they control. Whether it is extorting truckers at roadblocks, protection rackets, smuggling drugs, or control of the oil trade (as in the case of Da'esh), the control of territory gives terrorist organizations vast opportunities to shake down the population and acquire wealth to attract recruits, outfit fighters, and conduct terror operations.

The policy solution to the control of territory by terrorist criminal can require kinetic means, as the recent campaign against Da'esh illustrates. But those means alone are not sufficient. Removing the threat of terrorist groups seizing territory, over the long run, will take long and frustratingly slow efforts to improve governance, build infrastructure, and strengthen institutions that can contribute to stable societies.

Some 30 years ago, I remember conversations with the then Coordinator for Counterterrorism at the Department of State, Ambassador Robert Oakley, who made an impassioned appeal to members of Congress for additional tools beyond those of law enforcement to counter the growing terrorist threat. He was right. We did need new tools, and after 9/11 the U.S. government exercised them fully.

Today, we use a wide array of intelligence and military tools to counter terror organizations. But to protect our citizens, we should not forget the tools of law enforcement and the government's powerful ability to investigate crimes and criminal organizations. If we are successful in taking down terrorist criminal enterprises, we will go a long way to keeping our country safe and secure.

Christopher A. Kojm

Acknowledgments

First and foremost, we wish to thank the authors of the chapters and Christopher A. Kojm who penned the foreword. You all worked tirelessly to ensure the concept of terrorist criminal enterprises was brought to fruition. It truly has been wonderful working with each of you. We appreciate your dedication to research, your patience with our multiple directions (sorry), and your overall incredible scholarly expertise, integrity, and spirit of cooperation. Without you, this would not be the terrific book it is.

Our wonderful graduate students at the Elliott School of International Affairs, the George Washington University, and at Advanced Academic Programs, Johns Hopkins University, are also most deserving of thanks. You are ever a source of amazing and innovative thinking. Your suggestions and comments on the concept of terrorist criminal enterprises were not only thought provoking but also a great source of inspiration.

We also want to thank Steve Catalano who saw the potential for this book and helped to make it a reality with Praeger Publishers. Also at Praeger, we wish to thank Pat Carlin and Jennifer Hartmann who enabled its professional and timely publication.

Rollie would like to thank Jean-Cédric Janssens de Bisthoven, Minister Counselor at the Belgian Embassy, the Belgian Financial Intelligence Processing Unit (CTIF-CFI), and the Italian Department of Treasury for their support.

Finally, it goes without saying that we thank our families for their love and support. Rollie thanks her husband, Steven, and her daughter, Isis Valentina. You have been great listeners and support. You have also provided much-needed amusement that helped me continue each day anew with enthusiasm. Also to Chetna, Smita, Matt, Ani, Armaan, Mom, and Dad for your encouragement.

Kim thanks her husband, Joe, and her son, John Bee. Your patience and support kept me working day and night on this great book. You were both a fount of incredible enthusiasm, love, and encouragement. Also thank you, Mother, for your encouragement and Big Dad and Mr. S—you inspired me from afar. Happy Trails.

Terminology and Abbreviations

In the writing of this book, we noted that there are many versions of the spelling for well-known terrorist groups. To reduce the chaos, we decided to use the United Nations spelling of Da'esh in place of Daesh, Islamic State, ISIS, ISIL, and IS, and we used the United Nations spelling of Al-Qaida for al Qaida, Al Qaeda, and al-Qaeda throughout the book. All others are as noted next.

AMIA	Argentine Israelite Mutual Association
AQ/Al-Qaida	Al Qaeda, Al Qaida
AQAM	Al Qaeda and Associated Movements
AQAP	Al-Qaida in the Arabian Peninsula
AQI	Al-Qaida in Iraq
AQIM	Al-Qaida in the Islamic Maghreb (formerly GSPC)
ASG	Abu Sayyaf Group (Philippines)
AUC	United Self-Defense Groups of Colombia
BAC	Hezbollah's External Security Organization Business Affairs Component
BACRIM	Bandas Criminals (Colombia)
Bayat/Bay'at	oath of allegiance to a Muslim leader
BIF	Benevolence International Foundation
CE	Caucasus Emirate
ChRI	Chechen Republic of Ichkeria

CTIF-CFI	Belgian Financial Intelligence Processing Unit
Da'esh	Islamic State of Iraq and Syria, Islamic State, IS, ISIL, ISIS, Daesh
EMCDDA	European Monitoring Centre for Drugs and Drug Addiction
FARC	Revolutionary Armed Forces of Colombia
FATA	Federally Administered Tribal Area
FATF	Financial Action Task Force
FIS	Islamic Salvation Front
FLN	National Liberation Front
Foco	insurrectionalist armed enclave (Colombia)
GAML	Grupos a las Margines de la Ley
GIA	Armed Islamic Group (Algeria)
GSPC	Salafist Group for Preaching and Combat
HIFPA	Hezbollah International Financing Prevention Act
HQN	Haqqani Network
HT	Hizb ut-Tahrir
ICU	Islamic Courts Union
IIRO	Islamic International Relief Organization (Saudi Arabia)
IMU	Islamic Movement of Uzbekistan
INCSR	International Narcotics Control Strategy Report
IRGC	Islamic Revolutionary Guard Corps (Iran)
ISI	Directorate of Inter-Services Intelligence (Pakistan)
Jamaat	operational unit
KADEK	Kurdistan Freedom and Democracy Congress
KCK	Kurdistan Communities Union
KDF	Kenyan Defense Troops
KFR	Kidnapping for Ransom
KGK	Kongra-Gel (Turkey)
LBC	Lebanese Canadian Bank
LIFG	Libyan Islamic Fighting Group
Loya Paktia	collective name for the Afghan provinces of Khost, Paktia, and Paktika
MNLA	National Movement for the Liberation of Azawad (Mali)
MNLF	Moro National Liberation Front (Philippines)
MUJAO	Also MUJWA; Movement for Unity and Jihad in West Africa
OCG	Organized Crime Group
PIJ	Palestinian Jihad
PKK	Kurdish Worker's Party (Partiya Karkerên Kurdistanê)
PYD	Syrian Kurdish Democratic Union Party

SFKO	North Caucasus Federal District
Shabu	crystal methamphetamine (Southeast Asia)
TAK	Kurdistan Freedom Hawks (offshoot of the PKK)
TBA	Tri-Border Area (Argentina, Brazil, and Paraguay)
TCO	Transnational Criminal Organizations
TFG	Transitional Federal Government (Somalia)
TL	Turkish Lira
Ulama/Ulema	body of Muslim scholars with specialist knowledge of Islamic law
UNODC	United Nations Office on Drugs and Crime
Vilayat	territory/province
Wahhabism	an austere form of Islam based on a literal interpretation of the Koran
Zakat	religious voluntary contribution; a form of tax

CHAPTER 1

An Introduction to Terrorist Criminal Enterprises

Kimberley L. Thachuk and Rollie Lal

Terrorism has steadily gangsterized over the past several decades. This is a success story, after a fashion, demonstrating the adaptability of terrorist groups in the 21st century. Financing terrorist operations today, including the payment of clandestine operatives and the purchase of weapons and explosives, requires the types of transactions that only illicit operations can satisfy. As such, the evolution to terrorist criminal enterprises has not only enabled many terrorist groups to survive and expand, but it also has afforded them added resiliency and mobility.

What may be even more disturbing is the fact that any policy debate on this transformation has been largely absent, and governments have thus failed to create new strategies to confront these terrorist criminal enterprises. Dealing with the transformed terrorist threat in today's dynamic operating environment requires an understanding of why extremist groups turned to organized crime, how they embarked upon their burgeoning criminal businesses, and what policy makers can do to combat the new threat.

Many of these terrorist criminal enterprises transformed incrementally over several generations, sometimes in unwitting strategies of survival. Meanwhile, others adopted organized crime into their operations with remarkable ease.[1] Yet, these signs of entrepreneurship were often obscured by expressions of ideological fervor and outrageous terrorist attacks. And embracing illicit commerce also held consequences for the extremists. Often the vast sums of money gained in the criminal underworld corrupted their ideological purpose, nearly consuming some while irrevocably transforming others.

Another challenge in facing this transformation is competitive government bureaucracies. Most jealously guard their monopolies on thwarting terrorism and tend to endorse particularistic and outmoded definitions for defining it. Yet, rather than continuing to treat terrorists solely as zealots, such groups should be understood for their engagement in complex illicit commerce. Their uneven evolutionary trajectory and ideologically motivated violence should not obscure the fact that they act as terrorist criminal enterprises. Indeed, their criminal operations are now as diverse as the multiplicity of groups and include, among others, drug trafficking, human smuggling and trafficking, extortion, robbery, kidnapping for ransom, theft and sale of antiquities, illegal mining, and smuggling of commodities. The adaptation to a more profit-seeking mind-set has ultimately made combating terrorist criminal enterprises more complex, but it also may provide new opportunities for policy makers.

This book explores a number of terrorist groups that have transformed into terrorist criminal enterprises or which are in the process of doing so. Each case study was authored by a notable expert or experts, providing an incisive assessment of the nature of these groups and their ideology, operations, and, above all, criminal interests. One aim of the book is to discern each group's distinctive criminal modus operandi. It also seeks to document the nature and extent of their profitable illicit activities. Each chapter then explores how groups are connected to government entities, possibly via official corruption and collusion. Finally, the book offers policy options to address the threat posed by these groups that increasingly combine their malevolent terrorist ideals with criminal greed.

TERRORISTS NEED MONEY TOO

Most terrorist groups were initially propelled into the shadow economy by the counterterrorism measures undertaken by the states in which they were based, by the international community as it sought to interdict state-sponsored terrorist financing (particularly after September 11), or a combination of both. Whether by accident or design, one of the easier methods to augment the shortfall presented itself in the form of illicit commerce where terrorists could employ the same criminal tactics generally considered the domain of organized crime groups. Indeed, although each of these groups can certainly be termed terrorist in that their ideological goals remain to politically control people through acts of outrageous violence, their illicit transactions are the purview of organized crime. What may distinguish them from traditional organized crime is their motivation for raising the illicit funds and the manner in which the money is spent.

Yet, the influx of criminal cash and the appeal of immoderate criminal lifestyles corrupted some of the principles of terrorist organizations. The moral distortion led orthodox insurgents to mutate into transnational criminal enterprises whose motivations are not always evident or ideologically pure. What may continue to conceal this criminal trajectory is the fact that most groups have not lost their commitment to fanaticism. Despite their newfound wealth, they continue to make zealous pronouncements reinforced by violence. The criminal money now assists them in perpetrating audacious attacks and allows them to extend their aspirations internationally.

ENDING THE STOVEPIPES

Articulating the combined ideological goals *and* criminal activities of terrorist criminal enterprises will be necessary for governments to proceed with effective counterterrorism strategies. At present, policy continues to be made reactively, guided by largely outmoded and stovepiped conceptualizations that treat terrorism and organized crime as distinct entities. Moreover, with a few notable exceptions, academic and policy literature often provides imprecise definitions, concentrating on the "nexus" between these nonstate actors rather than identifying the fact that most terrorist groups' transformation to terrorist criminal enterprises is a fait accompli.[2] Although at one time there was significant evidence of a "nexus" with organized crime, or a terrorist-criminal continuum, such symbioses may have been largely transcended altogether.[3] Hence, breaking the false dichotomy that defines these groups as separate phenomena will provide a fresh perspective and have widespread policy implications for the manner in which states deter and dismantle terrorist groups.

THE EVOLUTION TO TERRORIST CRIMINAL ENTERPRISES

A number of groups lurched gradually into organized crime, while others launched into it rapidly, apparently viewing the benefits of illicit commerce as an opportunity to advance their ideologies, acquire new weapons, and grow their organizations. Despite overarching ideological motivations, the vast sums of illicit funds and the descent into criminal activity appealed to the avarice of both lower echelon operatives and their leaders. Nor once established was there any indication they would relinquish their newly acquired skills and high profits. Thus, over time, various terrorist groups became increasingly proficient at organized crime, in part by recruiting people with criminal capabilities to their number. Globalization also assisted in this endeavor. Many of the rapid developments in commerce, finances, telecommunications, and technology enabled them to exploit the sinister underbelly of increased global trade and engage more widely in smuggling, credit card fraud, trade-based money laundering, and even cybercrimes.[4] These opportunities were facilitated by porous borders, weak states, and an increasingly accessible global transportation system.

Much of the transition was not a huge leap. For numerous groups, mounting terrorist conspiracies in a post–September 11 world meant operating clandestinely with significant efficiency; they were experienced in the stealthy operational methods organized crime had perfected. Early on, extremist organizations like Al-Qaida began seeking reliable alternative sources of income to fund both short- and long-term operations. As a result, many extremists first began to delve into criminal enterprise through "nexus" or convergence relationships with more traditional organized crime groups.[5] Initially this involved guarding drug labs, providing security for airstrips, or paying counterfeiters to produce fake identity documents. Over time, recognizing they could make more money via their own illicit enterprises, some terrorist organizations began acquiring criminal competencies and soon were engaged in extortion, credit card fraud, bank robberies, and other street crimes. From there they graduated into arms, drug, and human trafficking; smuggling of contraband; kidnapping for ransom; and other crimes traditionally considered the purview of organized crime.

Terrorist groups such as Al-Qaida in the Islamic Maghreb (AQIM), the Islamic Movement of Uzbekistan (IMU), and the Taliban traditionally engaged in smuggling of contraband and other forms of organized crime such as kidnapping for ransom. AQIM emerged from tribal structures that for centuries trafficked humans for the transatlantic slave trade. It began as an insurgency against what it considers an "apostate" regime in Algeria. It now operates throughout the Sahelo-Saharan region where its criminal activity, including kidnapping Western nationals for ransom, trafficking of drugs and weapons, and smuggling of commodities such as cigarettes, may have earned it up to $100 million.[6]

In Central Asia, the now reconstituted IMU rose out of the ashes of the Civil War in Tajikistan (1992–1997) to launch a protracted insurgency against several of the region's governments, which it funded through narcotics trafficking. At the end of Tajikistan's Civil War, it was driven into Afghanistan and later to Pakistan where it merged in 2015 with other regional jihadist groups that pledged allegiance to Da'esh.[7] Its percentage of regional drug trafficking profits is low due to the competition from criminal-political clans that exercise near-monopolies over illicit narcotics. Yet, even these small drug trafficking operations net the IMU significant rewards. In turn, this criminality taints the ideals of many of its members who "drink alcohol, poach women, [and] survive on banditry."[8]

In Afghanistan and Pakistan, the Taliban long exercised feudal control over contract killings, kidnapping for ransom, arms and drug trafficking, and extortion campaigns on a local scale.[9] To counter coalition forces after the U.S.-led invasion of Afghanistan in 2001, its commanders became involved in "systematically promoting, financing, organizing, and protecting the drug trade."[10] The huge profits from narcotics are not always invested in terrorism, however. Rather, leaders often build flashy mansions and buy new Toyota Land Cruisers and other luxury items.

Finally, some revolutionary terrorist groups internationalized their criminal enterprises to realize greater profits. Organizations such as the Fuerzas Armadas Revolucionarias de Colombia (FARC), the Liberation Tigers of Tamil Eelam (LTTE), and the PKK/KONGRA-GEL (PKK) all maintain convincing guerrilla wings that sometimes engage in fierce battles against authorities, effectively camouflaging decades of criminal enterprise. They are highly successful, especially in Europe, where the latter two groups extort their respective diaspora communities and engage in drug trafficking, human trafficking and smuggling, and credit card fraud.

The vast profits illicit trade generates often far exceed what is needed for extremists' operational purposes. The windfall may have caught some groups off guard and over the long run may have harmed their cause with both open and tacitly sympathetic supporters. Certainly, many of the members of groups such as Abu Sayyaf, AQIM, the Caucasus Emirate, the Haqqani Network, and the IMU seem to have become as captivated by profit as ideology. For others, like Boko Haram, Da'esh, and al-Shabaab, there has been decidedly more fluctuation between professed ideological values and profit maximization. Ultimately, entire groups have lost many of their comprehensible ideals as members became wealthy beyond their wildest dreams. Yet, it is unlikely that most extremists wish to be viewed as common criminals; the pursuit of excessive enrichment is difficult to explain to followers who expect high degrees of moral turpitude from terrorists. Moreover, crimes such as drug trafficking often are viewed as antithetical to ideological and/or religious values.[11] Hence, in such cases, the more professionalized and business-minded the criminal operations, the less terrorists may be able to cling to their ideals.

IDEOLOGY AS A FAÇADE

For many terrorists, their evolution to terrorist criminal enterprises has comprised a careful balancing act to appear committed to ideology while at the same time generate revenue. Some of this stems from newer members being recruited into an organization that already is financially dependent on illicit activities and whose members enjoy lavish criminal lifestyles. Once introduced to such wealth, its lure often corrupts and supplants loftier ideals, leaving ideology to serve as little more than the group's façade.[12] Hence, for instance in some regions, "Islam is a convenient label hiding the joining of two bloodied hands: trafficking and terrorism. Global gang violence has been 'Islamised.'"[13]

Thus, sometime during their evolution, profit-making surpassed "political aspirations as the dominant operating rationale" for groups such as Abu Sayyaf Group (ASG), many Al-Qaida affiliates, the FARC, the Haqqani Network, Hezbollah, and the PKK.[14] To provide an idea of how money may become a dominant motivator for many terrorist organizations, the income realized in 2013 by the Italian mafia group 'Ndrangheta is instructive. That year the group's estimated profits, largely from narcotics trafficking, were €53 billion (approximately US$ 70.41 billion). This sum exceeded the combined incomes of Deutsche Bank and McDonald's.[15] If such wealth is any indicator of the fruits of illicit commerce, then certainly at some point money constitutes as much of a draw for some extremists as does ideology.

Yet, it may not have been until the March 11, 2004, Madrid train bombings that organized crime became a more permanent fixture of terrorist funding. These attacks showcased the new breed of terrorist criminal enterprises, with an independent Al-Qaida cell engaging in illicit enterprises to raise money for the attack.[16] Its military planner, a Moroccan drug trafficker named Jamal Ahmidan, led a "small, but effective drug trafficking group, which smuggled hashish from Morocco and ecstasy from Holland to Spain."[17] The proceeds paid not only for the weapons and matériel for the attack but also for transportation, phones, and safe houses for the bombers. Additionally, the 440 pounds of explosives stolen from a Spanish mine and used in the attacks were traded for 66 pounds of hashish. When the Guardia Civil raided the home of one of the terrorists, officers found 125,800 ecstasy tablets, which caused it to be one of the largest narcotics seizures in Spanish history. In total, Spanish authorities seized approximately $2 million in drugs and cash from the group. That its criminal profits far exceeded the cell's operational needs is indisputable. Its entire Madrid operation is estimated to have cost $50,000.[18]

Prior to the Madrid attacks, the 1993 Mumbai bombings are illustrative of a slight variation on the evolution of terrorist criminal enterprises or perhaps a precursor to present models in which members of organized crime groups turn their tradecraft to the cause of terrorism. In this instance, the decision to engage in terrorism demonstrated that organized crime can develop ideologically. Certainly, the fact D-Company and its operatives already formed a powerful Indian criminal syndicate foreshadowed the trend that developed more than 20 years later in Europe where many terrorists have backgrounds, if not steady careers, in at least petty crime that predates their terrorism.[19]

The Mumbai bombings that killed 257 people were masterminded by Sunni Muslim crime boss Dawood Ibrahim Kaskar. They were revenge for the destruction of the Babri Masjid (mosque) by Hindu nationalists in December 1992. Prior to the attack, his organization D-Company was a formidable criminal enterprise with a vast logistical network based in India. Hence, acquiring criminal skills to raise cash for terrorism was not needed by D-Company. Instead, Dawood Ibrahim successfully adapted the highly profitable organized crime group to a terrorist purpose, thereby demonstrating how useful this expertise is to extremists. No cost appears to have been spared. Operatives were recruited for training in using the AK-56, hand grenades, rocket launchers, and RDX explosive compounds in

Pakistan after first being sent to Dubai to acquire new identities and false passports.[20] Although the bombings caused the gang to fracture along religious lines, they pushed Ibrahim firmly into terrorism, which he continues to fund through criminal enterprise from an unknown location in Karachi.[21]

These incidents illustrate the genesis of a trend that gathered momentum over the next several decades with factions of groups like the FARC all but setting aside ideological honesty and turning their operational skills to organized crime. Meanwhile, the PKK and Hezbollah went so far as to alter their organizational structures to form specialized units that focus exclusively on organized crime rather than terrorist operations. Thus, the engagement in organized crime often altered the complexion of many terrorist groups. In some instances, over time and as immense profits were realized, many extremists' ideological goals became markedly subordinate to criminal enterprise.

CONCLUSION

The steady descent of terrorist groups into terrorist criminal enterprises may have produced more confusion than clarity for policy makers. Bureaucracies continue to compete with one another by supporting separate and functionally invalid definitions of terrorist and criminal organizations. Adding further complexity is the fact that despite morphing into terrorist criminal enterprises, most groups did not necessarily lose their ideological fervor. Rather, the money from illicit trade has complemented their terrorist goals.

As the chapters that follow demonstrate, some groups clearly are diverted from their ideals and take advantage of the opportunities afforded them by criminal enterprise for the profit of themselves and their cronies. Yet even these groups continue to use their ideological or religious values as a cover for their criminality rather than openly abandon them. Terrorist criminal enterprises differ from conventional organized crime only in their motivations for making and spending illicit funds. Otherwise, the criminal modus operandi is the same.

NOTES

1. The Federal Bureau of Investigation (FBI) defines organized crime as any group having some manner of a formalized structure and whose primary objective is to obtain money through illegal activities. Such groups disrupt financial markets, suborn public officials, and employ ruthless violence to guarantee themselves impunity and unimpeded criminal operations, many of which extend internationally.

2. For some notable exceptions, see, for example, Thomas M. Sanderson, "Transnational Terror and Organized Crime: Blurring the Lines," *SAIS Review* 24, no. 1 (2004), 49–61; Rollie Lal, "South Asian Organized Crime and Terrorist Networks," *Orbis* 49, no. 2 (Spring 2005), 293–302; Justine A. Rosenthal, "For-Profit

Terrorism: The Rise of Armed Entrepreneurs," *Studies in Conflict and Terrorism* 31 (2008) 481–498; Phil Williams, "Terrorist Financing and Organized Crime: Nexus, Appropriation or Transformation?" in *Countering the Financing of Terrorism*, ed. Thomas Biersteker and Susan Eckert (London: Routledge, 2008), 126–149; Louise Shelley, *Dirty Entanglements Crime Corruption and Terrorism* (New York: Cambridge Press, 2014); Colin Clarke, *Terrorism Inc: The Financing of Terrorism, Insurgency, and Irregular Warfare* (Santa Barbara, CA: Praeger, 2015).

3. Tamara Makarenko, "The Crime-Terror Continuum: Tracing the Interplay between Transnational Organised Crime and Terrorism," *Global Crime* 6, no. 1 (2004), 129–145.

4. Kimberley L. Thachuk, "Organized Crime and National Security: Globalization's Sinister Underbelly," in *The Global Century: Globalization and National Security*, ed. Richard Kugler and Ellen Frost (Washington, DC: National Defense University, 2000), 743–760.

5. See, for example, Phil Williams, "Terrorism and Organized Crime: Convergence, Nexus or Transformation," in *FOA Report on Terrorism*, ed. Gunnar Jervas (Stockholm: Swedish Defence Research Establishment, 1998), 69–91; Svante Cornell, "Narcotics, Radicalism and Armed Conflict: The Islamic Movement of Uzbekistan," *Terrorism and Political Violence* 17 (2005), 577–597; Lal, "South Asian Organized Crime and Terrorist Networks," 293–302; Louise I. Shelley, John T. Picarelli, Allison Irby, Douglas M. Hart, Patricia A. Craig-Hart, Phil Williams, Steven Simon, Nabi Abdullaev, Bartosz Stanislawski, and Laura Covill, *Methods and Motives: Exploring Links between Transnational Organized Crime and International Terrorism* (Washington, DC: National Institute of Justice, 2005); Chris Dishman, "The Leaderless Nexus: When Crime and Terror Converge," *Studies in Conflict and Terrorism* 28, no. 3 (2005), 237–252; John Rollins and Liana Sun Wyler, *International Terrorism and Transnational Crime: Foreign Policy Issues for Congress* (Washington, DC: Congressional Research Service, 2013); Vanessa Neumann, "Grievance to Greed: The Global Convergence of the Crime-Terror Threat," *Foreign Policy Research Institute* (Spring 2013), 251–267; John T. Picarelli, "Osama bin Corleone? Vito the Jackal? Framing Threat Convergence through an Examination of Transnational Organized Crime and International Terrorism," *Terrorism and Political Violence* 24 (2014), 180–198; Tamara Makarenko and Michael Mesquita, "Categorising the Crime–Terror Nexus in the European Union," *Global Crime* 15, nos. 3–4 (2014), 259–274; Tamara Makarenko, "Foundations and Evolution of the Crime-Terror Nexus," in *Routledge Handbook of Transnational Organized Crime*, ed. Felia Allum and Stan Gilmour (New York: Routledge, 2015), 234–249; Tuesday Reitano, Colin Clarke, and Laura Adal, *Examining the Nexus between Organised Crime and Terrorism and Its Implications for EU Programming* (Brussels: CT Morse—Counterterrorism Monitoring, Reporting and Support Mechanism, 2016). http://globalinitiative.net/wp-content/uploads/2017/04/oc-terror-nexus-final.pdf.

6. Abdelmalek Alaoui, "The Secret of Al Qaeda in Islamic Maghreb Inc.: A Resilient (and Highly Illegal) Business Model," *Forbes*, December 16, 2013, https://www.forbes.com/sites/kerryadolan/2013/12/16/the-secret-of-al-qaeda-in-islamic-maghreb-inc-a-resilient-and-highly-illegal-business-model/#23089116475e.

7. Annette Bohr and Gareth Price, *Regional Implications of Afghanistan's Transitions, Pakistan, Kyrgyzstan, and Tajikistan* (London: Chatham House, December 2015), 8.

8. "Pakistan's Militant Drift: Taliban All Over," *The Economist*, April 12, 2007, http://www.economist.com/node/9008911.

9. Lal, "South Asian Organized Crime and Terrorist Networks," 293–302.

10. Ron Moreau, "The Taliban's New Role as Afghanistan's Drug Mafia," *Newsweek*, June 12, 2013, http://www.newsweek.com/2013/06/12/talibans-new-role-afghanistans-drug-mafia-237524.html.

11. Rollie Lal, "South Asian Organized Crime and Linkages to Terrorist Networks," in *Transnational Threats: Smuggling and Trafficking in Arms, Drugs and Human Life*, ed. Kimberley L. Thachuk (Westport, CT: Praeger, 2007), 150.

12. Rosenthal, "For-Profit Terrorism," 481–498.

13. Hiba Khan, "Isis and al-Qaeda Are Little More Than Glorified Drug Cartels, and Their Motivation Is Money, Not Religion," *The Independent*, April 16, 2017, http://www.independent.co.uk/voices/isis-al-qaeda-drugs-trafficking-cartels-heroin-terrorism-a7684961.html.

14. John Rollins and Liana Sun Wyler, *Terrorism and Transnational Crime: Foreign Policy Issues for Congress* (Washington, DC: Congressional Research Service, June 11, 2013), i.

15. Giulio Rubino, "Mafia Boss: 'The State Is Me,'" *Organized Crime Corruption and Reporting Project*, July 19, 2017, https://www.occrp.org/en/blog/6740-mafia-boss-the-state-is-me.

16. Phil Williams, "In Cold Blood: The Madrid Bombings," *Perspectives on Terrorism* 2, no. 9 (2008), http://www.terrorismanalysts.com/pt/index.php/pot/article/view/50/html.

17. Sebastian Rotella, "Jihad's Unlikely Alliance," *Los Angeles Times*, May 23, 2004, http://articles.latimes.com/2004/may/23/world/fg-terrcrime23.

18. Kimberley L. Thachuk, "Countering Terrorist Support Structures," *Defence Against Terrorism Review* 1, no. 1 (Spring 2009), 17.

19. See, for example, Emilie Oftedal, "The Financing of Jihadi Terrorist Cells in Europe," Norwegian Defence Research Establishment (FFI), January 2015; Rajan Basra, Peter R. Neumann, and Claudia Brunner, "Criminal Pasts, Terrorist Futures: European Jihadists and the New Crime-Terror Nexus," *Perspectives on Terrorism* 10, no. 6 (2016). http://www.terrorismanalysts.com/pt/index.php/pot/article/view/554/html; Colin P. Clarke, *Crime and Terror in Europe: Where the Nexus Is Alive and Well* (The Hague: International Center for Counter-Terrorism, 2016). https://icct.nl/publication/crime-and-terror-in-europe-where-the-nexus-is-alive-and-well/.

20. Lal, "South Asian Organized Crime and Terrorist Networks," 293–304.

21. Reports by Indian sources state that the Pakistani Directorate of Inter-Services Intelligence (ISI) affords Ibrahim the impunity to pursue his organization's terrorist criminal ambitions from a safe haven in Pakistan. New Delhi has been unsuccessful in its requests to Islamabad for his extradition. See, for example, "Factbox: Wanted by India, Living in Pakistan," *Reuters*, December 2, 2008, http://www.reuters.com/article/us-india-mumbai-militants-sb-idUSTRE4B12I120081202; "ISI Promised Dawood Ibrahim Protection, Shelter If He Invested 30% of His Earnings to Fund Terror: Sources," *India Today*, August 27, 2013, http://indiatoday.in today.in/story/isi-promised-dawood-ibrahim-protection-shelter-if-he-invested-30percent-of-his-earnings-to-fund-terror-sources/1/304061.html; Rana Banerji, "Dawood's ISI Protection Shield Is Tighter Than Ever," *Daily Mail India*, October 27, 2014, http://www.dailymail.co.uk/indiahome/indianews/article-2810222/The-ISI-shield-Dawood-worry-India.html.

CHAPTER 2

The Gangsterization of Terrorism

Kimberley L. Thachuk

Although the transformation of terrorist groups into terrorist criminal enterprises was the consequence of numerous interrelated factors, it was largely motivated by the need for group survival. After September 11, not only did the international community pressure states to end their sponsorship of terrorism, but the global economic downturn also meant terrorists could no longer depend on their traditional supporters for funding. To make up the shortfall, most groups began joining forces with traditional organized crime in so-called nexus or convergence relationships to raise cash and equip teams of operatives.[1] These activities launched extremists on a new trajectory, which, while it gave them resiliency and financial independence, also altered the complexion and modus operandi of numerous groups.

For many terrorist groups, the initial criminal arrangements involved guarding drug labs, providing security for clandestine airstrips, or paying counterfeiters for fake identity documents. Yet, as they realized the advantages of engaging in organized crime, many extremists gradually began forging closer associations with career criminals and thereby acquired new underworld competencies. As a result, especially in criminal hubs, close-knit diaspora communities, prisons, and even conflict and postconflict environments, a "cross-pollination" of terrorist and organized crime groups transpired. Soon extremists were conducting their own illicit schemes traditionally considered the purview of organized crime. At first these were street crimes including extortion and shakedowns of local merchants, credit card fraud, and bank robberies. Later such transnational illicit enterprises as drug, arms, and human trafficking; kidnapping for ransom; and smuggling of commodities were added to their repertoire. They were wildly successful.

Yet many extremists miscalculated the extent to which their engagement in organized crime and subsequent predation on fellow citizens would diminish public approval. Citizen support is one of the more pernicious enablers of terrorist groups. As long as terrorists display moral rectitude and purity of goals, in many regions they can usually count on the public for a degree of financial support and at least benevolent shortsightedness for their violence. The withdrawal of public support was thus a serious blow to terrorist groups and may have hastened the metamorphosis that the loss of official state sponsorship began.

The role of cyberspace and the ability to launder and move money also played integral roles not only in the evolution of terrorist groups but also in ensuring their continued success as terrorist criminal enterprises. Both activities are difficult to quantify, and it may be impossible to know precisely the nature and extent of these critical enablers. Despite this, what is known is that terrorist messaging anonymously and effectively drafts new adherents. It draws recruits not only to fight in foreign conflicts but also to conduct terrorist attacks close to home. Likewise, the ability to move money around the globe and launder it is vital to operatives no matter their location. Although many terrorist attacks are relatively inexpensive to conduct, there are still a number of costs involved, including operatives' living expenses and the purchase of matériel. Moreover, when the money is derived from organized crime, formal channels need to be avoided due to international money-laundering agreements. Hence understanding how to move money dexterously by informal methods is an asset of successful terrorist criminal enterprises.

LOSS OF STATE SPONSORSHIP

Arguably the main impetus for extremists' descent into criminal enterprise occurred when successful antimoney-laundering initiatives combined with the global economic downturn led many state sponsors to withdraw financial support for terrorist groups. As the details of the planning for the September 11 terrorist attacks became known, substantial attention was paid to the manner in which the hijackers funded the operation. The subsequent counterterrorism policies and international agreements to stop terrorism financing were relatively swift and extensive. In particular, in 2001 UN Security Council Resolutions 1267 and 1373 called on states to criminalize monetary support for terrorists and report suspicious transactions. Included in these agreements was action against possible funding by nongovernmental organizations, including charities, as well as the use by terrorists of wire transfers, banks, and cash couriers.

Despite these measures, and the fact that the UN Terrorist Financing Convention[2] was concluded in 1999, several states continued to openly or covertly flout the international community and sponsor terrorism.

The most flagrant of these included Cuba, Iran, Iraq, Libya, North Korea, Sudan, Syria, and Yemen.[3] A decades-long, unrelenting public shaming campaign by the international community then saw this list whittled down to Iran, Sudan, and Syria. Indisputably, this loss of sponsorship caused many terrorist groups' mutation. They were forced not only to adapt and acquire criminal expertise for funding operatives and operations but also to recruit new members with competencies in a range of illicit transactions.

DIMINISHED CITIZEN SUPPORT

A secondary and more complex impetus for the gangsterization of terrorist groups is the loss of citizen support. Waning public acceptance for the tactics and methods of emergent terrorist criminal enterprises has compounded the monetary troubles caused by the loss of official state sponsorship. Although outrage and frustration with corrupt and arbitrary governments often spark increased public tolerance for the alternative leadership that terrorist groups offer, it may be short-lived. For instance, at first members of Da'esh were praised for being "more honest and efficient than either the Syrian or Iraqi Baathists or the democratically elected Iraqi governments."[4] Yet, once extremists adopt mafia practices, it does not take long for them to begin preying on local citizens. In a variety of locations controlled by terrorist criminal enterprises, including Da'esh and the Haqqani Network, the local people have been forced to pay protection money, taxes for public goods like roads and water, and ransom for kidnappings. Many are even sold into slavery.

Although such brutality and predation alone may be sufficient to diminish the public's charitable donations and tacit approval, the engagement in criminal enterprise also raises doubt whether the extremists' ideological objectives are as virtuous as they profess. In most places, there is great distaste for organized crime, especially if it is committed at the expense of the citizenry. The result has been for once heralded "freedom fighters" to be increasingly cut off from local populations' financial and moral contributions to the terrorist cause. In turn, this translates to extremists' increased reliance on both organized crime for needed cash and violent methods to control uncooperative citizens.

CROSS-POLLINATION OF GROUPS

A third factor contributing to many terrorist groups' evolution to terrorist criminal enterprises was the growth of close associations between members of terrorist and organized crime groups. There often is a "crosspollination" of groups as a result of their congregation in the same locations allowing them to share tradecraft, exchange contraband and weapons, and in numerous cases, be recruited. There are four general

settings in which this transpires. First, is in criminal hubs or "hubs of badness," often located in areas plagued by weak and corrupt governance in
the developing world;[5] second, in diaspora enclaves, which are located
especially but not exclusively in the West; third, prisons serve as "places
of vulnerability" for both radicals and criminals to influence and recruit
each other while sharing tradecraft;[6] and finally, the fourth category comprises conflict and postconflict zones to which foreign fighters and camp
followers gravitate.

Criminal Hubs

These were some of the first locales for organized crime and terrorists to
comingle and share tradecraft. They continue to be areas in which members of mafia syndicates are radicalized as well as locales where terrorists
acquire criminal expertise and recruit operatives. Often criminal hubs are
located in weak and failed states plagued by dysfunctional institutions,
pervasive corruption, the absence of the rule of law, factionalism, and economic stagnation. Terrorist criminal enterprises navigate such conditions
with ease, filling the void left by rapacious autocrats who prefer to "find
clever ways to benefit from impoverishment and misery," robbing citizens
of opportunities for economic advancement while at the same time often
virtually selling their sovereignty to the highest bidders.[7] The situation
enables illicit actors to thus insinuate themselves into daily public life,
promising the restoration of order, justice, and public services. Yet they
are anything but benevolent. Rather, their arbitrary rule is nasty and, over
time, increasingly brutish and predatory.

Criminal hubs range from remote areas such as the *despeje* (safe haven)
zone in Colombia[8] once exclusively controlled by the FARC to territories
in the Rasht Valley in Tajikistan frequently dominated by the remnants of
the Islamic Movement of Uzbekistan (IMU). These also include regions
such as Haqqani-controlled Loya Paktia[9] in eastern Afghanistan and parts
of Pakistan's Federally Administered Tribal Areas (FATA), and enclaves in
Iraq and Syria once controlled by Da'esh.

Likewise, sprawling "feral" megacities like Karachi, Lagos, Mogadishu, and Mumbai are urban metropolises where "the rule of law has long
been replaced by near anarchy in which the only security available is that
which is attained through brute power."[10] For instance, with a population
of approximately 18 million, Karachi is dominated by militant ethnic mafias, such as Pashtun tribesmen from the north. Linked to political parties,
each operates a criminal fiefdom arbitrarily controlling large sectors of
the city into which even the Pakistani Army is reticent to venture.[11] Feral
megacities also attract thousands of unemployed youth who flock there
seeing opportunities and who are quickly recruited into the membership
of terrorist criminal enterprises. Nor are the suburbs exempt. Often built
from criminal cash, satellites like "Cocainebougou"[12] in Mali also serve as

zones that support and perpetuate interaction and exchanges between terrorists and organized crime.

When combined with the presence of a major sea or river port, the lack of effective law enforcement and widespread corruption in urban criminal hubs allows for near-unimpeded international movement of goods and people. In some notable cities like Brasilia, Budapest, Dubai, Istanbul, Karachi, Lagos, Mumbai, Rio de Janeiro, and Sao Paolo, added attractions include logistical infrastructure services including warehousing facilities where contraband can be stored, redistributed, and repackaged for transportation. Moreover, usually these metropolises provide ready access to communications, fairly reliable electricity, Internet access, office space, and good international connections for both licit and illicit bulk shipments. Finally, one of the more attractive features of such large centers is the existence of money transfer services including banks and hawalas, which enable terrorists and criminals to fund international conspiracies quickly and seamlessly. Cities such as Istanbul and Karachi have hundreds if not thousands of hawalas. Using this traditional underground money transfer system, funds can be moved anonymously to such states as Dubai where criminal cash not only is laundered into licit businesses and luxury real estate, but where it can be used to pay for weapons and other needed supplies.[13]

Other notable "hubs of badness" where terrorists and organized crime congregate and share expertise are found along trafficking routes. These often are major nodes along transportation networks normally on well-traveled roads or commercial waterways. Many are preexisting trading centers that have rail links, port facilities, and airports. Towns or settlements along these routes also tend to spring up as a result of criminal activity. For example, along some of the larger established drug and human smuggling routes in Mali are criminal hubs such as Bamako, Gao, and Timbuktu. Meanwhile, In-Khalil, Tessalit, and Tin Essako also in Mali, and Agadez in Niger where the paved road ends, are growing as vital staging points and centers for criminal and extremist recruitment. As a result, warehousing and redistribution of illicit commodities, money laundering, and the recruitment of mules and other personnel occur in these locales. As the illicit trade intensifies, hostels, restaurants, and day markets appear. Hence, criminal hubs are not only important for terrorist and criminal exchanges, but they are also integral to local communities in which people have few options for economic advancement. In essence, economic necessity thus becomes a form of tacit public approval critical to terrorist criminal enterprises.

Many of the most frequented centers of illicit activity are located at international borders. Such borderland "spaces of engagement" ostensibly were developed as a result of regional trade but are largely ungoverned and encourage a wide range of illicit exchanges.[14] In market towns such as Karasu in Kyrgyzstan located along a major trafficking route between

Kyrgyzstan and Uzbekistan, drug traffickers trade weapons to jihadists in exchange for drugs.[15] Meanwhile, in Madama, Niger near the Libyan border, day markets serve traffickers and terrorists who congregate before the two-day journey across the open desert to Libya. Similarly, day markets opened by the Tajik government in Ishkashim, Khorogh, and Rushon that straddle the frontier with Afghanistan serve as meeting places where terrorist criminal enterprises recruit young, unemployed men who survive by engaging in petty crime.

Diaspora Enclaves

Terrorists and criminals often exchange expertise and co-opt each other in close-knit diaspora communities both in the developing world and the West. In Europe, for example, some of these districts continue to be relatively isolated from larger society and act as incubators of crime and disaffected youth. Such ethnic enclaves often maintain the linguistic, cultural, and social norms of their inhabitants' states of origin, despite the fact that many residents are second- or third-generation immigrants. Many tend to be places where resentful and segregated groups of unemployed or underemployed young men entrench themselves and become increasingly alienated from and scornful of the surrounding environs and populace.[16] Terrorists and organized crime often dominate these quasi-lawless locales because the police rarely venture into them. "It's an environment very favourable [sic] to radical branches. It's not so much poverty that leads to it, it's the decay of social order. There is extreme societal misery, but it's the fact that it has just been abandoned by the state."[17]

In the wake of the Syrian civil war and sporadic outbreaks of conflict in Afghanistan and Iraq, there has been a steady influx of large numbers of refugees into Europe. Many have settled in already burgeoning diaspora communities joining other migrants steadily leaving Sub-Saharan Africa and South Asia in search of economic opportunities. Often the newcomers have resettled in the satellite communities outside of Paris or in neighborhoods like Molenbeek in Belgium, where the November 2015 Paris attacks were planned. Unfortunately, these districts minimize immigrants' interaction with wider European civil society, and large numbers of migrants remain unemployed and isolated.[18] Many have resorted to petty crime to eke out a living and, once in that fraternity, eventually are also exposed to religious extremists in what amounts to a seamless underworld.

For many Muslims in these locales, feelings of alienation and being "stuck between cultures" have led to the "development of what might be best described as a countercultural movement that expresses a puritanical devotion to Islam" that is combined with derision and hatred for non-Muslims.[19] Not only has this blend of factors led many young Muslims to resort to criminal activities and engage in the black market, but also it may have caused them to be more receptive to messages of terrorist radicalization and recruitment via social media, discussed later in this chapter.[20]

Prisons

Prisons provide another opportunity for terrorists and organized crime to exchange ideas and influence each other. Prison culture is conducive equally to extremists' and organized crime's goals. Institutional life is similar to the outside operating environment where both groups conduct clandestine activity, face hostile security personnel, and create tight-knit groups to survive. Sometimes terrorists become adept at criminal enterprise as a result of being incarcerated alongside organized criminals.[21] Moreover,

> the environment can act as an incubator for religious radicalization and violent extremism . . . It also provides them with a worldwide network of connections and further develops their understanding of tactics, techniques and procedures to fund and conduct such attacks. It is in this environment that the transformation from small-time crook to terrorist occurs, creating an emerging profile of jihadists like Abdelhamid Abaaoud and Salah Abdeslam, two of the ringleaders of the Paris terror attacks.[22]

Extremist groups also regularly extend their influence among the convicts in order to successfully bolster their organizational structures and recruit new members. "A typical behaviour [sic] is for convicted terrorists to attempt to assume leadership roles among the wider prison population, for example by leading Friday prayers or taking the lead in negotiating concessions on behalf of particular prisoners or 'Muslim prisoners' as a whole."[23]

One of the more important elements terrorist groups learn from criminal gangs in prisons is how to establish command and control networks. These direct inmates' movements, interaction, and arguably, thought processes. Just as numerous organized crime groups establish a foothold in one prison and then extend that operating structure to others, so too do a number of terrorist groups. In particular, Islamic extremist groups as diverse as Abu Sayyaf, the Algerian Armed Islamic Group (GIA), Da'esh, the Palestinian Jihad (PIJ), Hamas, and Hizb ut-Tahrir (HT) have all targeted prison populations for recruitment. Specific targets include veterans of wars such as against the Soviets in Afghanistan, as well as hardened members of traditional organized crime groups, including the Russian *vor v zakone* (thieves-in-law), especially in Central Asia and the Caucasus. In every region, other potential recruits often are young petty criminals, drug addicts, marginalized ethnic minorities, and individuals from regions to which the terrorists plan to expand.

In Spain, terrorists recruited lower-level career criminals to assist with the 2004 Madrid train attacks.[24] One of the ringleaders of the bombings was Jamal Ahmidan, a major drug dealer who sold hashish and ecstasy in Western Europe. He first became radicalized in a Spanish prison in 1998 and later was influenced to engage in terrorism while serving time in a Moroccan jail between 2000 and 2003.[25] In turn, another Madrid attacker Rachid Aglif, a.k.a. "the Rabbit," incarcerated for 18 years for his role in the train bombings, may have helped radicalize the mastermind of the August 2017 Barcelona truck attack, Abdelbaki Es Satty. Satty reportedly was not religious prior to being jailed for two years for smuggling hashish between Morocco and Spain.[26] Shortly after the Barcelona attack, he was killed in an explosion in a bomb factory in the Catalan town of Alcanar.

In another instance, *Charlie Hebdo* attackers Amedy Coulibaly, who did three prison stretches for armed robbery, and Cherif Kouachi, who was twice imprisoned for attempting to travel to Syria to fight, met while serving prison sentences in 2007 in Fleury-Mérogis prison near Paris. They formed an alliance during the seven months they spent on the same wing.[27] They were incarcerated with Djamel Beghal, one of Al-Qaida's leading recruiters in Europe. He was serving a sentence for attempting to bomb the U.S. Embassy in Paris in 2001 and likely inspired these men to commit their terrorist attacks. Similarly, Abdelhamid Abaaoud, the mastermind of the Paris plot, and his coconspirator, Salah Abdeslam, both engaged in serial petty crime and armed robbery for which they were ultimately incarcerated in Belgium in late 2010 and early 2011.[28] In prison, they were purportedly radicalized by Fouad Belkacem who was the main recruiter for the organization Sharia4Belgium in Brussels.

Conflict and Postconflict Environments

Conflict and postconflict zones also serve as locales for the cross-pollination of extremist groups and organized crime. The conditions found in these zones mirror those in weak and failing states but with the added dimension of high levels of ethnic, religious, or political strife. The chaos perpetuates insecurity and enables robust war economies to flourish. As such, the existence of illicit and lootable resources serves to perpetuate ongoing conflict and restart waning ones.[29] For their part, traditional organized crime groups usually avoid conflict zones as the excessive time and expense spent protecting operations and personnel compromises illicit transactions and cuts into profits. Yet, Da'esh, the Haqqani Network, and some Chechen groups navigate conflict environments readily, largely because they possess both the combat and criminal skills necessary to realize a profit.

It is no coincidence that a wide range of terrorist sympathizers, criminals, veterans of conflicts, and adventure seekers flock to conflict zones. Due to the sporadic outbreaks of conflict in Afghanistan and Iraq and ongoing civil war in Syria, booming war economies combined with battles for power have enabled nimble strongmen to become significantly enriched. Infamous gangsters such as Abu Bakr al-Baghdadi in Iraq, as well as Jalaluddin Haqqani (now dead) and his son, Sirajuddin, who operate on the Afghan-Pakistan border, may have remained low-level warlords if these conflicts had not spiraled out of control. The resultant conditions of chaos and lawlessness proved ripe for them to seize power over large regions, and to engage in war profiteering, and reap other conflict spoils with relative ease.

In turn, their successes attracted a range of "jihad tourists," many of whom are young people under 30 years of age who express feelings of alienation from the societies in which they live.[30] As a result of what is likely a desire for adventure and a demonstration of profound rejection of their birth or adopted countries, they gravitate to conflicts often after being inspired by terrorist groups' ideological rationales.[31] What cannot be overlooked is that those who arrive to the conflict with large sums of cash are highly favored, which suggests that money comprises an integral part of extremists' operations.[32] Others who do not have money have brought with them criminal skills, which they use to engage in an array of illicit enterprises. "Often male recruits come from dysfunctional families or single-parent families (frequently without a father) and with multi-criminal backgrounds, having past convictions for drug offenses, theft, or violence. Many have operated together with territorial criminal gangs."[33] Thus, the 3,000 to 5,000 European Union (EU) nationals who flocked to Iraq and Syria by 2015 to become gangster jihadists were certainly welcomed both for the money they brought and for their future earning potential.[34]

Concurrently, hardened fighters also found their way to these zones. Many first joined the Afghan Mujahedeen to combat the Soviets in the 1980s or fought in Tajikistan's civil war (1992–1997). Even Chechen fighters living in Europe as refugees have traveled to the Middle East to once again take up arms. As such, all have become members of a "stateless, vagrant mob of religious mercenaries" who travel from fight to fight looking for a purpose.[35] They act as force multipliers in insurgencies sharing experience and ideological commitment with newer recruits. Their presence indisputably has helped more recent conflicts spiral quickly out of control.

The confluence of unchecked opportunism, people with criminal skills, and hardened fighters is a potent combination enabling groups to hijack entire regions and install themselves as the governing authorities. In fact, it is their "strategic vision to create lawless regions with acquiescent populations so they can maximize profit."[36] Nowhere was this phenomenon more evident than in the swathes of territory in Iraq and Syria captured by Da'esh where it demanded obeisance to its arbitrary regulations and institutions.[37] Moreover, to secure and extend their capricious tenure, groups often pay salaries to a wide range of people, including young men with few employment prospects. In Mali, for example, new members of militant groups such as Al-Qaida in the Islamic Maghreb (AQIM) receive a monthly salary of roughly $900, which is a terrific sum in a country where the GDP is $1,100.[38]

Substantial credit for numerous terrorist criminal enterprises' success in dominating these conflict and postconflict territories lies with former rulers who were incompetent and corrupt. In some cases, extremist and/or religious appeals only needed to be superimposed onto the absence of government legitimacy for entire cities to become subordinated to criminal purposes. Yet there were unintended consequences. In many regions, vicious gangland violence, including murders and suicide bombings, occurred as rival terrorist criminal enterprises battled for territorial control of illicit businesses, including extortion, smuggling, and kidnapping. Additionally, because institutions were destroyed or were deficient, trade was not closely scrutinized, and illicit transactions often merged with what licit commerce did exist. As a result, in many conflict and postconflict zones, there are few options for relief. Over time the opportunities for criminal enrichment only multiply while state authority shrinks.

CRITICAL ENABLERS

Cyberspace

One of two important enablers of terrorist criminal enterprises, cyberspace has been a highly effective tool for their growth and evolution. The cyber world fulfills a number of important roles. Not only it is used to gain and share information and tradecraft, advertise exploits, and recruit operatives, but money is also raised by some of the more tech-savvy groups through a variety of illicit online schemes. Prospective members gain much of their information from those terrorist criminal enterprises that run websites. New recruits may even add to those sites, which cause the media to transform as quickly as do the groups that run them. In this way, the radical spirit is maintained and spread efficiently. Even those living for sustained periods on battlefields, although they may not eat or bathe regularly, have access to an array of current information at their fingertips. Many are citizens of a globalized world and are conversant in such things as building websites, hacking others' accounts, streaming video, and even buying and selling contraband and stolen goods on the Dark Web.

Such capabilities add a somewhat nebulous character to both the radicals and their operations. Cyber skills assist them in circumventing law enforcement, regulations, and borders. Versatility with online tools also allows groups to communicate plans, inspire and recruit new followers, conduct illicit commerce, and move money around the globe. One of the more pernicious outcomes of such capabilities is that evidence of violent attacks may be immediately loaded onto websites and viewed by thousands of potential recruits before authorities manage to dismantle them. Moreover, radicals understand how to appeal to young, disaffected people across the globe with glossy messages sent on a variety of social media platforms. These include Twitter and Facebook that act as near real-time coverage of battlefield exploits and terrorist attacks. Other Internet tools include Kik and Skype that enable free communication with sympathizers and potential recruits.

Additionally, the moneymaking side of cyberspace cannot be discounted. It is an increasingly efficient method for terrorist criminal enterprises' illicit transactions. Not only can they be expedited, but a wide range of exchanges can also be conducted relatively anonymously. Moreover, web skills are used to commit a variety of profitable cybercrimes, including fraudulent loan applications, Social Security scams, and theft.[39] For at least a decade, several groups have conducted phishing attacks and purchased stolen credit card numbers. In 2006, U.K. hacker Younis Tsouli, known online as "Irhabi 007," helped generate £2.5 million (approximately $331 million) for jihadi operations by engaging in these cybercrimes.[40] Additionally, groups can buy or sell illicit products and services via the Internet. For instance, in 2015 Da'esh advertised two hostages for sale on its online magazine *Dabiq*, and several groups managed to procure weapons and other matériel on the Dark Web. Further, in what is unlikely to be a single instance, 57 people were arrested in France in 2015 for buying arms and ammunition on the Dark Web intended for attacks in Europe.[41]

Laundering and Moving Money

As terrorist criminal enterprises become increasingly adept at illicit commerce, the ability to launder and move money will be as critical to them as it is to conventional organized crime. Criminal activity generates vast sums of money, a great deal of which continues to be cash. At least in the West, extremists need to alter the complexion of illicit funds in order to use it for operational purposes as well as for such mundane matters as paying members.[42] Overall, there are various ways money is laundered, including basic bulk cash smuggling, trade-based money laundering, money laundering into real estate, money laundering through payment in conflict minerals, and the use of legitimate businesses to hide criminal proceeds.

Although some groups, especially those in the West, may use bank accounts and credit cards for smaller transactions and formal bank transfers, others use PayPal, Bitcoin, or nonbank mobile money transfer services like Orange Money. In particular, Bitcoin that once had a certain amount of transparency now is almost entirely anonymous making transactions virtually untraceable. As a result, it appears to be a popular cryptocurrency with several terrorist criminal enterprises, including Da'esh.[43]

Despite the availability of these instruments, many groups continue to prefer cash.[44] Illicit commerce including drug trafficking and kidnapping for ransom are cash businesses that generate small bills in the millions that are neither easy to conceal nor spend. AQIM, for instance, only accepts cash for kidnapping ransom payments. Yet, in remote places in the desert, its members may be hard pressed to spend millions of dollars, never mind launder it. As a result, they buy new equipment, weapons, and four-wheel drive jeeps and pay "wads of cash" as bonuses to members. Beyond that, they bury it and map its location using GPS devices, which is not a fail-safe method.[45] In one instance, Abd al-Hamid Abu Zeid, the leader of an AQIM katiba (brigade) and a main earner of kidnap for ransom money, buried a payment of €16 million (approximately $17,840,000) probably in northern Mali but was killed in a traffic accident before he could provide the cache's GPS coordinates to other AQIM members.[46] Hence, although terrorist criminal enterprises may generate a lot of money and their need to move it seamlessly is great, at present not all groups are sophisticated with regard to laundering it.

CONCLUSION

The evolution of extremist groups to terrorist criminal enterprises is the result of a confluence of circumstances and factors. Although the efforts by the international community to halt terrorist financing were one of the dominant factors promulgating the change, there were other pivotal drivers for this metamorphosis. Not only did the descent into criminality cause extremists to lose public support, especially when crimes were perpetrated against ordinary people, but over time, necessity often was surpassed by the profit motive, if not by greed. The resultant "cross-pollination" with organized crime in a variety of locales further hastened this trend. Indeed, once the process of gangsterization of terrorism began, it became increasingly unlikely to be reversed. Enabled by the Internet and a nimble approach to laundering the proceeds of crime, it was a winning strategy.

Although some terrorist groups clearly have become diverted from some of their more comprehensible ideals by the lure of large sums of criminal money, for others, organized crime complements their terrorist purpose and enables the more effective promulgation of esoteric goals. Yet even these groups often use their ideological or religious values as a cover for their criminality rather than openly abandon it. Thus, the large amounts of money realized through criminal activity allows terrorist criminal enterprises to prosper, increase their numbers, and buy matériel all in support of terrorist plots. Understanding the extent to which criminal entrepreneurship transformed and altered the strategic calculus of terrorist groups thus will be critical in formulating coherent policies to combating them.

NOTES

1. See, for example, Phil Williams, "Terrorist Financing and Organized Crime: Nexus, Appropriation or Transformation?" in *Countering the Financing of Terrorism*, ed. Thomas Biersteker and Susan Eckert (London: Routledge, 2008), 126–149; Tamara Makarenko, "The Crime-Terror Continuum: Tracing the Interplay between Transnational Organised Crime and Terrorism," *Global Crime* 6, no. 1 (2004), 129–145.

2. Formally, the International Convention for the Suppression of the Financing of Terrorism.

3. After diplomatic wrangling by the U.S. Department of State over whether Saudi Arabia should be named a State Sponsor of Terrorism, it was ultimately not included.

4. Bruce Hoffman, "Return of the Jihadi," *National Interest*, January/February 2016, 10.

5. Patrick Radden Keefe, "The Geography of Badness: Mapping the Hubs of the Illicit Global Economy," in *Convergence: Illicit Networks in the Age of Globalization*, ed. Michael Miklaucic and Jacqueline Brewer (Washington, DC: NDU Center for Complex Operations, 2013), 97–110; Richard J. Norton, "Feral Cities," *Naval War College Review* LVI, no. 4 (Autumn 2003), 97–106.

6. Peter R. Neumann, *Prisons and Terrorism Radicalisation and De-radicalisation, in 15 Countries* (London: International Centre for the Study of Radicalisation and Political Violence [ICSR], 2010), i.

7. Robert I. Rotberg, *When States Fail: Causes and Consequences* (Princeton, NJ: Princeton University Press, 2004), 22; Kimberley L. Thachuk, "Corruption and International Security," *SAIS Review* XXV (Winter 2005), 143.

8. In January 1999, following an agreement with the Colombian government, the FARC took control of a 15,000 square mile area, known as the *zona de despeje*, from which the government withdrew its security forces.

9. The mountainous Afghan provinces of Khost, Paktia, and Paktika are collectively known as Loya Paktia.

10. Norton, "Feral Cities," 97.

11. See, for example, Samira Shackle, "Gangsters and 'Mafia' Groups Add to Political and Ethnic Violence in Karachi—Pakistan's Most Affluent City," *The Independent*, January 31, 2013, http://www.independent.co.uk/news/world/asia/gangsters-and-mafia-groups-add-to-political-and-ethnic-violence-in-karachi-pakistans-most-affluent-8475246.html; Huma Yusuf, *Conflict Dynamics in Karachi* (Washington, DC: U.S. Institute of Peace, 2012).

12. As a result of the money earned in the cocaine trade, local drug lords erected mansions in neighborhoods known popularly as Cocaine City (Cité de Cocaine or "Cocainebougou") on the outskirts of Gao, Mali.

13. See, for example, "FBR to Start Scrutiny of Travel History of Frequent Visitors to Dubai to Check Outflow of Untaxed Money," *PKRevenue.com*, June 1, 2015, http://www.pkrevenue.com/inland-revenue/fbr-to-start-scrutiny-of-travel-history-of-frequent-visitors-to-dubai-to-check-outflow-of-untaxed-money/#more-1329.

14. Willem van Schendel, "Spaces of Engagement: How Borderlands, Illegal Flows, and Territorial States Interlock," in *Illicit Flows and Criminal Things*, ed. Willem van Schendel and Itty Abraham (Bloomington: Indiana University Press, 2005), 38–68.

15. Mariya Y. Omelicheva, *Mapping the Terrorism/Trafficking Nexus in Central Asia*, Paper Prepared for the Annual Conference of the Central Eurasian Studies Society, Princeton University, November 2016, 12. http://ipsr.ku.edu/trafficking/pdf/CESS2016_Omelicheva.pdf.

16. Kimberley L. Thachuk, Marion "Spike" Bowman, and Courtney Richardson, *Homegrown Terrorism: The Threat Within* (Washington, DC: National Defense University, 2008), 5–6.

17. Angelique Chrisafis, "Charlie Hebdo Attackers: Born, Raised and Radicalised in Paris," *Guardian*, January 12, 2015, https://www.theguardian.com/world/2015/jan/12/-sp-charlie-hebdo-attackers-kids-france-radicalised-paris.

18. See, for example, Thachuk, Bowman, and Richardson, *Homegrown Terrorism: The Threat Within*.

19. Ibid., 4.

20. Tuesday Reitano and Colin Clarke, *Examining the Nexus between Organised Crime and Terrorism and Its Implications for EU Programming* (Brussels: CT Morse Counter-Terrorism Monitoring, Reporting and Support Mechanism, April 20, 2017), http://globalinitiative.net/wp-content/uploads/2017/04/oc-terror-nexus-final.pdf.

21. See, for example, "Central Asia: Islamists in Prison," *International Crisis Group Asia Briefing*, no. 97, December 15, 2009, https://www.crisisgroup.org/europe-central-asia/central-asia/central-asia-islamists-prison.

22. Colin Clarke, "A Parochial Nexus? Crime and Terror in Europe," *Fletcher Security Review*, Winter 2016, https://www.fletchersecurity.org/winter-2016-web-exclusive.

23. Neumann, *Prisons and Terrorism Radicalisation and De-radicalisation*, 28.

24. Renwick Mclean, "Spanish Prisons Provide Pool of Recruits for Radical Islam," *New York Times*, October 31, 2004, http://www.nytimes.com/2004/10/31/world/europe/spanish-prisons-provide-pool-of-recruits-for-radical-islam.html; Renwick Mclean, "Common Criminals in Spain Transformed into Islamic Militant: Terrorists Recruiting in Prisons," *New York Times*, November 1, 2004, http://www.nytimes.com/2004/11/01/news/common-criminals-in-spain-transformed-into-islamic-militants-terrorists.html.

25. Dale Fuchs, "Spain Says Bombers Drank Water from Mecca and Sold Drugs," *New York Times*, April 15, 2004, http://www.nytimes.com/2004/04/15/world/spain-says-bombers-drank-water-from-mecca-and-sold-drugs.html; Phil Williams, "In Cold Blood: The Madrid Bombings," *Perspectives on Terrorism* 2, no. 9 (2008), http://www.terrorismanalysts.com/pt/index.php/pot/article/view/50/html.

26. James Rothwell and Martin Evans, "Imam behind Barcelona Terror Cell Had Links to Madrid Bomber," *Telegraph*, August 20, 2017. I am indebted to Jessica Schrimp for this point.

27. Angelique Chrisafis, "Charlie Hebdo Attackers: Born, Raised and Radicalised in Paris," *Guardian*, January 12, 2015, https://www.theguardian.com/world/2015/jan/12/-sp-charlie-hebdo-attackers-kids-france-radicalised-paris.

28. Mirren Gidda, "Belgian Prisons: Breeding Grounds for Islamist Extremists?" *Newsweek*, March 24, 2016, http://www.newsweek.com/brussels-attacks-forest-prison-belgian-prisons-radicalization-salah-abdeslam-440547.

29. See, for example, Michael L. Ross, "How Do Natural Resources Influence Civil War? Evidence from Thirteen Cases," *International Organization* 58 (Winter 2004), 35–67.

30. Thomas Hegghammer, "The Rise of Muslim Foreign Fighters: Islam and the Globalization of Jihad," *International Security* 35, no. 3 (Winter 2010/2011), 63.

31. David Malet, "Why Foreign Fighters? Historical Perspectives and Solutions," *Orbis*, Winter 2010, 109.

32. Elizabeth Braw, "Foreign Fighters Financing: The Very Non-Halal Ways Potential Jihadists Are Funding Their Work," *Foreign Affairs*, October 25, 2015.

33. Magnus Ranstorp, "Microfinancing the Caliphate: How the Islamic State Is Unlocking the Assets of European Recruits," *CTC Sentinel* 9, no. 5 (May 2016), 11.

34. Rob Wainwright, "Counter-terrorism in Europe," Oral Evidence before the Home Affairs Committee, House of Commons, London, January 13, 2015. http://data.parliament.uk/writtenevidence/committeeevidence.svc/evidencedocument/home-affairs-committee/counterterrorism-in-europe/oral/17575.html.

35. Lawrence Wright, *The Looming Tower: Al-Qaeda and the Road to 911* (New York: Knopf, 2006), 163.

36. Justine A. Rosenthal, "For-Profit Terrorism: The Rise of Armed Entrepreneurs," *Studies in Conflict and Terrorism* 31 (2008), 485.

37. Aaron Zelin, "The Islamic State of Iraq and Syria Has a Consumer Protection Office," *The Atlantic*, June 13, 2014, https://www.theatlantic.com/international/archive/2014/06/the-isis-guide-to-building-an-islamic-state/372769/.

38. Valeri Melnikov, "Cocaine, Islam, Nomad Pride: The Roots of Mali's Crisis," *Sputnik International*, February 6, 2013, https://sputniknews.com/analysis/2013 0206179263782-Cocaine-Islam-Nomad-Pride-The-Roots-of-Malis-Crisis/.

39. Ranstorp, "Microfinancing the Caliphate," 13.

40. Beatrice Berton and Patryk Pawlak, "Cyber Jihadists and Their Web," *European Union Institute for Security Studies*, January 2015, 2. https://www.iss.europa.eu/sites/default/files/EUISSFiles/Brief_2_cyber_jihad.pdf; Rita Katz and Michael Kern, "Terrorist 007 Exposed," *Washington Post*, March 26, 2006, http://www.washingtonpost.com/wp-dyn/content/article/2006/03/25/AR2006032500020.html.

41. Colin Freeman, "Inside the 'Ant Trade'—How Europe's Terrorists Get Their Guns," *Telegraph*, November 23, 2015, http://www.telegraph.co.uk/news/worldnews/europe/12010458/Inside-the-Ant-Trade-how-Europes-terrorists-get-their-guns.html.

42. Michael Freeman and Moyara Ruehsen, "Terrorism Financing Methods: An Overview," *Perspectives on Terrorism* 7, no. 4 (2013), http://www.terrorismanalysts.com/pt/index.php/pot/article/view/279/html.

43. Olivia McCoy, "Bitcoin for Bombs," *Micah Zenko Blog*, Council on Foreign Relations, August 17, 2017, https://www.cfr.org/article/bitcoin-bombs.

44. For instance, in 2010 a formal bank transfer was used by Nasserdine Menni to send £5,725 (approximately $8,400) to the bank account of a suicide bomber, Taimour Abdulwahab, in Stockholm.

45. Rukmini Callimachi, "Paying Ransoms, Europe Bankrolls Qaeda Terror," *New York Times*, July 29, 2014, https://www.nytimes.com/2014/07/30/world/africa/ransoming-citizens-europe-becomes-al-qaedas-patron.html.

46. Camille Tawil, "Al-Qaida in the Islamic Maghreb Calls on North African Jihadists to Fight in Sahel, Not Syria," *Jamestown Foundation Terrorism Monitor* 11, no. 6 (March 20, 2013).

CHAPTER 3

Da'esh in Iraq and Syria: Terrorist Criminal Enterprise

Colin P. Clarke and Phil Williams

INTRODUCTION

From the summer of 2014 and well into 2016, Da'esh[1] was not only the strongest and most successful terrorist organization in history but also the richest one. Moreover, most of its wealth was not the result of external state support but was generated through a comprehensive set of criminal activities based largely on territorial control.[2] Indeed, Da'esh developed a portfolio of criminal activities that surpassed anything previously done by terrorist organizations. Hezbollah has long been described as "the Gambinos on steroids."[3] If this really is the case, then Da'esh should be seen as the Gambinos on a potent cocktail of steroids, testosterone, and human growth hormone.

Does this mean that Da'esh transformed into a criminal organization? Clearly, under some circumstances, terrorist organizations can become commercialized and lose their ideological, religious, or nationalist fervor. There are also hybrid organizations that combine an extremist agenda and quest for power, with a desire to make profits through illegal activities in pursuit of both political and financial objectives. Yet to see Da'esh either as simply a criminal or even a hybrid organization is to underestimate its strength and singularity of purpose. For Da'esh, organized crime is best understood as a methodology or a set of activities that are used to obtain funds to further the cause. The ultimate ends remain political, ideological, and religious, but organized crime methodologies are appropriated as a means of funding this broad agenda. In other words, the defining characteristic is not the activity so much as the purpose—and organized crime is simply an instrumental activity. In this sense, the use of organized crime activities by Da'esh has to do with both Mohammed and Machiavelli: the creation, maintenance, and expansion of a new Caliphate are the ends that justify any means, including the appropriation of organized crime methods or the adoption of what one of the authors previously termed "do-it-yourself" organized crime.[4] Nevertheless, Da'esh, like other organizations examined in this volume, has clearly become a terrorist criminal enterprise par excellence with a portfolio of criminal activities that would put Al Capone to shame.

If Da'esh has taken the use of organized crime by terrorist organizations to new levels, the adoption of crime was neither novel nor unprecedented. Many years ago, Paul Clare referred to the Irish Republican Army's extortion activities to fund its cause as its "Capone discovery";[5] the Tamil Tigers engaged in drug trafficking and people smuggling as well as extortion in the Tamil diaspora, especially in Canada;[6] and, as suggested earlier in the chapter, Hezbollah has made extensive use of criminal activities to fund both its terrorist activities and its social welfare programs.[7] Closer to home, Al-Qaida in Iraq (AQI—which gradually morphed into Da'esh) developed a broad portfolio of criminal activities, establishing the funding framework within which Da'esh subsequently operated. Indeed, for almost every criminal activity pursued by Da'esh—drug trafficking, human trafficking, kidnapping for ransom (KFR), oil theft and diversion, and extortion—AQI had blazed the trail.[8] And as evidenced by the extensive list of illicit activities, Da'esh inherited a true criminal enterprise that encompassed a range of lucrative funding streams.

What Da'esh potently added to the mix was a monopoly of extensive territorial control. By declaring the Caliphate and providing governance in the parts of Syria and Iraq that it had conquered—including key cities such as Raqqa and Mosul—Da'esh was able to extract rents from the population through both taxation and extortion. It also took control over the local economy, transforming what in other circumstances has been referred to as a "resource curse" into a resource blessing and a source of wealth, strength, and resilience. Whereas some terrorist organizations drift into criminality as a fund-raising mechanism, Da'esh simply inherited such an approach—and then systematically refined it and expanded its scope. The entry barriers for organized crime are low, thereby ensuring its attractions for terrorist organizations. Even allowing for this, Da'esh grasped the criminal opportunities available with singular focus, ruthless enthusiasm, and remarkable skill.

Against this background, this chapter explores the range of criminal activities from which Da'esh benefits financially.[9] It identifies oil smuggling, extortion and taxation, KFR, antiquities trafficking, drug trafficking, and human smuggling and trafficking as the main revenue streams and explores each of these in turn. The range of activities is explained in large part by the degree of territorial control that Da'esh exerted for about two and a half years over 8 million people. It became a de facto and highly predatory government over large parts of Syria and Iraq. Yet, before the bombing campaign and the subsequent loss of territory, Da'esh provided governance that, although brutal, was, in some respects and for some people, an improvement on what had gone before. This was especially true when compared to the provision of goods and services offered by the Iraqi government and, even more obviously, by the Assad regime in Syria. After looking at specific criminal revenue flows, the chapter considers how Da'esh is organized to carry out its criminal enterprises. The final section of the chapter contends that for Da'esh loss of territory and the degradation of its financial capacity are directly related—and equally to be welcomed.

OIL SMUGGLING AND TRAFFICKING

A significant portion of the money raised by Da'esh smuggling activity comes from the smuggling and trafficking of oil and oil-related products. AQI had been involved in the theft, diversion, and smuggling of oil, but Da'esh turned it into an art form. The group captured key oil fields and refineries in northeastern Syria and northern Iraq between June 2014 and September 2014 and took control of key roads and other centers of commerce.[10] When Da'esh gained control over Deir-ez-Zor in 2014, it laid claim to Syria's largest oil field, al-Omar, in addition to several smaller but still significant oil fields, including Tanak, Jafra, and Ward.[11] It also developed relationships with traditional smuggling organizations, such as the Berri clan in Aleppo, that were critical in moving gasoline into Turkey where prices are among the highest in the world.[12]

By mid-2016, Da'esh still controlled approximately 60 percent of the oil wells in Syria and 5 percent of the oil wells in Iraq, although this control continued to be degraded throughout 2017.[13] Da'esh assigned much value to those operating its oil-related equipment; skilled workers received more money than regular fighters. In a December 2015 report, an oil field technician confirmed receiving $675 per month, up from an initial $450—well above his $150 Syrian government salary, although it should also be noted that many of these workers remain under the threat of coercion and death.[14]

Da'esh has sold oil, oil products, and gas to a range of buyers, including dealers in Syria and Iraq, who then go on to resell to the local market and the Assad regime.[15] Da'esh derives most of its oil revenue from local sales, which can be taxed multiple times along the supply chain—from oil field to refinery to local markets. Estimates of Da'esh oil revenue from mid-2016 ranged from $250 million per year to nearly $365 million per year, although these revenues are estimated to have declined.[16] The decline has been especially steep in Iraq; as of late 2016, Da'esh reportedly no longer controlled any oil wells in that country.[17] Assistant Secretary of the Treasury Daniel L. Glaser noted that Da'esh's revenue from oil had been halved from $500 million in 2015 to approximately $250 million.[18] These successes have stemmed from military and territorial gains against Da'esh.

Figures from IHS Jane's assert that Da'esh's monthly revenue was diminished by as much as 30 percent over the course of 2016, from roughly $80 million per month to $56 million per month (equivalent to $960 million per year and $672 million per year, respectively).[19] This included a 26 percent drop in revenue earned from oil and gas.[20] Likewise, Combined Joint Task Force—Operation Inherent Resolve (CJTF-OIR), the command heading the multinational counter-Da'esh Coalition, has said that Tidal Wave II air operations, starting in October 2015, reduced Da'esh's oil production from 45,000 barrels per day to 34,000 barrels per day— a 24 percent decrease. Before the operation, the group was making roughly $40 million per month.[21]

The targeting of Da'esh's oil and natural gas supply chain includes air strikes against oil fields, refineries, and tanker trucks—the entire Da'esh oil and gas supply chain.[22] The Coalition has destroyed hundreds of trucks, disrupted fuel supply lines across and outside Da'esh territory, and hit key infrastructure at oil fields and other oil production sites. Overall, this has diminished Da'esh's capability to sell oil and the capacity of Da'esh and purchasers to make and sell refined products, such as gasoline.

Turkey has finally increased its efforts to stop the flow of oil and oil-related products from traversing its borders, thereby restricting Da'esh's access to the black market.[23] Securing the border is a daunting task, but one the Turks seem more firmly committed to in the wake of terrorist attacks in some of their major cities. While the border will likely never be fully secure, more earnest efforts to deploy military and police along the border have clearly helped deter smugglers from moving contraband back and forth.

Air strikes have successfully targeted high-ranking individuals, including Da'esh's minister of oil, Abu Sayyaf, in May 2015. In some areas where Da'esh is losing territory, it has adopted a scorched-earth strategy, destroying gas field installations as it retreats.[24] Revenues from oil will be further squeezed if the anti-Da'esh Coalition can retake the Deir-ez-Zor oil fields from the group. Da'esh began shifting critical resources from Raqqa to protect this stronghold in the summer of 2017.[25]

EXTORTION, TAXATION, AND APPROPRIATION

It has become fashionable, and is often appropriate, to make a distinction between extortion and taxation. From a Da'esh perspective, however, this is a distinction without a difference: as a protostate it taxes the population in the territory it controls; as a mafia, it extorts the population in the areas it governs. Indeed, Da'esh enjoys all the power of a traditional mafia organization—which is to say it is in the business of private protection or extortion—but since it is also the government, it faces neither any competition for control of rents nor any constraints on its predatory behavior. Da'esh has an unchallenged monopoly that extends to both licit and illicit businesses and enables it to appropriate whatever property it wants. Indeed, not just oil but other natural resources as well, including grain and a host of agricultural products, are all "lootable resources" for Da'esh.[26] A 2015 report by the Financial Action Task Force (FATF) noted that Da'esh "manages a sophisticated extortion racket by robbing, looting, and demanding a portion of the economic resources in areas where it operates, which is similar to how some organized crime groups generate funds."[27] The extortion encompasses a wide variety of goods and activities, ranging "from fuel and vehicle taxes to school fees for children."[28] The report added that although all of this "is done under the auspices of providing notional services," it is "underwritten by the threat of force" and amounts to "a sophisticated protection racket where involuntary 'donations' purchase momentary safety or temporary continuity of business."[29]

In addition, Da'esh has imposed transit taxes on goods moving into and through territory it controls. These include "a road tax of 200 USD in northern Iraq and an 800 USD 'customs' tax on trucks entering Iraq along the Syrian and Jordanian borders."[30] Da'esh has also proved to be quite entrepreneurial. In Mosul, for example, it turned a former police station "into a market, with 60 shops selling fruits and vegetables. The annual rent for a market stall is . . . roughly $2,500."[31] In Raqqa, Da'esh has an Office of Services that collects "a cleaning tax" from market shops of "$7 to $14, per month depending on the size of the shop."[32] Residents go to collection points to pay their monthly electricity and water bills: $2.50 for electricity and $1.20 for water.[33] In addition, Da'esh imposes a 4 or 5 percent income tax on salaries.[34] The income tax was particularly effective in Iraq as the central government in Baghdad continued to pay salaries to government employees in Da'esh-controlled areas until July 2015. Even after the cessation of the payments, however, Da'esh members reportedly forced "some employees to leave IS controlled territory to collect their salaries, holding their property as collateral, only to retroactively tax them" on their return.[35] This created a serious dilemma for the government in Baghdad.

Da'esh also controls the banks in its territory. When it took Mosul in the summer of 2014, there were multiple reports of the largest ever bank robbery amounting to around $500 million.[36] Although the reports portrayed Da'esh actions as a heist, it seems more likely to have been an assertion of control over the bank and everything in its vault.[37] Indeed, since then, Da'esh has treated "state-owned and private banks differently."[38] The state banks have effectively been appropriated by the Caliphate. At the private banks, Da'esh imposed a "tax of 5 percent on all customer cash withdrawals," thus providing another form of extortion.[39] In addition, Da'esh imposed fines for any kinds of behavior that violated the societal and behavioral norms it imposed.[40]

Da'esh also established control over businesses, agriculture, and industry throughout the territory it controlled in Syria and Iraq. As the Center for the Analysis of Terrorism noted, "ISIS exerts its authority over a wide range of industrial and commercial activities, natural resources and raw materials, from oil to agricultural products, including minerals."[41] Da'esh's control over agricultural production and products is extensive. Da'esh governs areas in the "Nineveh, Salaheddine, and Al-Anbar provinces that make up 40% of Iraq's annual wheat production and 53% of the barley production."[42] In addition, it oversees cement plants, phosphate mines, and manufacturing facilities that produce sulfuric and phosphoric acid as well as a major Syrian salt mine.[43] In short, the territorial control Da'esh enjoys gives it access to enormous resources. As the *New York Times* observed, "Its biggest source of cash appears to be the people it rules, and the businesses it controls."[44] Funds are both raised and spent locally, obviating counterthreat finance policies put in place by the West.

Moreover, by setting up "a predatory and violent bureaucracy that wrings every last American dollar, Iraqi dinar and Syrian pound it can from those who live under its control or pass through its territory," Da'esh has exploited its territorial resources to the utmost.[45] As it has faced continued military setbacks and territorial losses, however, it has tried to compensate by cutting services and subsequently even reducing salaries for its fighters. At the same time, it has adopted an even more predatory approach: extortion accounted for 12 percent of Da'esh revenue in 2014 but increased to a third in 2015.[46] The highly predatory nature of Da'esh has also been evident in its kidnapping activities, although in this area of activity financial considerations have not invariably dominated.

KIDNAPPING FOR RANSOM

Kidnapping is an ideal terrorist weapon as it can be used for political purposes or as a fund-raising activity. KFR in Iraq became a staple of AQI during the four years or so following the U.S. occupation.[47] It included Iraqi citizens and foreigners, although the latter were given much more attention in the Western media. The Iraqi kidnappings began with the targeting of Assyrian Christians and children of "middle income or wealthy families."[48] Another Christian sect, the Sabean Mandeans, was also targeted, in part because the community included goldsmiths and jewelers and had a reputation for wealth. The target pool was subsequently extended to professionals including doctors, scientists, and university professors as well as businessmen. In a number of cases, the victims were released but told to leave the country. The kidnapping of Iraqis probably peaked in 2006 and then diminished as NGO workers left and the security situation stabilized.

Kidnapping of foreigners began in earnest in April 2004 when 43 people were abducted.[49] In some instances foreign hostages were beheaded and their executions recorded—something that began with the release of a video showing the execution of Nicholas Berg.[50] U.S. and British citizens, as opposed to French, Italian, or Swiss nationals, were more likely to be killed because their governments refused to negotiate. In other circumstances hostages were killed as a warning, highlighting the dangers facing foreign contractors working in Iraq and eroding logistic support for the Coalition. The abduction and subsequent killing of 12 Nepalese in 2004 was a case in point.[51] In many other cases, however, ransoms were demanded and paid. Reports suggested that France, Germany, and Italy paid about $45 million for the release of 11 hostages.[52] Other countries such as Japan, Jordan, the Philippines, Sweden, and Turkey are also believed to have paid significant ransoms for release of their hostages. In addition, multiple companies paid for the release of their employees. Within Iraq, connections were established between kidnapping gangs and groups such as AQI with the gangs conducting subcontracting operations, selling the kidnapped victims to the highest bidder.

Many of these patterns were replicated under Da'esh, which has used kidnapping as a weapon against its enemies—particularly the United States and Britain, neither of which pays ransoms for the release of its citizens—and as an important fund-raising method. Indeed, the great virtue of kidnapping is that it can be used symbolically to spread fear and deliver a message of defiance. This was done with U.S. journalist James Foley who was captured in 2012; a video of his execution was released in August 2014. Although Da'esh in an e-mail communication with Foley's family had demanded millions for his release, how serious this was remains uncertain. After Foley was executed, Da'esh, in what Cragin and Padilla contend was an attempt to embarrass and humiliate the United States, claimed that Obama was to blame.[53] Yet the profit motive might also have been present: the killing of Foley certainly increased the pressure to pay for the release of hostages from other countries to ensure they did not share the same fate.

Although there was a high degree of opportunism in its kidnapping activities, Da'esh also seems to have adopted a strategic approach to kidnapping and reportedly has an entire unit known as the "Intelligence Apparatus" specializing in kidnappings.[54] According to a BBC report, some Da'esh members pretending to be Syrian refugees in Turkey would befriend journalists and encourage them to go to Syria to do interviews; the journalists were then kidnapped.[55] Once they were held by Da'esh, the leaders of the organization determined that "the political value of some of the hostages was far higher if they were executed, whereas for others it was higher if they were exchanged for a ransom."[56] At the same time, Da'esh took a calculating approach to ransoms. This was evident in negotiations for the release of the 25 hostages "held by the Islamic State from the end of 2012 until the summer of 2014. The first ones to be released belonged to countries that pay the highest ransoms."[57] One negotiator even noted that "in 2013 the market for Western hostages in northern Syria was very well developed. Foreigners were traded according to their nationality and profession."[58] The result was the release of around two-thirds of the hostages after ransom payments were made, totaling somewhere between 60 million and 80 million Euros.[59] In other cases, however, hostages were killed. For example, in September 2015, the Da'esh online magazine, *Dabiq*, included photographs of a Chinese and a Norwegian prisoner and advertised them for sale. In the November issue of the magazine, their bodies were shown.

If kidnapped foreigners provided a lucrative revenue stream for Da'esh, the organization, following the AQI model, also kidnapped locals "including many Yezidis, releasing them for sums of up to 4,000 dollars."[60] In 2015, Da'esh engaged in a mass kidnapping of 230 Assyrian Christians in Syria. Facilitated by contributions from the global community of Assyrian Christians, ransom payments were subsequently made and the hostages were gradually freed, with the last 42 of them released in February 2016.[61] Reports of how much had been paid in ransom varied from around $9 million to between $25 and $30 million.[62] This lack of precision about the profits from KFR is not unusual, and official estimates of the revenue stream from KFR vary considerably.

Most criminal organizations engaged in kidnapping activities are concerned almost exclusively with the ransom payments. What distinguishes Da'esh from a traditional kidnapping gang or organized crime group is that its kidnapping activities, in addition to being part and parcel of its broader criminal enterprise, serve a political agenda. At the same time, the concern with maximizing ransom payments from countries or companies willing to pay is consistent with the notion of a terrorist criminal enterprise. It is also likely that, as with AQI, kidnapping gangs are responsible for at least some abductions and then sell the victims to Da'esh.

ANTIQUITIES TRAFFICKING

Da'esh appears to be involved both indirectly and directly in the looting and trafficking of antiquities. Once again, this is about exploiting readily available criminal opportunities since the territory Da'esh controls includes 2,500 archaeological sites in Iraq and 4,500 sites in Syria, including some UNESCO World Heritage Sites.[63] The indirect involvement involves the issuing of permits to looters and the subsequent taxing of looted artifacts being moved through Da'esh territory. There is also some direct involvement, with Da'esh itself engaged in both excavations and the subsequent smuggling and sale of items. Al Azm, a Syrian scholar based in the United States, has argued that this "shift toward institutionalization occurred" once Da'esh "realized the potential profit in antiquities . . . By the end of summer 2014 . . . they were employing their own people, conducting their own excavations, and were bringing in their own equipment and resources—they would not be doing this unless there is a lot of profit at stake."[64] It is entirely possible that the destruction of cultural heritage sites such as Palmyra was little more than an attempt by Da'esh to obfuscate the trade in antiquities, although there is clearly antipathy toward anything that does not fit the strict confines of the Caliphate.[65] Whatever the case, direct involvement in the antiquities business probably became even more attractive to Da'esh as U.S. air strikes reduced revenue from other activities within its criminal enterprise.[66]

There is still a lot of uncertainty, however, about the profits Da'esh accrues from the illicit antiquities trade, with estimates ranging from the tens of millions of dollars to a hundred million or more. As with all illicit markets, the uncertainty is irreducible. There are arguments for the proceeds being modest and other arguments for them being substantial. The argument for modest profits is that Da'esh is simply feeding the trafficking networks, which link to buyers and collectors worldwide. Moreover, it is much later in the smuggling chain that the prices really increase, particularly after looted artifacts are laundered by being given false provenance.[67] On the other hand, it seems likely that Da'esh members are directly involved in smuggling antiquities into Turkey, Lebanon, and Jordan and selling them to antiquities dealers and even some dealers from Europe. Some of the artifacts are moved to Dubai, which is another important outlet and trading center for licit and illicit antiquities. Moreover, even though Da'esh involvement is confined to the early market where prices are lowest, the looting is on such a scale that the profits remain substantial and likely in the tens of millions. In the final analysis, antiquities trafficking provides an important revenue stream but one that is far behind those generated by oil sales, and by extortion, taxation, and appropriation.

HUMAN SMUGGLING AND HUMAN TRAFFICKING

One area of activity that has been discussed a great deal, but very little in terms of Da'esh profit-making, is human smuggling of refugees. Napoleoni, however, claimed that "in the summer of 2015, the tax on human cargo crossing into Turkey generated about half a million dollars a day for the Islamic State."[68] She also argued that Da'esh forces in Libya are regulating and taxing refugee boats leaving to cross the Mediterranean, limiting the number of passengers to 120 per boat.[69] "Traffickers pay 50 percent of their profits to Da'esh in exchange for the right to sail, so counting the migrants also establishes the amount of tax each boat must pay. In 2015, this tax generated about $20 million for every ten thousand migrants."[70] This was at the height of the refugee crisis, and it seems likely that since then, this revenue stream has declined somewhat.

In addition to the taxation of human smugglers, Da'esh has subsequently become involved in human trafficking and, according to one report, "has set up prostitution businesses in certain towns and cities in which they occupy using primarily teenage girls that they force to work in such businesses."[71] In 2014, Da'esh abducted over 5,000 Yazidi women, whom its members used to conduct "slave auctions."[72] The primary thrust of these auctions, however, seemed to be aimed at rewarding their own fighters—who reportedly buy women—rather than accruing profits. Nevertheless, the human trafficking and prostitution elements are typical of a criminal enterprise, especially as humans are a renewable resource—the women could be sold over and over by fighters within the organization.

DRUG TRAFFICKING

As discussed throughout this chapter, Da'esh has diversified its funding portfolio to ensure a steady supply of financing to support its operations and organization.[73] And as its territory is further squeezed in Iraq and Syria, it will increasingly turn to opportunistic methods of raising money, including drug trafficking.[74] One major consequence of the Arab Spring and follow-on geopolitical tumult has been a shift in smuggling and trafficking networks throughout the Middle East and North Africa, with criminal groups and terrorist organizations taking advantage of continued instability in key geographic hubs throughout the Mediterranean region.[75] Da'esh fighters are cognizant of the benefits that this instability affords, even stressing in a 2017 issue of *Rumiyah* that conflict zones such as Ukraine and Syria provide ample opportunities for connections to underground criminal networks.

In September 2016, Rukmini Callimachi and Lorenzo Tondo reported in the *New York Times* on a new drug trafficking route discovered by the Italian Navy, stretching from Sicily to Libya.[76] The new route is thought to be a response to increased surveillance along the Spanish coastline and the opportunity provided by the implosion of Libya, where drugs can now transit en route to Egypt and the Middle East, before entering Europe through the Balkans.[77] An investigation by Italy, which also included other European countries and the U.S. Drug Enforcement Administration, revealed that, at least for a time, drugs were transiting through the territory in Libya controlled by Da'esh, and likely taxed by the group that conducted similar procedures in Iraq and Syria. Other reports have detailed a transactional relationship between Da'esh militants in Libya and the Calabrian 'Ndrangheta, which is working with the Neapolitan Camorra.[78]

There was also a report that a shipment containing 26 million tablets of the synthetic opiate Tramadol was intercepted by Greek authorities, originating in India and destined for Libya, bound for entities associated with the Da'esh.[79] A Da'esh-linked group operating in North Africa, Jund al-Khilafah, has allegedly profited from providing armed protection to cocaine traffickers operating in North Africa, while a report in *Asharq Al-Awsat* noted that Da'esh has been profiting from the trafficking of cannabis, moving it from Iraq through Syria and Turkey into Europe.[80]

And Da'esh militants are not just in the business of profiting from drugs but are apparently taking them too. Myriad reports suggest that terrorists are widely using Captagon, also known as "jihad pills," an amphetamine that suppresses feelings of pain, induces euphoria, and allows fighters to remain awake for extended periods of time during intense battles.[81] The Global Initiative Against Transnational Organized Crime estimates that the Captagon market could be worth approximately $1.39 billion.[82] Criminal gangs from Syria and Bulgaria and other terrorist groups, including Hezbollah, are thought to be involved with the production and sale of Captagon throughout the Middle East, which could potentially bring them into contact with Da'esh militants as fighters flee the collapsing Caliphate.[83]

MONEY LAUNDERING

There is another important way in which the Da'esh criminal enterprise closely resembles traditional criminal organizations—the use of schemes to protect and launder its criminal proceeds. This has become increasingly urgent and important as Da'esh has come under siege and lost territory. As Renad Mansour noted, "The loss of administrative territory not only signals the end of the state mind-set, but it also jeopardizes Da'esh's position in the war economy. It will no longer be able to offer security to smuggling networks. As such, the organization must now adjust to new realities to maintain its position and economic interest-based relationships."[84] Da'esh has moved to do this by focusing on moving its money into "legitimate business via third parties, which are the profit-driven businesses and tribal elites. . . . These middlemen agree to terms with their funder without many questions asked. . . . This allows ISIS to maintain liquidity and therefore relevance in the war economy."[85] Mansour noted further that Da'esh is using these middlemen to purchase "businesses in Baghdad and elsewhere."[86] These businesses "include electronic companies, car dealers, private hospitals and the food and beverage industry. The third party business owner then shares his revenues with his ISIS contact."[87] A second strand has been to use currency exchange companies to exchange Iraqi dinars for U.S. dollars.[88] Da'esh has also used currency auctions held by the Central Bank of Iraq to acquire dollars.[89] In effect, these schemes involve the use of front companies that are either complicit or unwitting tools of Da'esh as it seeks to maintain, protect, and diversify at least portions of the massive wealth it obtained from 2014 to 2016.

ORGANIZING FOR CRIME

How a terrorist or insurgent group structures its organization has implications for how it conducts operations, how it maintains cohesion, and how it raises funds, especially through criminal activities. Much like its predecessor, AQI, Da'esh adopted a top-down approach that maintained hierarchical control over and a high degree of accountability for its financial assets as it worked to keep an ironclad grip over the money it earned from a series of rackets.[90]

Da'esh may be wealthy, especially when compared to other terrorist groups, but it also maintains a vast human resources–type network to deal with medical expenses for fighters (and their families), legal support, safe houses, administrative expenses (e.g., utilities) in the areas under its control, and other logistical requirements of clandestine organizations.[91] In what may be a sign that Da'esh has learned from AQI's mistakes in Anbar Province during the "Awakening," when Da'esh has removed civil servants from their leadership positions, it has consistently compelled mid-level bureaucrats and technocrats to remain in order to ensure continuity.[92] Da'esh's use of former Assad regime loyalists displays a pragmatism that has been vital to its success holding onto the territory it has captured and connecting with other entities in Syria that can provide it with opportunities to make money.[93]

A Da'esh department "the Diwan al-Rikaz," or the Office of Resources, oversees oil production and smuggling, the looting of antiquities, and a long list of other businesses now controlled by the militants. It operates water-bottling and soft-drink plants, textile and furniture workshops, and mobile phone companies, as well as tile, cement, and chemical factories, skimming revenues from all of them.[94] The group also set up a financial committee consisting of a "finance minister" who oversees its financial affairs and exerts authority over local financial councils accountable to governments in the provinces under Da'esh control. This finance minister is on equal footing with the other members of the "cabinet" of eight ministers, each of whom has his own specific field, under the direct authority of Abu Bakr al-Baghdadi, the group's political and religious leader. The primary function of the finance minister is to ensure collection of tax revenue.

Just as the organization is structured to capitalize on criminal opportunities, this same vertical structure lends itself to state-building, in line with the Da'esh's declared goal of establishing an Islamic caliphate. In August 2014, as one of the authors has written elsewhere, "ISIS paid municipal salaries, provided public works, maintained electric, trash and sewage services, offered health care and education to its supporters and even attempted to enforce parking laws and regulations in areas it controlled or claimed to control."[95] In these same areas, it ensured the availability of basic necessities like gas and food.[96] In Mosul, Da'esh has held a "fun day" for kids, distributed gifts and food during Eid al-Fitr, held Koran recitation competitions, started bus services, and opened schools.

CONCLUDING ASSESSMENT

Although Da'esh remains predominantly a terrorist organization, it has used its territorial control to establish a variety of criminal enterprises with a series of funding streams—some extremely lucrative and others more modest.[97] Indeed, one former official has argued that after oil and taxes, everything else is a rounding error.[98] The implication, however, is that, unlike more networked organizations that have a high degree of transnational flexibility, Da'esh is critically dependent on maintaining its territorial control to ensure its continued fund-raising. Consequently, territorial losses and a reduction in its revenue streams are synonymous. The loss of control over Raqqa, and even more obviously over Mosul, will impact significantly on Da'esh's criminal enterprises and the money the organization is able to accrue. This does not mean that Da'esh will rapidly be transformed from a wealthy terrorist organization to one that is poverty stricken. The money-laundering activities discussed in this chapter will help ensure that it has continued access to funding. Nevertheless, the loss of territorial control marks the beginning of the effective dismantling of Da'esh's criminal enterprises, if not its ability to continue terrorist attacks.

POLICY OPTIONS

Since early 2016, Coalition forces have conducted targeted, intelligence-driven strikes on Da'esh's oil operations and its bulk-cash stores in Iraq and Syria. To continue crippling the group's main sources of wealth, it will remain necessary to continue these operations. As Da'esh continues to lose territory, it will seek to compensate for losses in certain revenue streams by increasing revenue generation in other areas, all of which should be considered for targeting or sanctioning—especially pertaining to an increase in taxation and extortion of the local population. Still, it will be crucial for Coalition forces to dedicate more resources in training Iraqi and other law enforcement entities, beyond advising, assisting, training, and equipping their military efforts. These forces can focus on combating Da'esh's renewed efforts to earn revenue through taxation and extortion.

As territory is reclaimed from Da'esh, much of the counter-Da'esh mission will need to shift from military force to law enforcement tools in order to address Da'esh's ongoing efforts to and tax local populations. As such, there is a dire need to invest more resources in training Iraqi and other law enforcement entities; the situation in Syria is far more difficult, since Assad remains in power and there is no semblance of state security services capable of policing large swaths of eastern Syria. To date, Da'esh has eschewed relying on external actors for financing, but this trend might not continue indefinitely. Traditional counterterrorism financing tools must continue to keep the group isolated from external patrons and potential state sponsors of terrorism. The Coalition should continue to track financial flows into Da'esh-held territory to monitor whether changes are occurring and keep an especially close watch on financial flows from countries where wealthy individuals have historically funded jihadist causes, including, but not limited to, Saudi Arabia, Kuwait, Qatar, and other Gulf countries.

NOTES

1. Also known as ISIS—Islamic State in Iraq and Syria or ISIL—Islamic State of Iraq and the Levant.

2. Colin P. Clarke and Phil Williams, "The Islamic State of Iraq and Syria: Paper Tiger or Sustainable Insurgency?" in *The Future of Counterinsurgency*, ed. Lawrence E. Cline and Paul Shemella (Santa Barbara, CA: ABC-CLIO, 2015).

3. Jo Becker, "Beirut Bank Seen as Hub of Hezbollah's Financing," *New York Times*, December 14, 2011, http://www.nytimes.com/2011/12/14/world/middleeast/beirut-bank-seen-as-a-hub-of-hezbollahs-financing.html?_r=1&hp.

4. Phil Williams, "Terrorist Financing and Organized Crime: Nexus, Appropriation, or Transformation?" in *Financing Global Terrorism*, ed. T. Bierstecker and S. Eckert (London: Routledge, 2007), 130.

5. James Adams, *The Financing of Terror* (New York: Simon and Schuster, 1986).

6. Human Rights Watch, *Funding the "Final War:" LTTE Intimidation and Extortion in the Tamil Diaspora* (Toronto: Human Rights Watch, March 2006). https://www.hrw.org/report/2006/03/14/funding-final-war/ltte-intimidation-and-extortion-tamil-diaspora.

7. See, Matthew Levitt, "Hezbollah's Transnational Organized Crime," *Policywatch* 2609, The Washington Institute, April 21, 2016, http://www.washingtoninstitute.org/policy-analysis/view/hezbollahs-transnational-organized-crime.

8. See Phil Williams, *Criminals, Militias and Insurgents: Organized Crime in Iraq* (Carlisle, PA: Strategic Studies Institute, U.S. Army War College, 2009). Monograph Series.

9. For a balanced and incisive analysis, see, Andrew J. Williams, "The Dark Economy: Examining the Practices and Policies of the Islamic State," *ASSC-2017*, Grove City College. http://austrianstudentconference.com/wp-content/uploads/2017/02/ASSC-2017-Andrew-Williams.pdf.

10. Tom Keatinge, "How the Islamic State Sustains Itself: The Importance of the War Economy in Syria and Iraq," *RUSI Analysis*, August 29, 2014, https://rusi.org/commentary/how-islamic-state-sustains-itself-importance-war-economy-syria-and-iraq.

11. Rachel Kreisman, "Raqqa and the Oil Economy of ISIS," *The Atlantic Council*, May 15, 2017, http://www.atlanticcouncil.org/blogs/syriasource/raqqa-and-the-oil-economy-of-isis.

12. Financial Action Task Force, *Financing of the Terrorist Organization Islamic State in Iraq and the Levant (ISIL)*, 14. www.fatf-gafi.org/topics/methodsandtrends/documents/financing-of-terrorist-organisation-isil.html.

13. Joby Warrick and Liz Sly, "U.S.-Led Strikes Putting a Financial Squeeze on the Islamic State," *Washington Post*, April 2, 2016, https://www.washingtonpost.com/world/national-security/us-led-strikes-putting-a-financial-squeeze-on-the-islamic-state/2016/04/02/e739a7be-f848-11e5-a3ce-f06b5ba21f33_story.html?utm_term=.42acb1c68517.

14. Ben Hubbard, "ISIS Promise of Statehood Falling Far Short, Ex-Residents Say," *New York Times*, December 1, 2015, https://www.nytimes.com/2015/12/02/world/middleeast/isis-promise-of-statehood-falling-far-short-ex-residents-say.html.

15. Daniel L. Glaser, remarks delivered at Chatham House, London, February 8, 2016; Jay Solomon and Benoit Faucon, "An Energy Mogul Becomes Entangled with the Islamic State," *Wall Street Journal*, May 8, 2016, https://www.wsj.com/articles/an-energy-mogul-becomes-entangled-with-islamic-state-1462734922.

16. Yeganeh Torbati, "Islamic State Yearly Oil Revenue Halved to $250 Million: U.S. Official," *Reuters*, May 11, 2016, http://www.reuters.com/article/us-mideast-crisis-islamic-state-revenue-idUSKCN0Y22CW; Benoit Faucon and Margaret Coker, "The Rise and Deadly Fall of Islamic State's Oil Tycoon," *Wall Street Journal*, April 24, 2016, https://www.wsj.com/articles/the-rise-and-deadly-fall-of-islamic-states-oil-tycoon-1461522313; "ISIS Revenues from Smuggled Oil Decline after Sharqat Liberation," *Iraqi News*, September 24, 2016, http://www.iraqinews.com/iraq-war/isis-revenues-from-smuggled-oil-decline-after-sharqat-liberation/.

17. "ISIS No Longer Controls Any Iraqi Oil," *Rudaw*, September 27, 2016, http://www.rudaw.net/english/kurdistan/270920164.

18. "Remarks by Assistant Secretary for Terrorist Financing Daniel Glaser at Chatham House," U.S. Department of the Treasury, February 8, 2016.

19. IHS Inc., "Islamic State Revenue Drops to $56 Million, IHS Says," April 18, 2016.

20. Ibid.

21. Patrick B. Johnston, Jacob N. Shapiro, Howard J. Shatz, Benjamin Bahney, Danielle F. Jung, Patrick Ryan, and Jonathan Wallace, *Foundations of the Islamic State: Management, Money, and Terror in Iraq, 2005–2010*, RR1192-DARPA (Santa Monica, CA: RAND Corporation, 2016).

22. Adam Szubin, "Remarks of Acting Under Secretary Adam Szubin on Countering the Financing of Terrorism at the Paul H. Nitze School of Advanced International Studies," U.S. Treasury, October 20, 2016.

23. Ayla Albayrak and Dana Ballout, "U.S., Turkey Step Up Border Campaign against Islamic State," *Wall Street Journal*, April 26, 2016, https://www.wsj.com/articles/u-s-turkey-step-up-border-campaign-against-islamic-state-1461684454.

24. James Burgess, "Scorched Earth Strategy? ISIS Blows Up Several Al Shaer Gas Field Installations," *OilPrice.com*, May 17, 2016, http://oilprice.com/Latest-Energy-News/World-News/Scorched-Earth-Strategy-ISIS-Blows-Up-Several-Al-Shaer-Gas-Field-Installations.html.

25. Anne Barnard, "Beyond Raqqa, an Even Bigger Battle to Defeat ISIS and Control Syria Looms," *New York Times*, June 10, 2017, https://www.nytimes.com/2017/06/10/world/middleeast/syria-raqqa-islamic-state-isis-deir-al-zour-iran-russia-united-states.html.

26. For an excellent guide to the notion of lootable resources, see, "Natural Resources: Definitions and Conceptual Issues" at www.peacebuildinginitiative.org/index818b.html?pageId=2097.

27. Financial Action Task Force, *Financing of the Terrorist Organization Islamic State in Iraq and the Levant (ISIL)*, 12. www.fatf-gafi.org/topics/methodsandtrends/documents/financing-of-terrorist-organisation-isil.html.

28. Ibid., 12.

29. Ibid.

30. Ibid., 17.

31. Dave Jolly, "ISIS Making Hundreds of Millions of Dollars through Extortion," *Godfather Politics*, December 7, 2015, http://godfatherpolitics.com/isis-making-hundreds-of-millions-of-dollars-through-extortion/.

32. Ibid.

33. Ibid.

34. Associated Press, "The Al-Qaeda Way: ISIS Resorts to Extortion Kidnapping for Money," *The Quint*, October 19, 2016, https://www.thequint.com/world/2016/10/19/the-al-qaeda-way-isis-resorts-to-extortion-kidnapping-for-money-mosul-iraq-foreign-donations.

35. Ibid.

36. Robert Tait, "ISIS' Half-a-Billion-Dollar Bank Heist Makes It World's Richest Terror Group," *The Telegraph*, June 14, 2014, http://www.telegraph.co.uk/news/worldnews/middleeast/iraq/10899995/ISIS-half-a-billion-dollar-bank-heist-makes-it-worlds-richest-terror-group.html.

37. Borzou Daragahi, "Biggest Bank Robbery That 'Never Happened'—$400m ISIS Heist," *Financial Times*, July 17, 2014, https://www.ft.com/content/0378d4f4-0c28-11e4-9080-00144feabdc0.

38. FATF, 12.

39. Ibid., 13.

40. Center for the Analysis of Terrorism, *ISIS Financing 2015*, 17.

41. Ibid., 4.

42. Ibid., 14.

43. Ibid., 12–13.

44. Matthew Rosenberg, Nicholas Kulish, and Steven Lee Myers, "Predatory Islamic State Wrings Money from Those It Rules," *New York Times*, November 29, 2015, https://www.nytimes.com/2015/11/30/world/middleeast/predatory-islamic-state-wrings-money-from-those-it-rules.html.

45. Ibid.

46. Center for the Analysis of Terrorism, *ISIS Financing 2015*, 15.

47. This paragraph draws heavily on Williams, *Criminals, Militias and Insurgents*.

48. Ibid., 118.

49. Ibid., 125.

50. Ibid., 127.

51. Ibid., 128–129.

52. Ibid., 144.

53. R. Kim Cragin and Phillip Padilla, "Old Becomes New Again: Kidnappings by Daesh and Other Salafi-Jihadists in the Twenty-First Century," *Studies in Conflict & Terrorism* 40, no. 8, (2016), 10–11.

54. "Inside the Islamic State Kidnap Machine," *BBC Magazine*, September 22, 2015, http://www.bbc.com/news/magazine-34312450.

55. Ibid.

56. Loretta Napoleoni, *Merchants of Men* (New York: Seven Stories Press, 2016), Kindle Edition Location 3157.

57. Ibid., Location 1803.

58. Ibid., Location 2164.

59. Ibid., Location 1803.

60. Center for Analysis of Terrorism, *ISIS Financing 2015*, 19.

61. "ISIS Collects Millions in Ransom for Abducted Christians," CBS News, February 22, 2016, http://www.cbsnews.com/news/isis-collects-millions-in-ransom-for-abducted-christians/.

62. Ibid.

63. Center for Analysis of Terrorism, *ISIS Financing 2015*, 19.

64. Quoted in Russell D. Howard, Marc D. Elliott, and Jonathan R. Prohov, *IS and Cultural Genocide: Antiquities Trafficking in the Terrorist State*, JSOU Report 16–11 (Florida: MacDill Air Force Base, November 2016), 34.

65. Ibid. See for a good discussion of this.

66. Center for Analysis of Terrorism, *ISIS Financing 2015*, 19.

67. E.A.J.H. Tijhuis, "The Trafficking Problem," in *Crime in the Art and Antiquities World*, ed. S. Manacorda and D. Chappell (Switzerland: Springer, 2011), 87–97.

68. Loretta Napoleoni, *Merchants of Men: How Jihadists and ISIS Turned Kidnapping and Refugee Trafficking into a Multi-Billion Dollar Business* (New York: Seven Stories Press, 2016), Kindle Edition Locations 3564–3570.

69. Ibid., Location 3563.

70. Ibid., Location 3569.

71. Christine Duhaime, "Terrorist Financing and the Islamic State," http://www.duhaimelaw.com/wp-content/uploads/2015/04/White-Paper-Terrorist-Financing-Methods-2.pdf.

72. FATF, 13.

73. Eric W. Schoon, "ISIS, Ideology, and the Illicit Drug Economy," *Political Violence @ a Glance*, July 24, 2015, http://politicalviolenceataglance.org/2015/07/24/isis-ideology-and-the-illicit-drug-economy/; see also, Colin P. Clarke, "Drugs & Thugs: Funding Terrorism through Narcotics Trafficking," *Journal of Strategic Security* 9, no. 3 (Fall 2016), 1–15; Colin P. Clarke, "ISIS Is So Desperate It's Turning to the Drug Trade," *Fortune*, July 25, 2017, http://fortune.com/2017/07/24/isis-mosul-defeated-news-territory-islamic-state-drugs/.

74. Dominic Dudley, "Why Defeat in Mosul Could Push Islamic State into Drug Trafficking," *Forbes*, November 4, 2016, https://www.forbes.com/forbes/welcome/?toURL=https://www.forbes.com/sites/dominicdudley/2016/11/04/isis-defeat-mosul-drug-trafficking/&refURL=https://www.google.com/&referrer=https://www.google.com/.

75. Giacomo Persi Paoli and Jacopo Bellasio, *Against the Rising Tide: An Overview of the Growing Criminalisation of the Mediterranean Region*, RAND Europe, January 26, 2017.

76. Rukmini Callimachi and Lorenzo Tondo, "Scaling Up a Drug Trade, Straight through ISIS Turf," *New York Times*, September 13, 2016, https://www.nytimes.com/2016/09/14/world/europe/italy-morocco-isis-drug-trade.html.

77. Frederick Deknatel, "New Drug Routes through Lawless Libya Raise Questions about ISIS' Role," *World Politics Review*, September 23, 2016, http://www.worldpoliticsreview.com/trend-lines/20011/new-drug-routes-through-lawless-libya-raise-questions-about-isis-role.

78. Barbie Latza Nadeau, "Italian Mob Trades Weapons for Looted Art from ISIS in Libya," *Daily Beast*, October 18, 2016, http://www.thedailybeast.com/italian-mob-trades-weapons-for-looted-art-from-isis-in-libya.

79. Tess Owen, "The Islamic State May Have Gotten Caught Smuggling a Huge Shipment of Opiates to Libya," *Vice News*, June 7, 2016, https://news.vice.com/article/the-islamic-state-may-have-gotten-caught-smuggling-a-huge-shipment-of-opiates-to-libya.

80. On cocaine trafficking, see Tom Porter, "Cocaine Funding ISIS: Drug Smuggling Profits Islamic-State-Linked Jihadists in North Africa," *International Business Times*, November 20, 2014, http://www.ibtimes.co.uk/cocaine-funding-isis-drug-smuggling-profits-islamic-state-linked-jihadists-north-africa-1475824; on cannabis, see Asharq Al-Awsat, "ISIS Resorts to Selling Drugs in Iraq, Syria For Funding," April 26, 2017, https://english.aawsat.com/theaawsat/news-middle-east/isis-resorts-selling-drugs-iraq-syria-funding.

81. "'Jihad Pills' Found by Dutch and Italian Police," BBC, May 10, 2017, http://www.bbc.com/news/world-europe-39870180; see also, Mirren Gidda, "Drugs in War: What Is Captagon, the 'Jihad Pill' Used by Islamic State Militants?" *Newsweek*, May 12, 2017, http://www.newsweek.com/drugs-captagon-islamic-state-jihad-war-amphetamines-saudi-arabia-608233.

82. Ben Crabtree, "The Nexus of Conflict and Illicit Drug Trafficking—Syria and the Wider Region," The Global Initiative against Transnational Organized Crime, November 27, 2016.

83. Chavala Madlena and Radwan Mortada, "Syria's Speed Freaks, Jihad Junkies, and Captagon Cartels," *Foreign Policy*, November 19, 2015.

84. Renad Mansour, "ISIS and the New War Economy" (London: Royal Institute for International Affairs, June 8, 2017).

85. Ibid.

86. Ibid.

87. Ibid.

88. Ibid.

89. Ibid.

90. Benjamin Bahney, Howard J. Shatz, Carroll Ganier, Renny McPherson, and Barbara Sude, *An Economic Analysis of the Financial Records of al-Qa'ida in Iraq* (Santa Monica, CA: RAND Corp., 2010); for more microlevel data on the group's financial bureaucracy, see Benjamin W. Bahney et al., "Insurgent Compensation: Evidence from Iraq," *American Economic Review* 103, no. 3 (2013), 518–522.

91. Howard J. Shatz, "To Defeat the Islamic State, Follow the Money," *Politico*, September 10, 2014, http://www.politico.com/magazine/story/2014/09/to-defeat-isil-follow-the-money-110825.

92. Janine Davidson and Emerson Brooking, "ISIS Hasn't Gone Anywhere—And It's Getting Stronger," Council on Foreign Relations, Defense in Depth, July 24, 2014.

93. Mariam Karouny, "In Northeast Syria, Islamic State Builds a Government," Reuters, September 4, 2014, http://www.reuters.com/article/us-syria-crisis-raqqa-insight-idUSKBN0GZ0D120140904.

94. Rosenberg, Kulish, and Myers, "Predatory Islamic State Wrings Money from Those It Rules."

95. As one of the authors has previously referenced, see Colin P. Clarke, *Terrorism, Inc.: The Financing of Terrorism, Insurgency and Irregular Warfare* (Santa Barbara, CA: ABC-CLIO), 2015; see also, Megan A. Stewart, "What's So New about the Islamic State's Governance?" *Monkey Cage* (blog), *Washington Post*, October 7, 2014, https://www.washingtonpost.com/news/monkey-cage/wp/2014/10/07/whats-so-new-about-the-islamic-states-governance/.

96. "The Anatomy of ISIS How the 'Islamic State' Is Run, from Oil to Beheadings," CNN, September 18, 2014, http://www.cnn.com/2014/09/18/world/meast/isis-syria-iraq-hierarchy/index.html.

97. Patrick B. Johnston and Colin P. Clarke, "Can the Islamic State Survive Financially?" *Lawfare*, May 14, 2017, https://www.lawfareblog.com/can-islamic-state-survive-financially.

98. Daniel Benjamin quoted in Rosenberg, Kulish, and Myers, "Predatory Islamic State Wrings Money from Those It Rules," *New York Times*, November 29, 2015, https://www.nytimes.com/2015/11/30/world/middleeast/predatory-islamic-state-wrings-money-from-those-it-rules.html.

CHAPTER 4

Da'esh and Al-Qaida in Europe

Rollie Lal

Da'esh in Europe is a wide-ranging network of terrorists operating to fund and organize terror attacks both inside Europe and in Iraq and Syria. The attackers in the majority of cases have been citizens or residents of European countries with roots in the Middle East and South Asia.[1] In contrast to terror groups in other regions, Da'esh in Europe is comprised of a disparate group of individuals who are not well unified or coordinated. Most are simply inspired by the same radical ideology.

Many Da'esh supporters in Europe have traveled to join the fight in Syria and then returned with a new vision. Some have been intercepted en route and prevented from entering the war front. Other adherents to Da'esh have simply remained in Europe to uphold the goals of the group there, without ever venturing to the battlefield. However, most have dealt in illegal activities to support their goals. Without connection to a unified organizational structure, many Da'esh supporters in Europe resort to small-scale drug trafficking and welfare fraud to support themselves. More extreme criminals with experience in the organized crime arena are valuable Da'esh recruits who bring skills in crime and violence as part of the package.

Ultimately, the goal of the attackers is more amorphous than that of Da'esh in Iraq and Syria. While Da'esh supporters in Iraq and Syria are fighting to conquer territory and claim the region as their caliphate, Da'esh in Europe has little direction for its ire. Attackers equip themselves in Europe with anything available: bombs, guns, cars, trucks, knives, and so forth in order to terrorize and destabilize Europe in any place. While some may dream of overthrowing Europe and replacing the governing structures with the caliphate, few likely believe that their attacks are closing in on that goal. Rather, they feel that creating terror and chaos in these Western countries is a worthy goal in itself.

Much of this resentment stems from a disenchantment with their adoptive countries. After two, three, or more generations in Belgium, France, the United Kingdom, or elsewhere, many Muslims are not yet integrated into the larger society. Both the Muslim communities and the "native" communities have strong tendencies to segregate themselves. Over time, this has led to a Muslim community whose members no longer feel a legitimate claim to their country of origin, but who are not yet accepted in their adoptive country.[2] The hostility that has arisen from this sense of alienation is a rich source for Da'esh.[3] The Tsarnaev brothers responsible for the Boston marathon bombings were ethnic Chechens partially raised in Russia and Kyrgyzstan. The discrimination and alienation their family faced in these countries and the U.S. may have been part of the attraction to radical Islam.[4] According to Iris Oppelaar, Chechens in Moscow recruit from Central Asian communities, on building sites or mosques.[5] The Chechen recruiters approach individuals with offers of funding to go to Syria. As the migrant workers are generally facing financial difficulties, they provide ripe pickings.

Individuals who are dysfunctional with a criminal bent or people who simply hate their country of residence are able to channel their sentiment into a ready ideology packaged by Da'esh. Critically, immigrant communities face higher unemployment rates and are incarcerated at higher rates—a situation that has led to a fertile environment for terrorism recruitment. Inmates share their extremist ideology with newcomers and pass on terrorism contacts as well. Prisons in Belgium, France, Spain, and the United Kingdom have taken petty criminals and returned them to the streets of Europe as hardened supporters of Da'esh and Al-Qaida.[6]

BLURRED LINES OF DA'ESH AND AL-QAIDA IN EUROPE

While Da'esh has come to the forefront in major attacks that have occurred in Europe in recent years, it does not have exclusive domain in the terror arena. Al-Qaida remains a force to be dealt with in Europe and has an organized infrastructure separate from Da'esh. The number and frequency of terrorist attacks in Europe have increased since 2015, and responsibility for attacks is sometimes taken by Al-Qaida rather than Da'esh, complicating an already dispersed terror situation. Violent attacks have spread across the continent. Belgium, Germany, Sweden, and the United Kingdom have sustained several attacks, many of which may have only been inspired by Da'esh or Al-Qaida, rather than coordinated by them.

While Da'esh and Al-Qaida have made clear statements regarding their animosity to and competition with each other, the two organizations have much in common in their European operations. The role of the two organizations in inspiring attacks in Europe, as well as the illicit methods of funding and supporting the attackers, is almost indistinguishable. The spectacular 2015 attack on *Charlie Hebdo* in Paris was planned and funded to the tune of $20,000 by Al-Qaida in the Arabian Peninsula (AQAP).[7] However, the foot soldiers conducting the attack were French citizens of Algerian descent, and one claimed allegiance to Da'esh. Mohamed Lahouaiej-Bouhlel conducted the attack in Nice by commandeering a truck to mow down pedestrians in support of Da'esh. However, a search of his computer revealed photos of Da'esh fighters, Osama bin Laden, and the *Charlie Hebdo* attack.[8] While the terror organizations may draw clear lines between themselves, individuals fighting for Islamic jihad in Europe perceive a blurred line, if one exists at all.

STRATEGY: KILL ANY DISBELIEVER

The pattern to the violence indicates increasing complexity in terms of strategy and operations. The use of inspiration instead of explicit direction now allows terror attacks to take place seemingly from nowhere. Da'esh followers who have been frustrated by their inability to arrive at the war zone in Syria can still join in the fight as respected terrorists inside the Da'esh community, even without military training. Leaders inside Da'esh simply expanded the fight by indicating that individuals and groups should kill any disbelievers. The propaganda magazine *Rumiyah* gives detailed advice on how to undertake these killings. "One need not be a military expert or a martial arts master, or even own a gun or rifle in order to carry out a massacre or to kill and injure several disbelievers and terrorize an entire nation."[9] This has had the effect of moving the battle from Afghanistan, Iraq, and Syria to Europe. Thus, individuals residing in Europe do not need to travel to the war zone to contribute to the fight. They can operate close to home. The increased hostility toward Muslims in Europe has the added benefit of assisting in their recruitment. The strategy allows for unexpected attacks in any location, increasing the impact on civilian populations accustomed to a relatively peaceful and organized daily life. The massive attacks on France indicate that Da'esh has been effective in bringing the war zone to the continent. The November 2015 Paris attacks that killed 130 included a suicide bombing at a stadium, as well as coordinated explosions and shootings at other locations. The July 2016 Bastille Day attack in Nice that killed 86 was undertaken by a single Tunisian-born French citizen driving a lorry into crowds of revelers.

Law enforcement was unable to predict these massive attacks, and due to the political landscape of Europe, they faced severe obstacles in tracking the terrorists afterward. Da'esh operates in Europe across borders, and so Salah Abdeslam, one of those responsible for the Paris attacks, quickly fled across the border into Belgium. He was assisted in escaping by his friend Mohamed Abrini, a man involved in the 2016 bombings in Brussels that killed 32. Open national borders allow Da'esh militants to slip across country boundaries with ease to conduct attacks. At the same time, security forces that are nationally based create a cumbersome landscape for information sharing. In other words, terrorists have the upper hand.

The directive also allows for extremely decentralized decision making and the ability of Da'esh to claim responsibility for almost any attack. The effect is both chilling and headache inducing. Tactically, Da'esh is similarly advantaged. Running on shoestring budgets, terrorists have constructed suicide bombs, commandeered vehicles for road attacks, and shot civilians. In contrast, security forces in Belgium, France, and the United Kingdom are forced to be on the defensive, patrolling streets and underground stations waiting for an attacker to become visible. Because Europe is not a war zone, governments can only take the initiative in tracking and arresting individuals with suspect motives and activities. As a result, Da'esh operatives usually appear to be normal civilians until the moment of attack.

TERRORISTS OR CRIMINALS?

Da'esh in Europe has a strong interest in criminal activities, however, that could allow authorities to track and inhibit their progress. The group relies on a diverse income stream including drug revenues, weapons trafficking, human trafficking, petty theft, social welfare fraud, VAT fraud, passport fraud, trafficking in archaeological artifacts, and bank fraud. In many cases, the traffickers may not be in the direct employ of terrorist groups such as Da'esh and sometimes may be unaware of the terror connection. In the case of the Bakraoui brothers responsible for the Brussels attacks in 2016, their passport and documents were provided by a Bulgarian criminal network. According to Belgian officials, the Bulgarians may not be so helpful to them any longer, now that their terrorist goals are clear.[10] To avoid this complication, Da'esh is now often using cars and guns already in their possession.

Inside Europe, terror groups have turned to small-time drug dealing to garner income. The low costs of bombing, shooting, and vehicle attacks have meant that a surprisingly small amount of criminal activity is enough to sustain most terror initiatives. Salah Abdeslam, a café owner in Molenbeek, Belgium, and one of those responsible for the 2015 Paris attacks, sold drugs from the café and simultaneously pocketed €19,000 in unemployment benefits from the Belgian government.[11] Amedy Coulibaly and the Kouachi brothers undertook low-cost coordinated attacks in Paris on a kosher grocery and the *Charlie Hebdo* offices using small arms. Their affiliations were mixed—Coulibaly had pledged to Da'esh and the Kouachi brothers to AQAP.[12] The rise of lone-wolf attacks and the lack of coherent line of command to the attackers have made tracking people and their funding incredibly complex. The inefficiency in attempting to trace such minute amounts of cash has led officials to change their strategy. According to Belgian officials, "Before, we were looking to take away funding from the terror networks. But now that the lone wolf attack is more popular, we are finding the links between people through their money. For example, Salah Abdeslam used a prepaid credit card, so we were able to track him. We can map and link people." Moreover, the lone-wolf attackers' lack of structure is also their weakness. "These organizations are not so organized, they didn't have a strategy for financing the attack, and they didn't care if they were tracked. In Paris, Abaaoud was on the run and he got a transfer from Brussels through his niece. This is how he was tracked. It was not well thought through. He didn't have enough cash with him, so he was caught."[13]

However, as the illegal product must be smuggled through militant-held territory, Da'esh or Al-Qaida profits from taxing the movement of the goods that traverse it. In this way, the traffickers can plausibly deny their connection to terror, and the terror groups can deny involvement in the sales of drugs, while both profit from the relationship. According to an Italian Treasury official, the taxing of others' illicit activities is well documented. "In the case of Somali hijackings of vessels, while al-Shabaab was not a part of the hijacking, they still received part of the payoff. Similarly, Da'esh and Al-Qaida are not organizing the sale of archaeological goods abroad. They are simply taxing the goods being smuggled. Either legal or illegal; they take their cut."[14]

While Da'esh has focused its attacks on Western Europe, its operations include members of North African origin, as well as experienced criminals from Balkan organized crime groups. The diversity of the individuals involved in the European terror and criminal network makes tracking Da'esh's activity particularly difficult.

DRUG TRAFFICKING

Of Da'esh's income streams, illegal drugs alone are a treasure trove for traffickers. Europeans spend approximately €24 billion per year on illegal drugs. Of this, an estimated €9.3 billion goes to cannabis, €6.8 billion to heroin, and €5.7 billion is spent on cocaine.[15] Amphetamines, ecstasy, and other drugs make up the remainder. Strong hubs for the trade exist, with the Netherlands and Spain taking the lead in trafficking cannabis and cocaine, and Belgium and the Netherlands leading in ecstasy and amphetamines. The ports of Antwerp and Rotterdam are main transit points.

CANNABIS

Cannabis remains the main drug of choice in Europe, and as such is a straightforward source of income for Da'esh. Along the Balkan route, Da'esh is involved in the production and distribution of cannabis after seizing control of existing organized crime assets.

The Case of Lazarat

In 2014 the town of Lazarat in Albania was at the center of drug operations, growing almost €5.9 billion in cannabis—Europe's largest producer. Albania's application to enter the European Union (EU) was denied based on the drug and disorder situation multiple times. For years the police near Lazarat feared entering the town, as the criminals were better armed than local law enforcement. In June 2014, the government made a more concerted effort. The interior ministry told residents to stay indoors as 800 police officers swept through with helicopters and armored personnel carriers. The gangsters defended the booty with rocket-propelled grenades, heavy mortars, and machine guns, but ultimately the police destroyed half a million plants and seized 102 tons of marijuana.[16]

In the aftermath of the spectacular raid, the marijuana economy returned. As a primary source of income for the locals, there was little other option. In Albania, 1 kg drug sells for €100 to 200, but in Italy the price rises to €1,500.[17] According to a local grower, the police takes 20 percent to look away.[18] The cannabis industry in Albania is sustained only by outside support; there is little demand for the drug inside the country. To reach the lucrative markets of Europe, Albanian marijuana travels out north through Montenegro, south through Greece, or west to Italy.

In the years since the seemingly effective raid, Da'esh militants have seized production and trade in cannabis, recruiting workers from the economically devastated area. Adding insult to injury, cocaine and heroin are now also produced in Albania and Kosovo.

As a neighboring country with a strong interest in taming the trade, Italy works with the government of Albania. Italy's paramilitary force flies over Albanian territory to inform the Albanian government of the coordinates of the cannabis plantations.[19] According to Italy's top prosecutor, Franco Roberti, Da'esh and the Italian mafia cooperate in smuggling hashish into Europe.[20] The cannabis originates in Morocco, traveling through Algeria and Tunisia to Tobruk in Libya. Da'esh is able to profit from the sale of the hashish over a part of that route. Roberti states that the Italian mafia nets more than $32 billion per year from all drug trafficking.

For distribution, Albanian cannabis travels by air to Italy, where the Italian and Albanian mafia work together to move the product to demand cities. While Albania provides a critical source of cannabis into Europe, the seizures from other sources indicate that the trade is flourishing across the continent. Fouad Belkacem, a dual Moroccan Belgian citizen and the leader of the terror group Sharia4Belgium, is believed to have brought 5.3 tons of cannabis from Morocco into Belgium.[21] Salah Abdeslam, a Belgian participant in the Paris attacks, was dealing hashish and other drugs from his café. In October 2016, Spanish police intercepted a boat with 20 tons of hashish headed to Libya from Turkey. The crew consisted of 11 Ukrainians and 1 Uzbek. The police noted that in many counter-hashish operations, nationals of Morocco, Spain, and Syria are netted. Some of the intercepted boats carried drugs, the rest carried weapons.[22] The mixture of arms and drugs destined for a location harboring militias indicated to the authorities the terrorist nature of the traffickers.

From 2013 to 2015, Italian authorities intercepted 20 ships carrying 280 metric tons of hashish, worth $3.2 billion, headed for Libya.[23] The ultimate destination for the cargo was not Libya, which does not have the appetite for hashish. The drug shipments were found to travel overland from Libya through Egypt and into the Balkans. They crossed Da'esh-held territory, where authorities found they were taxed by the terror group.

CAPTAGON

Illegal drugs can play a broader role within terror groups than simply as moneymakers. Amphetamine-type stimulants such as Captagon allow fighters to go into combat situations with an expanded sense of invulnerability, impaired judgment, and less fear. Users ultimately feel impervious to pain, leading to its nickname the "jihadi drug."[24] However, the drug was not initially intended as a combat-support upper. Captagon is a brand name for fenethylline, a drug that relaxes the muscles around the lungs and can treat breathing problems. As an alertness-enhancing drug, fenethylline is also prescribed for attention deficit hyperactivity disorder (ADHD). For decades, fenethylline was used by athletes as a performance enhancement drug in West Germany.

As realization dawned that Captagon was highly addictive, it became an internationally controlled substance. Because the drug had legitimate medicinal purposes, its use spread through Saudi Arabia and other countries of the Middle East. Now Captagon has become the drug of choice for Da'esh. The stimulant is useful in both steeling Da'esh militants for missions and for filling the coffers of the group with cash. Produced in Syria, the small white pills are transported inside the war zones, and through the country to waiting consumers in Europe. In January–February 2017, French officials seized a total of 135 kg of Captagon at Paris' Charles de Gaulle airport on two occasions. The tablets originated in Lebanon and were headed through the Czech Republic and Turkey to Saudi Arabia.[25] While this was a first for France, a Captagon laboratory and hundreds of thousands of pills were also discovered in the Netherlands in April 2017. As a primary export of Da'esh in Syria, the seizure heightened fears that the group is spreading its tentacles throughout Europe. However, Syria is not the only country churning out Captagon pills. According to the European Monitoring Centre for Drugs and Drug Addiction (EMCDDA), Bulgaria and Turkey are prime producers with export destinations in the Middle East.[26] The high profits and ease of production have made Captagon a critical resource for terrorist criminal enterprises operating in Europe.

HEROIN

Heroin trafficking remains a major source of income for Da'esh operations across Asia to Europe. According to the UN Office on Drugs and Crime (UNODC), Afghanistan remains the source of 95 percent of the global supply of opium. Since the start of U.S. military operations in Afghanistan, the drug has only boomed in production, as the Taliban funds its insurgency through sales of heroin. While Da'esh is primarily in competition with the Taliban as a terror group, it is able to skim off profits from the transit of the heroin produced by the Taliban. The relationship between the drug and the terrorist groups has become closely intertwined, with the drug traffickers providing weapons and funding, while the Taliban provides protection for the drug routes, fields, laboratories, and trafficking.[27] As the heroin transits through Da'esh-controlled territory in Iraq and Syria, Da'esh is able to pocket payments as well.[28] However, Da'esh is no longer limiting its profits to a tax on the drugs as they pass through. According to Iraqi sources, Da'esh has also been producing heroin at the laboratories of the University of Mosul and other Iraqi areas under Da'esh control.[29] Iraqi forces have burned opium poppy fields in Iraq to drain Da'esh's profits, while news reports indicate that the majority of individuals involved in the Iraqi production were Afghan nationals working for Da'esh.[30]

Heroin from Afghanistan and Da'esh-controlled regions is often transported through Iran into Turkey for processing. In the next stage, between 50 and 60 metric tons of the heroin transit Greece and Serbia along the Balkan Route. Most of the heroin moved through this region then transits into other countries in the EU.

Inside Afghanistan and Pakistan, the Haqqani Network and the Taliban control much of the heroin production and trade, yet Da'esh also controls production in Nangarhar Province. In this regard, it may be competing with the other two terrorist criminal enterprises. Different aspects of the heroin trade allow the Haqqani Network to profit from precursor chemicals and the Taliban to produce the heroin. According to the United Nations, farmers in Afghanistan produce about 3,300 tons of raw opium. Once processed, the heroin moves into Pakistan, where its progress is not tracked, and into Iran. Iran carries the weight of intercepting the drugs, and according to a U.S. State Department report, Iran has intercepted around a third of all heroin seized globally since 2007.[31] The head of Iran's police anti-narcotics squad stresses, "For you, drug smuggling is an illicit business. For us, it is war. A war in which we protect Europe, the destination of all that rubbish. How does the West want to fight terrorism when it doesn't target drug smugglers?"[32]

COCAINE

Colombian cocaine finds its way into Europe via multiple routes. Authorities from Spain and Morocco jointly uncovered a trafficking network operating across three continents. The cocaine originated in Colombia, was transferred to a Moroccan fishing vessel near Cabo Verde, and was intercepted off the coast of the Western Sahara.[33] The group's headquarters were in Spain.

The Albanian arm of Da'esh has become a powerful link between organized crime and Da'esh in Europe via its networks in Albania, Kosovo, and Macedonia. The former leader of the Albanian group, Muhaxheri, recruited Albanians to join jihad and was designated a global terrorist by the U.S. Department of State in 2014. He worked at a NATO training camp in Afghanistan and then returned to Kosovo. He was killed in Syria in mid-2017, but only after strengthening the ties of Albania to Da'esh. According to a former military intelligence officer, "There is no doubt that the best recruits for the jihadists are those that were in the mafia. Already schooled in violence, they even pay their own way because the dirty money that the jihadists then gain when they recruit mafia recruits helps to further swell the jihadist coffers."[34]

Drugs form the basis of terrorist criminal enterprises in Belgium and often provide a small but necessary income for terror cells. At the same time, larger criminal syndicates based in Morocco and the Netherlands operate a strong cocaine trade through Amsterdam and Antwerp. In recent years the demand for cocaine has boomed in Antwerp, so it is now considered the cocaine capital of Europe. Drug tests of the water supply indicate that the city releases the most cocaine into wastewater of any European city. However, while Antwerp is a destination, it is also a transit point for the drugs. The drug is smuggled in through the port of Antwerp, hidden in cargos of marble slabs and wooden beams in shipping containers.[35] There, the Albanian mafia enters the picture, shipping the rest of the cocaine into the United Kingdom.[36] Much of the drug is brought in containers from Colombia, Ecuador, and Venezuela. As its coffers swell, Da'esh recruits from the Albanian mafia, and many other Albanians are increasingly joining Da'esh.[37]

Cocaine finds another route into Europe via West Africa. Approximately $2 billion of cocaine transits West Africa en route to Europe, according to the UNODC.[38] Boko Haram is a major player in this trade route, offering logistics and security protection to traffickers bringing the product from South America through Cameroon, Chad, and Nigeria.[39] From West Africa, cocaine is smuggled into Portugal and Spain, as well as Belgium, France, Italy, the Netherlands, and the United Kingdom.[40]

A critical factor connecting the drug trade and radicalization is the prison system. In Belgium and France, the penalty for drug use or dealing is incarceration. Muslim youth imprisoned for drug offences find that the prisons are well primed for recruitment and radicalization.[41] Many perpetrators of attacks were later found to have spent time in prisons, including Cherif Kouachi, Amedy Coulibaly, and Mohammed Merah.[42] According to EU counterterror chief Gilles de Kerchove, "We know that prisons are a massive incubator for radicalization." Resentment toward hostile treatment of Islam through suspicion of religious behavior and poor access to halal food creates an atmosphere that draws criminals toward radicalization and political violence.

HUMAN AND OIL SMUGGLING

The continuing conflict in Afghanistan, Iraq, and Syria has provided a lucrative profession for Da'esh and its criminal faces. The devastated areas struck by military offensives have created a refugee surge of massive proportions. And in the shadow of this outflow is a thriving trade in smuggled oil. The millions of people fleeing bloodshed are all traveling west, with an ultimate goal of reaching Germany, Sweden, or the United Kingdom. If unable to reach these final destinations, they are at least attempting to arrive somewhere in Western Europe. In 2014, 170,000 people were picked up by Italian authorities trying to cross from Libya into Europe through the Mediterranean Sea.[43] However, the route is not easy, nor is it free. This is where criminal gangs enter the equation.

Once refugees enter Turkey, they pay smugglers anywhere from $1,750 to $4,500 just to reach as far as Albania or Greece.[44] Da'esh profits from the immigration, taking a cut of this along the way.[45] There are two primary routes exiting Turkey, the Eastern Balkan route and the Western Balkan route. The eastern route travels over land from the border of Turkey into Bulgaria but requires crossing a border fence between the nations. The Western Balkan route goes over sea in what are known as "death balloons" or inflatable boats. This route traverses Albania or Greece into Macedonia and then on to Serbia. The two routes meet again there, and the refugees attempt to go forward into Hungary and Western Europe.[46]

A robust illicit trade in oil is supported by the flow of trafficked humans. Reports indicate that while human smugglers are charging $2,128 to smuggle a person from Tunisia to Libya, 2.6 million liters of smuggled oil is entering Tunisia daily moved by the same mafia.[47]

The disarray and general attention to human trafficking have led to opportunities for small-scale oil smugglers. Many companies want the cheap oil available by smugglers. These consumers provide business for trading companies who can charge large markups for the oil. Among other routes, oil is smuggled to Italy from Iran, Iraq, and Syria through Turkey. According to an Italian Treasury official, "All the oil from Syria and Iraq can't just disappear. It also goes to Western countries."[48]

WELFARE BENEFITS AND FRAUD

Social welfare benefits have risen as an unexpected source of income for terrorist groups and terrorist individuals inside the EU. The availability of easy income from the government has created an incentive for members of Da'esh and Al-Qaida to sign up for a mix of both legal and fraudulent welfare benefits in order to support terrorist activities. In 2013, British preacher Anjem Choudary was filmed urging his followers to stop working and claim unemployment benefits in order to better plot jihad against non-Muslims, a "Jihad Seeker's Allowance." He claimed that the welfare payments are a form of jizya, or tax, on non-Muslims. For years, he had been claiming welfare benefits in the United Kingdom amounting to $40,000 per year to support his family, including four children.[49] He assisted in establishing the group Sharia4Belgium in Belgium and continued drawing followers to fight in Syria and launch jihad in Europe.[50] In 2015, he was arrested for recruiting people into Da'esh.

According to CTIF-CFI, "In Belgium, an unemployed man can receive 800 Euros per month indefinitely. If five guys band together, they can receive 4000 Euros, and they can do a lot with that. But it's purely administrative, civil servants do this."[51] As a result of their status as a domestic–civil affairs issue, the benefits receive minimal oversight from a counterterrorism perspective. Vehicle assaults on pedestrians by Da'esh reveal the minimal levels of cash needed to carry out an attack. The CTIF-CFI noted that rather than directly financing an attack, social welfare benefits provided the Paris and Brussels attackers with "livelihoods and indirect support for their terrorist activities."[52]

POLICY OPTIONS

Currently, European governments are working rapidly to counter the threat from the financial angle as well as through counterterror operations. The attacks of 2001 pushed the importance of terror finance to the front of the agenda, and governments began to view money laundering and terror finance as related categories. In more recent years, the decentralized nature of new networks has changed the way European governments approach the threat. Earlier, governments were looking to deny funding for terror networks. While this is still a goal, the rise of the lone-wolf attacker requires new thinking.[53] The government of Belgium is increasingly investigating and discovering the links between people by following the money. It found that Salah Abdeslam used a prepaid credit card, which was trackable. Using information such as prepaid cards, officials are able to map and link people in a network. Surprisingly, officials in Belgium note that the terrorists inspired by Da'esh lacked a strategy for financing—they do not necessarily care if they are being tracked. According to the CTIF-CFI, "In Paris, Abaaoud was on the run, he got a transfer from Brussels through his niece, and this is how he was tracked. It was not well thought through; he didn't have enough cash with him, so he was caught."[54]

However, coordination between intelligence agencies is still quite basic and leaves much to be desired. While there is much cooperation between Belgium and the United States for instance, glitches can occur when there is lack of agreement on the operational goals. In the past, when Belgium gave the Pentagon information regarding a target, the Pentagon proceeded to bomb it. However, the collateral information from the target site was then classified so that U.S. and European prosecutors did not have access to this critical information. This type of uncoordinated attack can be counterproductive, and the United States should undertake a more coherent strategy in dealing with targets. It is clear that European governments need to have access to the material discovered from these targets, such as cell phones, documents, and passports. Phone numbers and messages on the phones can be critical in cracking open networks.

Similarly, coordination inside Europe can be found to be lacking. Countries patrolling the Mediterranean Sea for smuggled refugees often encounter vessels holding smuggled oil instead. However, as their intention is to locate refugees, the smuggled oil is left unhindered.[55] These bureaucratic holes in the policing of common areas must be addressed.

The Internet provides another arena for future cooperation. Drug smuggling, recruitment, and communication are increasingly enabled by the Internet and the Dark Web. Inside Europe, extremists use the Internet to disseminate information that legitimates their actions, bolstering the ideological side of their operations.[56] This creates a powerful advantage for terrorist criminal networks if governments do not take the initiative to equally emphasize the criminal elements of extremist operations. Exposing the dual nature of terrorist criminal enterprises to supporters would undercut the force of their ideological communications.

In terms of domestic policy, European governments have their hands full as well. This issue of social welfare benefits is a difficult one for governments to face, politically. Whereas generous welfare benefits are supported as a mode of reducing poverty and integrating immigrants as well as criminals back into society, the tool has clearly been abused by individuals working for Da'esh and Al-Qaida. More stringent regulations on who can receive benefits and stronger oversight on abuse of benefits are necessary. The length of time of benefits available should also be reconsidered. Currently, the law is lax, and many individuals have been found to be receiving benefits while trafficking drugs or while residing in another country. Greater manpower to conduct oversight will be necessary to strengthen controls against abuse by terror and criminal groups.

Critical for curbing the recruitment of terrorists and criminals across Europe, European governments need to consider options to better integrate Muslim communities into the broader society and economy. That will require changes in how education and employment are provided, as well as new approaches to forming national identity for disadvantaged minorities. These changes are not simple but have the possibility of limiting the threat from both criminal and terrorist activity across Europe.

NOTES

1. Akbar Ahmed, "Why Are European Muslims Joining ISIS?" *Huffington Post*, November 17, 2014, http://www.huffingtonpost.com/akbar-ahmed/why-are-european-muslims-_b_6175334.html.

2. Interviews with Muslim residents and citizens in Belgium, 2015.

3. Angel Rabasa and Cheryl Benard, *Eurojihad: Patterns of Islamist Radicalization and Terrorism in Europe* (New York: Cambridge University Press, 2015), 54.

4. Asel Kalybekova, "Kyrgyzstan: Boston Bombing Suspects' Hometown Skeptical," *Eurasianet*, April 22, 2013. http://www.eurasianet.org/node/66857.

5. Interview with Iris Oppelaar, researcher and author of "Central Asia and the Islamic State: The Russian Connection," August 29, 2017.

6. Rabasa and Benard, *Eurojihad*, 110–117.

7. Charlie Winter, "AQAP vs. ISIS: Who Was Really behind the Charlie Hebdo Attacks?" *Middle East Eye*, January 15, 2015, http://www.middleeasteye.net/columns/aqap-vs-isis-who-was-really-behind-charles-hebdo-692115745; Rukmini Callimachi and Jim Yardley, "From Amateur to Ruthless Jihadist in France," *New York Times*, January 17, 2015, https://www.nytimes.com/2015/01/18/world/europe/paris-terrorism-brothers-said-cherif-kouachi-charlie-hebdo.html. *Charlie Hebdo* attackers Cherif and Said Kouachi claimed allegiance to AQAP, while Amedy Coulibaly claimed allegiance to Islamic State.

8. "Attack on Nice: Who Was Mohamed Lahouaiej-Bouhlel?" BBC, August 19, 2016, http://www.bbc.com/news/world-europe-36801763.

9. Nick Gutteridge, "New Terror Tactic: ISIS Orders Western Jihadis to Become Serial Killers to Spread Fear," *Express*, October 6, 2016, http://www.express.co.uk/news/world/718279/Islamic-State-ISIS-propaganda-urges-Western-lone-wolf-jihadis-to-carry-out-knife-attacks.

10. Interviews with the Belgian Financial Intelligence Processing Unit (CTIF-CFI), June 28, 2017, Belgium.

11. Mark Maremont and Valentina Pop, "Terrorist Suspects in Europe Got Welfare Benefits While Plotting Attacks," *Wall Street Journal*, August 4, 2016, https://www.wsj.com/articles/terrorist-suspects-in-europe-got-welfare-benefits-while-plotting-attacks-1470350251.

12. Michael Pizzi, "From Lone Wolf to Wolf Packs, What Paris Says about a New Model of Terror," *Aljazeera.com*, January 13, 2015, http://america.aljazeera.com/articles/2015/1/13/paris-attacks-affiliation.html.

13. Interview with the CTIF-CFI, June 28, 2017.

14. Interview with official from the Department of Treasury of Italy, July 11, 2017.

15. European Monitoring Centre for Drugs and Drug Addiction (EMCDDA), *European Drug Report 2016: Trends and Developments*, 2016, http://www.emcdda.europa.eu/system/files/publications/2637/TDAT16001ENN.pdf.

16. Allan Hall and Dan Warburton, "ISIS Seizes £4bn GBP Drug Ring from the Mafia to Fund Its Brutal Terror Campaign," *Mirror*, January 16, 2016, http://www.mirror.co.uk/news/uk-news/isis-seizes-4bn-drug-ring-7191800; "Albanian

Cannabis Growers and 800 Police Battle in Lawless Village of Lazarat," *Guardian*, June 17, 2014, https://www.theguardian.com/world/2014/jun/17/albanian-cannabis-growers-800-police-battle-lazarat; Elvis Nabolli, "An Albanian War on Drugs," *Balkan Insight*, November 16, 2016, http://www.balkaninsight.com/en/article/an-albanian-war-on-drugs-11-15-2016.

17. Linda Pressly, "Europe's Outdoor Cannabis Capital," BBC News, December 1, 2016, http://www.bbc.com/news/magazine-38111945.

18. Ibid.

19. "Hash and Burn," *Economist*, September 22, 2016, http://www.economist.com/news/europe/21707556-albania-seeks-contain-spread-cannabis-plantations-hash-and-burn.

20. Steve Scherer, "Decriminalizing Cannabis Would Hurt Islamic State, Mafia-Italy Prosecutor," Reuters, April 18, 2016, http://www.reuters.com/article/us-italy-mafia-islamic-state-cannabis-idUSKCN0XF11D.

21. "Trafic de Drogue: Nouvelle Peine de Prison Pour Fouad Belkacem?" *7Sur7.be*, March 11, 2015, http://www.7sur7.be/7s7/fr/1502/Belgique/article/detail/2248050/2015/03/11/Trafic-de-drogue-nouvelle-peine-de-prison-pour-Fouad-Belkacem.dhtml.

22. "Spain Seizes Drugs Shipment Destined to Fund Terrorism," *The Local*, October 12, 2016, https://www.thelocal.es/20161012/spain-seizes-drugs-shipment-to-libya-in-global-operation.

23. Rukmini Callimachi and Lorenzo Tondo, "Scaling Up a Drug Trade, Straight through ISIS Turf," *New York Times*, September 13, 2016, https://www.nytimes.com/2016/09/14/world/europe/italy-morocco-isis-drug-trade.html.

24. Mirren Gidda, "Drugs in War: What Is Captagon, the 'Jihad Pill' Used by Islamic State Militants?" *Newsweek*, May 12, 2017, http://www.newsweek.com/drugs-captagon-islamic-state-jihad-war-amphetamines-saudi-arabia-608233.

25. Jenny Awford and Peter Allen, "Massive Shipment of Captagon—a 'Euphoria' Drug Used by ISIS Fanatics in Battle—Found at Paris' Charles de Gaulle Airport Sparking Fears of a New Terror Cell," *The Sun*, May 30, 2017, https://www.thesun.co.uk/news/3681894/massive-shipment-of-captagon-a-euphoria-drug-used-by-isis-fanatics-in-battle-found-at-pariss-charles-de-gaulle-airport-sparking-fears-of-a-new-terror-cell/.

26. "Bulgaria—Key Captagon Producer: EU Drug Markets Report," Sofia News Agency Novinite.com, January 31, 2013, http://www.novinite.com/articles/147429/Bulgaria+-+Key+Captagon+Producer%3A+EU+Drug+Markets+Report.

27. Keegan Hamilton, "The Golden Age of Drug Trafficking: How Meth, Cocaine, and Heroin Move around the World," *Vice News*, April 25, 2016, https://news.vice.com/article/drug-trafficking-meth-cocaine-heroin-global-drug-smuggling.

28. William Watkinson, "ISIS Could Make Billions from Heroin Trade to Mount Attacks against the West," *International Business Times*, December 1, 2015, http://www.ibtimes.co.uk/isis-could-make-billions-heroin-trade-mount-attacks-against-west-1531211.

29. Wassim Bassem, "Is Iraq Turning into a Drug-Producing Country?" *Al-Monitor*, January 2, 2017, http://fares.al-monitor.com/pulse/originals/2016/12/krystal-drug-iraq-narcotics-heroin.html.

30. Amr Ibraheem, "Iraqi Forces Burn ISIS Poppy Fields to Curtail Heroin and Opium Revenue," *Iraqi News*, October 5, 2016, http://www.iraqinews.com/iraq-war/iraqi-forces-burn-land-belong-isis-planted-opium-poppies/.

31. Hanne Coudere, "Tracing Heroin's Destructive Path from Afghan Poppy Fields to British Needles," *Vice News*, April 27, 2016, https://www.vice.com/en_us/article/from-afghan-poppy-fields-to-the-english-needle-the-heroin-trail.

32. Ibid.

33. Mimi Yagoub, "Spain and Morocco Bust Colombia Cocaine Trafficking Ring," *Insight Crime*, December 7, 2016, http://www.insightcrime.org/news-briefs/spain-and-morocco-bust-colombian-cocaine-trafficking-ring.

34. Hall and Warburton, "ISIS Seizes £4bn Drug Ring from the Mafia to Fund Its Brutal Terror Campaign."

35. Patrick Hill, "Gangs Overwhelm the Cocaine Capital of Europe That Used to Be Famed for Its Diamonds," *Mirror*, December 23, 2016, http://www.mirror.co.uk/news/world-news/gangs-overwhelm-cocaine-capital-europe-9508753.

36. "Albanians Are among the Biggest Traffickers of Heroin in Europe," Independent Balkan News Agency (IBNA), June 4, 2016, http://www.balkaneu.com/albanians-biggest-traffickers-heroin-europe/.

37. "Daesh Money Grows on Albanian Mafia Marijuana Trees," *Albawaba.com*, January 17, 2016, http://www.albawaba.com/editorchoice/daesh-money-grows-albanian-mafia-marijuana-trees-793992.

38. Daniel Wheeler, "Is Europe's Coke Habit Funding Terrorism?" *African Herald Express*, January 12, 2017, http://africanheraldexpress.com/blog8/2017/01/12/is-europes-coke-habit-funding-terrorism/.

39. Robert Rotberg, "The War of Drugs Is Fueling Islamist Terrorism," *Newsweek*, February 17, 2016, http://www.newsweek.com/war-drugs-fueling-islamist-terrorism-427716.

40. Christopher Woody, "Spanish and Moroccan Police Seized 5,700 Pounds of Cocaine in the Middle of a High Seas Trafficking Corridor," *Business Insider*, December 6, 2016, http://www.businessinsider.com/spanish-police-seize-cocaine-morocco-2016-12.

41. Patrick Hilsman, "How Decriminalizing Drugs Could Reduce Islamic Terrorism in France and Belgium," *Vice News*, March 23, 2016, https://www.vice.com/en_us/article/how-decriminalizing-drugs-could-reduce-islamic-terrorism-in-france-and-belgium.

42. Ibid.

43. Kathleen Caulderwood, "Drugs and Money in the Sahara: How the Global Cocaine Trade Is Funding North African Jihad," *IBT*, June 5, 2015, http://www.ibtimes.com/drugs-money-sahara-how-global-cocaine-trade-funding-north-african-jihad-1953419.

44. Simona Sikimic, "From Syria to Serbia: The Migrants' Balkan Backdoor," *Middle East Eye*, May 28, 2015, http://www.middleeasteye.net/news/syria-serbia-migrants-balkan-backdoor-1184791364#block-disqus-disqus-comments.

45. Interview with official from the Department of Treasury of Italy, July 11, 2017.

46. Sikimic, "From Syria to Serbia."

47. Javier Martin, "Libya, A Smuggling Hypermarket," *Euractiv.com*, June 15, 2017, https://www.euractiv.com/section/politics/news/libya-a-smuggling-hypermarket/.

48. Interview with official from the Department of Treasury of Italy, July 11, 2017.

49. Melanie Hall, "Muslim Preacher Urges Followers to Claim 'Jihad Seeker's Allowance,'" *Telegraph*, February 17, 2013, http://www.telegraph.co.uk/news/9875954/Muslim-preacher-urges-followers-to-claim-Jihad-Seekers-Allowance.html.

50. Vikram Dodd, "Anjem Choudary: A Hate Preacher Who Spread Terror in UK and Europe," *Guardian*, August 16, 2016, https://www.theguardian.com/uk-news/2016/aug/16/anjem-choudary-hate-preacher-spread-terror-uk-europe.

51. Interview with the CTIF-CFI, June 28, 2017, Belgium.

52. Mark Maremont and Valentina Pop, "Terrorist Suspects in Europe Got Welfare Benefits while Plotting Attacks," *Wall Street Journal*, August 4, 2016, https://www.wsj.com/articles/terrorist-suspects-in-europe-got-welfare-benefits-while-plotting-attacks-1470350251.

53. Interview with the CTIF-CFI, June 28, 2017, Belgium.

54. Ibid.

55. Ibid.

56. Rabasa and Benard, *Eurojihad*, 118.

CHAPTER 5

The Industry of Terror: Criminal Financing of the North Caucasus Insurgency

Yuliya Zabyelina

INTRODUCTION

With the abundance of studies on the terrorist insurgency in the North Caucasus and its ideological transformation,[1] the financial underpinnings of terrorism in the region remain poorly understood. The significance of terrorism financing, however, cannot be overstated. Like any other human enterprise, terrorist activity requires funding. Funds are needed to purchase weapons and supplies; provide training, propaganda materials, and financial incentives for recruits; and cover travel and other logistical expenses. There exists some consensus among both scholars and practitioners that the individuals engaged in terrorism or violent extremism often participate in organized or ordinary crime activities.[2] This crime–terror nexus, however, is not a static phenomenon. It may transform over time.

This chapter will discuss the dynamics of fund-raising through crime by the terrorist insurgency from the North Caucasus region since the 1990s with a focus on the activities of the Caucasus Emirate (CE)—a militant jihadist organization active in the region since 2007. The analysis herein demonstrates that the insurgency has continuously relied on all sorts of criminal activities, including drug trafficking, oil smuggling, and extortion rackets. While the first two revenue streams were significant during the first and the second Russo-Chechen wars, control over oil fields and drug trafficking routes significantly diminished with the brutal but rather effective counterinsurgency campaign led by the incumbent head of the Chechen Republic Ramzan Kadyrov. Faced with a lack of liquidity and being no longer able to control cross-border movements, CE leaders turned to exploit the local population through extortion of businesses, kidnapping, and other activities reminiscent of organized crime. By plaguing local businesses for protection payments, they reaffirmed control over certain territories, mainly in wooded areas and hard-to-access terrain, often striking mutually beneficial deals with the local authorities and the police. Being unable to run illicit businesses under Kadyrov, CE jamaats engaged in extortion rackets, often in collaboration with the location authorities. This caused an internal divide in the CE between those who continued working with the authorities and sought financial enrichment via economic crime and those who chose a more ideological and thus morally justifiable path in the fight against the enemies of Islam.

This split has opened an opportunity for Da'esh to establish a presence in the North Caucasus. Starting in November 2014, a group of commanders of the CE began publicly switching their allegiance to Da'esh. In this way, militant groups from the North Caucasus became once again integrated into the global jihadist revolutionary movement. This transformation provided them with access to foreign sources of funding, including the North Caucasian Diaspora and other kinds of support groups abroad. The new revenue streams are decentralized and inconsistent and shift based on the availability of economic resources and the progress of national and, more important, multilateral counterterrorism efforts.

FROM A CRIMINAL RACKET TO THE WAR FOR INDEPENDENCE

Chechens were well represented in the Soviet-era organized crime landscape. Their early activities included extortion and robbery of street traders, moving on to racketeering of larger enterprises and profiting from the sales of goods and services on the black market.[3] By the late 1980s, Chechen organized crime groups (OCGs) consolidated and developed into a well-organized and brutal *obschina* (community). They seized control over the illicit trade in foreign cars in Moscow's Yuzhnyi Port and considerably expanded racketeering activities. They also assumed a central role in hotel, entertainment, and gambling businesses.[4] This position owed a great deal to the fact that, unlike "Slavic" criminal groups, Chechens had much stricter lines of internal discipline and cohesion, often built around kinship and blood ties. They were also known for using excessive violence, which was often outsourced by the political elites or other criminal groups against their enemies. In addition, some members of Chechen OCGs did not stay in Moscow permanently. They were the so-called gastrolery—"touring" criminals. Secure refuge in Chechnya and other North Caucasian republics often made them inaccessible to law enforcement and rival OCGs, for whom traveling to Chechnya was a risky move in light of the region's sociopolitical, linguistic, and cultural dissimilarity with Russia.

When Moscow's predominantly "Slavic" OCGs nevertheless made progress in ousting some Chechen OCGs out of the capital (largely due to their close collaboration with the police), Chechens moved some of their activities to Russia's Far East and Western Europe with its members involved in various criminal activities ranging from automobile theft and human smuggling to trafficking in drugs and radiological materials.[5] When the first Russo-Chechen conflict started in 1994, some Chechen OCGs returned to Chechnya and joined the mounting separatist movement led by Major General Dzhokhar Dudayev.

The general environment of impunity and institutional hemorrhage of the post-Soviet transition was favorable for the appointment of individuals with criminal pasts to leading positions in the Chechen pro-independence movement. Some of them were closely associated with a well-known *vor v zakone* (thief-in-law) Khozh-Ahmed Nukhayev. He enjoyed considerable authority in criminal circles in Russia and other post-Soviet states as one of the founding members of the Lazanskaya gang serving as a liaison between the Chechen community in Moscow and Chechnya's political elites. In particular, he was responsible for directing *obschak* (criminal proceeds) from Chechen OCGs in Russia to Chechnya in support of the separatist movement.

The first Russo-Chechen War (1994–1996) left nothing but destruction and economic decay in its wake. During Aslan Maskhadov's regime (1997–2005) that followed the Dudayev administration, virtually nothing was done for the republic's economic and social revival. The newly proclaimed Chechen Republic of Ichkeria (ChRI; 1991–2000) embarked on the road toward consolidation of antigovernment sentiments. The salience of lawlessness and unemployment along with the preexisting anti-Russian sentiment and Salafist ideology created an environment in which the rising Chechen field commander, Shamil Basayev, and al-Khattab, Saudi Arabian–born foreign fighter, managed to consolidate leadership over the most radical and violent *bandformirovaniya* (bandit formations) and guerilla factions, triggering *jihadization* of the Chechen (and to some extent the pan-Caucasian) cause and its integration into the global terrorist network, at the time associated with Al-Qaida (AQ). With some internal reluctance to join the ranks of the global jihad, the radicalization of the Chechen resistance movement and its representation as part of AQ were instrumental in resolving internal struggles and securing human and material capital from Salafi supporters abroad.[6]

CRIME AS AN EXTENSION OF TERRORIST IDEOLOGY

Following the Moscow theater siege in 2002, Al Jazeera broadcasted Bin Laden's message, in which the internationalization of the Chechen insurgency was mentioned. "If you were distressed by the killing of your nationals in Moscow, remember ours in Chechnya," he warned, underscoring the prominence that the Chechens had gained in the global jihadi network.[7] "Why should fear, killing, destruction, displacement, orphaning and widowing continue to be our lot, while security, stability and happiness be your lot? This is unfair. It is time that we get even," he continued. Declassified U.S. intelligence documents (e.g., "Swift Knight Report"[8]) reveal AQ's plans and methods for supporting training camps and terrorist cells in Chechnya and other parts of the Caucasus, including states in the South Caucasus, including Georgia and Azerbaijan. The report, for instance, suggested that Amir al-Khattab was at the origins of the "terrorist fundamentalist political organization 'Al-Kaida.' "[9] He was referred to in the report as Usama Bin Laden's "personal friend."[10]

Al-Khattab was sent to Chechnya to coordinate training camps and secure the transfer of foreign funds to the region in support of the terrorist insurgency. In a well-recorded case, Enaam Arnaout, director of a nonprofit organization Benevolence International Foundation (BIF), pled guilty for diverting charity funds raised through the BIF, allegedly connected to al-Khattab, to various terrorist groups around world, including the Chechen insurgency.[11] MADLEE, a BIF-affiliated nonprofit Georgian organization missioned to provide humanitarian aid in the Pankisi Gorge,[12] was used to transfer funds to the Chechen underground. These funds were used to procure X-ray machines, antimine boots, camouflage military uniforms, and other supplies.[13]

Apart from receiving external support from Islamic organizations, there was a strong connection between the Chechen insurgency and organized crime.[14] According to Shelley, Shamil Basayev was in contact with an international car-theft ring located in Los Angeles.[15] Members of the ring purchased luxury vehicles and shipped them from the port of Houston to Georgia's Black Sea ports. While the vehicles were sold in Georgia and elsewhere in the region by individuals loyal to the Chechen insurgency, vehicles were also declared stolen to insurance companies in the United States. Fraudulent claims of theft allowed additional profits to be collected by the criminal group.[16] Although 8 individuals of the ring were arrested by the Los Angeles Police Department (LAPD) and 11 others were placed on the wanted list, none of the suspects was prosecuted for terrorism financing. Despite prosecution's preference for ordinary crimes, the U.S. intelligence agencies and State Department officials familiar with the case recognized the LAPD's breakup of the ring as an important "setback to international terrorists."[17] In April 2009, however, Russian Prosecutor-General Yury Chaika reiterated the problem of couriers entering the Russian Federation from Georgia and Azerbaijan with cash designated for the Chechen insurgency.[18]

Similar to Mexican and Colombian cartels, the Chechen insurgency turned to drug trafficking as a fund-raising activity. Chechnya became an important segment of a heroin trafficking route from Afghanistan to Russia and Western Europe. According to the investigation by Lt. Colonel

Aleksandr Alekseyev, a Federal Security Service (FSB) officer in Grozny during the first Russo-Chechen War, Chechnya developed into an essential hub for transporting narcotics from Afghanistan. Throughout the 1990s, opium poppy and morphine shipments from Afghanistan were transferred on trucks or helicopters to the Uzbek towns of Termez and Samarkand. From there, drug consignments were loaded into private aircraft that delivered them to Chechnya.[19] Chechen groups did not limit their activities to Chechnya and operated in neighboring republics. More specifically, drugs were transported from the airport in the Ingush town of Sleptsovsk to Vilnius and Šiauliai in Lithuania. From the Lithuanian port of Klaipėda, drugs were shipped to Rügen—a German island in the Baltic Sea—from where Sicilian and Albanian OCGs smuggled them to England. Seeking profit maximization, Basayev also controlled several drug laboratories that processed opium poppy and morphine into heroin exported from Afghanistan and Pakistan. Some laboratories also processed the poppy straw, an agricultural by-product, into a concoction known in Russia as *kompot*. Due to the poor quality of *kompot* compared to heroin produced from seed pods, it was sold primarily in the Russian market.

In addition to Shamil Basayev, another Chechen field commander Ruslan Gelayev coordinated several international drug trafficking operations. From the end of the 1990s until 2004 when Gelayev was killed, he was the key figure in drug trafficking from Afghanistan to Russia and Europe via the Pankisi Gorge.[20] He also ran plantations of opium poppy and hemp in Chechnya located in forested areas. Given Gelayev's contacts with several Georgian political leaders, businessmen, and Georgian organized crime, he was able to transform the Pankisi Gorge into one of the major gateways for drug trafficking into Russia. Lawlessness in the gorge contributed to the deployment of U.S. forces to launch a train and equip program for the Georgian military. Up to 70 U.S. service members were sent to Georgia for a 21-month mission to help Georgian counterparts improve their ability to deny safe haven or transit to terrorist organizations.[21]

Finally, it is worth mentioning that drug trafficking was not the only source of criminal revenue for the Chechen insurgency. A portion of income was generated from the illicit trade in oil. Oil deposits in Chechnya are found at shallow depths. Their close proximity to the surface prompted a boom in illicit oil refineries during the Chechen conflicts. These low-tech mini oil refineries processed illicitly extracted crude oil into petroleum products. According to some sources, as soon as oil contraband reached the Black Sea ports Novorossiysk and Tuapse, it was mixed with legitimate Russian oil and traded internationally.[22]

FINANCING OF THE CE

After Russian forces seized control of Chechnya, Akhmad Kadyrov was appointed acting head of the Republic's administration by President Putin in 2003. Following his assassination in May 2004, his son, Ramzan Kady-rov continued to head the pro-Russian militia *kadyrovtsy* (literally "Kady-rov's followers"). He was committed to his father's pro-Kremlin policies and managed to establish an informal control over the governing institutions in the Republic until he reached the minimum legal age (30 years) to become the head of the Chechen Republic in 2007.

With pro-Russian forces fervently engaging in the counterinsurgency operation aimed at isolating the remaining terrorist formations from the rest of the world, the Chechen insurgency underwent substantial changes. One of Russia's most wanted rebels, Doku Umarov (a.k.a. Abu Usman) consolidated the fading insurgent force into a jihadist movement with a distinct pan-Caucasian identity. In October 2007, he publicly announced the creation of the CE—an independent Islamic emirate governed by *sharia* law. Territories of current Chechnya, Ingushetia and North Ossetia, Adygea and a southern part of Krasnodarsky Krai, Dagestan, Kabardino-Balkaria, and Karachay Cherkessia were proclaimed *vilayats* (Arabic for province or territory) of the CE.

Internally, the CE was a highly decentralized organization yet with a distinct governing hierarchy headed by the supreme emir. He appointed *valiyami* (leaders) of each constituent *vilayats* (territory) in exchange for an oath of allegiance or *bayat*. Each *vilayat* subsequently consisted of sectors, which in turn contained multiple operational units or *jamaats*. Each jamaat within the organization was responsible for raising funds, recruiting supporters, and carrying out operations, in accordance with the overall strategy of the Emirate's leadership. The largest *jamaats* (up to 50 members), such as the Makhachkala/Shamilkala *jamaat* and the Khasavyurt/Jundullah *jamaat*, operated primarily in cities and suburban areas.

Despite the disorganized structure and the general strategy of underground hideouts, which made the organization a hard target for law enforcement, the Umarov-led CE experienced severe fractures. The organization relocated from Chechnya to other North Caucasian republics, mainly Dagestan and Kabardino-Balkaria, and revised its funding strategies. Isolated from foreign financial injections, the CE leadership turned to domestic sources of financing.

JAMAAT-BASED OCGS

From late 2010 to 2015, the CE underwent substantial organizational changes and revisited its sources of financing. The CE leadership shifted from illicit cross-border trade (e.g., drug trafficking and oil smuggling discussed earlier) that was commonplace during the Russo-Chechen conflicts to domestic sources of financing. Then presidential envoy to the North Caucasus Federal District (SKFO) Aleksandr Khloponin noted in September

2011 that 90 percent of the CE's funding came from within the region and the remaining 10 percent was provided by unspecified international sources.[23]

Amir Seyfullah (a.k.a. Anzor Astemirov), one of the main ideologists of the CE and its *quadi*, stated in 2007:

> First, Russia entered into an agreement with the United States on a joint fight against terrorism. Then, King Abdullah (. . .) concluded a similar agreement with Russia. Abdullah promised Putin that he would block the financing channels for the Chechen jihad. But the lack of assistance from abroad did not stop the mujahideen. Many units switched to self-financing, ceasing to depend on foreign donations.[24]

During this time, criminalization of the North Caucasus region took a somewhat different form compared to the warlord era of Shamil Basayev and his followers. This time, the principal method of operation relied on extortion, kidnapping, and robberies. It should be noted that many CE members had a criminal background. "They [were] cynical, pragmatic and practical. And they operate[d] as organized crime groups: they extort[ed] money, buil[t] 'obshchak' and then redistribute[d] its funds," explained Sergei Chenchik, then chief of the Internal Affairs Ministry Directorate for the North Caucasus.[25]

Interestingly, the CE leader Doku Umarov was once known in the criminal scene of the 1990s before he joined the Chechen pro-independence movement in 1994. The fact that he was involved in organized crime was later acknowledged by the CE hagiographer Said Buryatsky, who stated, "Before the first jihad, Abu Usman Doku Umarov was a racketeer in Russia, and this is not a secret to anybody. But when fighting broke out, he went to Chechnya, leaving everything he had behind to take up jihad in the way of Allah."[26]

With considerable past experience in the criminal circles in Russia, the vast extortion network organized by Umarov functioned as a system of voluntary payments know as *zakat* payments—a form of a tax dating back to the times of the Prophet Mohammed. The accumulated funds were described as donations collected to help "brothers in the woods" and those sitting in prison, as well as cover other expenses. The importance of domestic sources of CE funding was stressed by Amir Seyfullah in his "televised" YouTube address. He acknowledged that financial contributions to the jihad cause were absolutely obligatory for those Muslims who did not participate in jihad themselves.[27] "And the fact that the man gave money to the enemies of the Muslims simply made him even more of a sinner—only contributions to the cause of jihad could save him" explained Seyfulla.[28] This obligation particularly applied to those with substantial income. Local entrepreneurs often received USB memory sticks with threatening messages recorded on them. In the recording, a speaker in a mask juxtaposed against a flag with jihadist symbols would demand they "donate" a couple of million rubles for "the needs of a holy war with infidels." Payments were also required from non-Muslims as a form of *jizya* or "tax on infidels."

The practice of taking from the rich by threat and coercion is not new in the North Caucasus. Schaefer refers to the early 1900s as the time when a cohort of highwaymen attacking travelers, trains, farms, factories, and even state institutions, emerged.[29] They called themselves *abreks* and were often perceived by the locals as avengers and protectors. *Abrecestvo* became integral to popular understanding of crime control, in which *abreks* acted as rule makers and law enforcers and facilitated the formation of the resistance of the Caucasian peoples against the Russian incursion. Some *abreks* were devoted Muslims and therefore rejected *hiraba* (gangsterism) or attacks against fellow Muslims. Beyond intimidation and violence, concerted activities by *abreks* constituted "the first organized form of jihad in early Islamic warfare."[30] Similar to those times, *jamaats* associated with the CE mainly attacked local businesses dealing in alcohol, casinos, saunas, or entertainment businesses associated with sex services, as well as enterprises run by foreigners and non-Muslims. By doing so, they presented themselves to the population as righteous Muslims and guardians of traditional Islamic values.

It is worth noting that *jamaat* leaders often collaborated with the regional political and business elites. This collaboration is in some ways the outcome of preexisting kinship-based networks, which have always been a significant source of social capital in the Caucasus region. Therefore, in situations when state officials, the police, and *jamaat* members came from the same family or belonged to the same kin, reliance on kinship structures and intranetwork bonding was more important than serving in formal institutions. Businesses affiliated with *jamaats*, for instance, received profitable state contracts. One of the most prominent groups in this respect is the Gimry *jamaat*. It is known that a business affiliated with a notorious field commander Ibrahim Gajidadayev, leader of the Gimry *jamaat*, received several state construction tenders, including the reconstruction of the Gimry Tunnel—a 4,000 meter road tunnel, the longest in Russia, located in Dagestan.[31] Souleimanov notes that *jamaat* leaders also found ways to make arrangements with the police.[32] Following a "good cop, bad cop" scenario, the police complicit in extortion rackets themselves turned to jihadists for collaboration. The latter used brutal violence and intimidation to collect the rents—a portion of which would be paid back to the authorities. In this way, although the local authorities had a share in the extortion market, attacks on businesses were always framed as crimes committed by jihadists. Worth mentioning is also that some initially criminal organizations, being unable to collect rents, pretended to be *jamaats*. By then, *jamaats* already had a reputation of being extremely violent and dangerous groups—most were feared by the population. Residents therefore were more likely to pay up to *jamaats* than regular extortionist criminals.

FOREIGN FINANCIAL INJECTIONS

Although the true nature of the involvement of the Chechen (and more broadly North Caucasian) Diaspora in providing support to the CE is unknown, some recent cases shed important light on the existence of some financial injections to the North Caucasus insurgency from abroad. The Kadyrov administration has always been quite sensitive about the limited access to Chechens whom they consider to be ex-combatants or individuals supporting the jihadi movement. During a press conference on March 31, 2016, Ramzan Kadyrov noted:

> They fled in the first days of the war, and now, sitting in Vienna, Paris or London, are trying to please their masters, expressing some kind of threats against Chechnya, shouting at rallies with their miserable donkey voices something about Chechnya and its people. There will be no return to Ichkerian lawlessness. Chechnya has begun a new life in union with Russia. And we will not allow anyone, especially those buffoons, to interfere with this life.[33]

It is known for instance that a Belgian group, Shariah4Belgium, comprised of ethnic Moroccans and Chechens, provided recruitment and financing for several terrorist organizations, including the CE. The criminal trial of Faisal Errai that took place in Spain in 2011 revealed that the group registered and maintained a website for the purposes of spreading jihadist propaganda and recruiting sympathizers to join violent jihad. The website was also used to collect donations for terrorist formations in Chechnya. "Their obsession with the group even led them to launch an initiative to translate into Russian the publications of Al Sahab, the propaganda wing of Al-Qaida, 'because many [of our brothers in Chechnya] are mistaken about the wise men and Hamas.' "[34]

In a similar case in the Czech Republic, Bohemian counterterrorism officers disrupted a cell connected to the CE. Individuals of Bulgarian, Chechen, Dagestani, and Moldovan origin participated in arms smuggling, counterfeiting legal documents, and planning terrorist attacks associated with the CE. "Profits made from the falsification of passports and other documents were sent to Dagestan and presumably used to purchase the weapons and explosives sent there by the cell."[35]

DECLINE OF THE CE

After the decay of the CE leadership following the death of Doku Umarov in 2013 and many of his associates, midlevel commanders of the North Caucasian insurgency, especially those supportive of a more radical Salafi agenda, pledged allegiance to Da'esh leader Abu Bakr Al-Baghdadi. Accepting the call, Da'esh established Vilayat Kavkaz—an active branch of Da'esh in the North Caucasus, appointing Rustam Aslidarov (a.k.a. Abu Muhammad al-Qadari, killed in 2016) as its leader. Despite loyalists of the

CE denouncing Vilayat Kavkaz, and accusing Rustam Aslidarov and his supporters of betrayal, the presence of fighters from the Caucasus in the ranks of Da'esh expanded. Europol alleged that Russian became the third language in Da'esh after Arabic and English.[36] In 2015, Russian passport holders accounted for up to 8 percent of Da'esh fighters with North Caucasians making up the majority of foreign terrorist fighters in Syria and Iraq.[37] In this way, the founding idea of the CE to unite all the Muslim-populated territories in southern Russia was revived, yet in a very different form. Now Da'esh served as an ideal magnet for "wanna be jihadists" and militants in Chechnya and elsewhere in the Caucasus.

This new wave of jihadists from the Caucasus quickly integrated into the global network of Da'esh cells. They thrived off loose affiliations with groups or individuals from a variety of locations in Europe and the Middle East and relied on flexibility and initiative to conduct action in support of global jihad—now led by Da'esh. Importantly, Europol data suggest that the majority of Chechens and other North Caucasians involved in the armed conflict in Syria traveled there from the European Union (EU), oftentimes after moving there as refugees.[38]

One of the recent Da'esh-claimed terrorist attacks, the assault on Istanbul airport that killed 43 in 2016, sheds an important light on the integration of the Northern Caucasian Diaspora, mainly from Europe and Turkey, into global jihad. According to a press statement by the European Parliament, the attack was perpetrated by a Da'esh cell from Chechnya, which also executed attacks in Russia and then established its base in Turkey in the 1990s. The assailants were nationals of Kyrgyzstan, Russia (Chechnya), and Uzbekistan. Akhmed Chatayev (a.k.a. Akhmed Shishkani), a Chechen combatant in the ranks of the Da'esh, masterminded the attack.

Chatayev, who fought in the Second Chechen War between 1999 and 2000, was known for his close ties with Doku Umarov. Wanted in the Russian Federation since 2003, he managed to attain refugee status in Austria. In 2008, Chatayev and several other Chechen nationals attracted the attention of the Swedish police in Trelleborg, where they were arrested with assault rifles, ammunition, and explosives. Chatayev spent one year in a Swedish prison and, upon his release in 2010, was again arrested in Ukraine. The Ukrainian police found him in possession of a mobile phone with demolition technique instructions. The Russian Federation requested his extradition. The European Court of Human Rights, which has "advisory status only," ruled against the extradition of Chatayev, claiming that he might receive an unfair trial and could be at risk of torture and ill-treatment.[39]

From 2012 to 2015, Chatayev lived in Georgia, where he allegedly joined terrorist groups and served a prison sentence on terrorism-related charges. In 2015, he left Georgia for Syria where he joined Da'esh. The same year he was designated a foreign terrorist by the UN Security Council and the U.S. Department of State. According to the former, Chatayev provided financial and logistical support to militants operating in the North Caucasus. "In September 2007, Chataev organized a delivery to the Chechen Republic, Russian Federation, consisting of US$12,000, military uniforms, a personal computer and audio equipment for the terrorists operating in the Northern Caucasus."[40] Further, it is alleged, "[h]e directly commands 130 militants and calls on Muslims to join the armed fight against the official authorities in Syrian Arab Republic, Iraq, and other countries with the aim of establishing a caliphate."[41]

Chatayev's case is not an isolated example of insurgents from the North Caucasus joining or otherwise assisting Da'esh.[42] Without supportive empirical evidence at the moment, it is very likely that Da'esh will be playing a key role in controlling and financing the insurgency in the North Caucasus, thus requiring closer collaboration between the Russian and foreign, mainly U.S. and European, counterparts. And, despite Russia's efforts, these returning fighters will be sufficiently funded by their Da'esh associates to give new life to the terrorist cause.

CONCLUDING REMARKS AND POLICY RECOMMENDATIONS

This chapter examined the financing of the North Caucasus insurgency from the last decade of the Soviet Union to the formation of the pan-Caucasian jihadist organization CE and its decline. It provides a primer on the confluence of ideological and economic considerations, shedding light on the transitioning of the North Caucasus insurgency along the crime-terrorism continuum over time.

Moreover, it highlighted the fact that Chechen OCGs that operated in Moscow provided some start-up funds for the Chechen independence movement. Some individuals, when appointed to high-ranking positions in the self-proclaimed Chechen government, maintained their presence in the criminal world and directed ill-gotten profits for the needs of the unrecognized Chechen state. As the armed conflicts in the North Caucasus were taking on an increasingly ideological as opposed to a nationalistic tone in the early 2000s, the emerging terrorist criminal enterprises turned to drug trafficking, making Chechnya (also the wider Caucasus area) a major regional hub for narcotics flows from Afghanistan to Europe. The Chechen insurgency also forged ties with Al-Qaida, which provided it with funds and operational support.

In the early 2000s, the Putin administration vested the powers in a pro-Russian Chechen leader Ramzan Kadyrov who was tasked to suppress the terrorist groups at any cost. Kadyrov's aggressive campaign against the insurgency pushed the remaining terrorist groups into the criminal underground. Similar to how some OCGs generate funds, the CE ran a sophisticated extortion network. The militant jihadist organization was thus both embedded in society and predatory upon it. Once introduced to criminal business, the appeal of illicit enrichment made some *jamaats* evolve into largely criminal enterprises. This metamorphosis caused them not only to adapt many of their tactics and strategies but also to recruit new members with competencies in crime, including extortion and underground banking. At this stage, CE *jamaats* used their ideological or religious agenda as a cover for ordinary crimes. This situation fed corruption and impunity, stripping the CE of its much-needed public support—the environment that provided Da'esh with an opportunity to expand its influence in the Caucasus region.

The case of the North Caucasian insurgency teaches several policy lessons. First, any successful response against the insurgency, at least in the North Caucasian context, should provide protection to regular citizens and incorporate a counter-corruption strategy. With regard to the latter, the conditions conducive to the spread of collusion between insurgents and political and economic elites in Chechnya and Dagestan should be addressed. In light of public dissatisfaction with high crime levels, mainly extortion, confidential channels for public victimization should be established. Whistle-blowers should be rewarded and provided with adequate protection from retaliation. Second, given the complex nature of terrorist organizations, it is important to address not only the ideological underpinnings of terrorism but also the criminal incentives that contribute to the expansion of terrorist organizations and their continuity. While international legal foundations for counterterrorism are yet to be strengthened and a global counterterrorism regime still lacks a central global body dedicated to terrorist prevention and response, countering terrorist organizations with measures that focus on prosecution of nonterrorism-related offenses, such as extortion, smuggling, or immigration violations, may turn out to be more productive.

NOTE ON TRANSLITERATION AND TRANSLATION

All translations from Russian and Ukrainian are my own except where otherwise indicated. The American Library Association/Library of Congress (ALA-LC) transliteration system (http://www.loc.gov/catdir/cpso/roman.html) is used throughout the text. The names of authors whose names were written in Latin script appear the same as in the original.

NOTES

1. See, for example, Robert W. Schaefer, *The Insurgency in Chechnya and the North Caucasus: From Gazavat to Jihad* (Santa Barbara, CA: Praeger, 2010); Elena Pokalova, *Chechnya's Terrorist Network: The Evolution of Terrorism in Russia's North Caucasus* (Santa Barbara, CA: Praeger, 2015).

2. See, for example, Tamara Makarenko, "The Crime-Terror Continuum: Tracing the Interplay between Transnational Organised Crime and Terrorism," *Global Crime* 2, no. 1 (2004), 129–145; Rajan Basra, Peter R. Neumann, and Claudia Brunner,

"Criminal Pasts, Terrorist Futures: European Jihadists and the New Crime-Terror Nexus," Report of International Center for the Study of Radicalisation and Political Violence, London, 2016.

3. Svante E. Cornell, "The Narcotics Threat in Great Central Asia: From Crime-Terror Nexus to State Infiltration?" *China and Eurasia Forum Quarterly* 4, no. 1 (2006), 37–67.

4. Louise Shelley, John T. Picarelli, Allison Irby, Douglas M. Hart, Patricia A. Craig-Hart, Phil Williams, Steven Simon, Nabi Abdullaev, Bartosz Stanislawski, and Laura Covill, "Methods and Motives: Exploring Links between Transnational Organized Crime and International Terrorism," Report for the National Criminal Justice Reference Service (NCJRS), U.S. Department of Justice, September 2005, https://www.ncjrs.gov/pdffiles1/nij/grants/211207.pdf.

5. Tamara Makarenko, "Europe's Crime-Terror Nexus: Links between Terrorist and Organised Crime Groups in the European Union," Study for the LIBE Committee. Directorate-General for Internal Policies, European Parliament's Committee on Civil Liberties, Justice and Home Affairs, October 2012, http://www.europarl.europa.eu/thinktank/en/document.html?reference=IPOL-LIBE_ET (2012)462503.

6. Emil Souleimanov and Ondrej Ditrych, "The Internationalisation of the Russian-Chechen Conflict: Myths and Reality," *Europe-Asia Studies* 60, no. 7 (August 2008), 1199–1222.

7. "Full Text of Bin Laden's Message," BBC, November 12, 2002, http://news.bbc.co.uk/2/hi/middle_east/2455845.stm.

8. DIA, "Intelligence Information Report (IIR) Concerning Usama Bin Laden's Current and Historical Activities," Report prepared for the Defense Intelligence Agency (Declassified), Document No. 3095345, 1998.

9. Ibid., 3.

10. Ibid.

11. U.S. Department of Treasury, "Treasury Designates Benevolence International Foundation and Related Entities as Financiers of Terrorism, Press Center," November 19, 2002, https://www.treasury.gov/press-center/press-releases/Pages/po3632.aspx.

12. Pankisi is a 30-kilometer-long valley in northeastern Georgia. It is adjacent to the Chechen Republic and is populated by Kists—a Chechen subethnos in Georgia.

13. *United States of America vs. Enaam M. Arnaout* (2005), U.S. District Court, Northern District of Illinois Eastern Division. No. 02 CR 892; Timothy Wittig, *Understanding Terrorist Finance* (London: Palgrave Macmillan, 2011).

14. Louise Shelley, *Dirty Entanglements: Corruption, Crime, and Terrorism* (New York: Cambridge University Press, 2014).

15. Ibid.

16. Ibid.

17. Robert Block, "An L.A. Police Bust Shows New Tactics for Fighting Terror," *Wall Street Journal*, December 29, 2006, n.p., https://www.wsj.com/articles/SB116736247579862262.

18. "Russia Accuses Azerbaijan and Georgia of Abetting Transfer of Funds to the North Caucasus Resistance," Radio Free Europe, May 4, 2009, http://www.rferl.org/content/Russia_Accuses_Azerbaijan_Georgia_Of_Abetting_Transfer_Of_Funds_To_North_Caucasus_Resistance/1621351.html.

19. Aleksandr Alekseyev, "Commonwealth of Independent Narco-Barons" (Sodruzhestvo nezavisimykh narko-baronov), *Spetsnaz Rossii*, 2002, http://www .specnaz.ru/gosudarstvo/121/.

20. Glenn E. Curtis, *Involvement of Russian Organized Crime Syndicates, Criminal Elements in the Russian Military, and Regional Terrorist Groups in Narcotics Trafficking in Central Asia, the Caucasus, and Chech*nya (Washington, DC: Library of Congress/ Federal Research Division, October 2000). https://www.loc.gov/rr/frd/pdf-files/RussianOrgCrime.pdf.

21. Kathleen T. Rhem, "American Troops Training, Equipping Georgian Military," American Forces Press Service, U.S. Department of Defense, March 30, 2002, http://archive.defense.gov/news/newsarticle.aspx?id=43997.

22. Yuliya Zabyelina, "Energy Sapping: Oil Theft in Russia's North Caucasus," *Jane's Intelligence Review*, January 16, 2013.

23. Kommersant, "Khloponin: There Are a Thousand Terrorists Left in the North Caucasus (Khloponin: Na Severnom Kavkaze ostalas tysyacha terroristov)," *Kommersant*, September 30, 2011, https://www.kommersant.ru/doc/1786046.

24. "Amir Sayfullah: How We Prepared the Declaration of the Caucasus Emirate," Kavkaz Center, November 20, 2007, n.p., http://www.kavkazcenter .com/russ/content/2007/11/20/54479/amir-sejfulla-o-protsesse-podgotovki-k-provozglasheniyu-kavkazskogo-emirata.shtml.

25. Elena Brezhytskaya, "Exclusive Interview with the Head of the Main Directorate of the Ministry of Internal Affairs of the Russian Federation for the North Caucasus Federal District (SKFO) Sergey Chenchik," *Rossiyskaya Gazeta*, December 16, 2013, https://rg.ru/2013/12/16/reg-skfo/chenchik.html.

26. Buryatskiy cited in Michael Fredholm and Nelly Lahoud, "Doku Umarov, Founder of the Caucasus Emirate: From Secularism to Jihadism," Jihadi Bios Project (West Point: Combatting Terrorism Center, August 2016), https://ctc.usma. edu/doku-umarov-founder-caucasus-emirate-secularism-jihadism/.

27. "Amir Seyfullah Answers Questions Asked by Muslims," Kavkaz Center, August 28, 2006, http://www.kavkazcenter.com/russ/content/2006/08/28/46749/ otvety-amira-sejfullakh-na-voprosy-musulman.shtml.

28. Ibid.

29. Schaefer, *The Insurgency in Chechnya and the North Caucasus*.

30. Ibid., 83.

31. Brezhytskaya, "Exclusive Interview with the Head of the Main Directorate of the Ministry of Internal Affairs," 2013.

32. Emil Souleimanov, "Making Jihad or Making Money? Understanding the Transformation of Dagestan's Jamaats into Organised Crime Groups," *Journal of Strategic Studies*, Online first, 2015, https://doi.org/10.1080/01402390.2015.1121871.

33. Mairbek Vatchagaev, "Kadyrov at Loggerheads with Chechen Diaspora in Europe," *Eurasia Daily Monitor* 13, no. 44 (March 4, 2016), n.p., https://jamestown .org/program/kadyrov-at-loggerheads-with-chechen-diaspora-in-europe-2/.

34. Manuel R. Torres-Soriano, "The Hidden Face of Jihadist Internet Forum Management: The Case of Ansar Al Mujahideen," *Terrorism and Political Violence* 28, no. 4 (September 2014), 744.

35. Gordon M. Hahn, *Getting the Caucasus Emirate Right*, CSIS Report, Russia and Eurasia Program (Washington, DC: Center for Strategic and International Studies, 2011), 12.

36. Europol, "North Caucasian Fighters in Syria and Iraq and ISIS Propaganda in Russian Language," O41 Counter Terrorism and O47 EU Internet Referral Unit (Declassified) (The Hague: The European Union Agency for Law Enforcement Cooperation, September 2015).

37. Ibid.

38. Ibid.

39. European Parliament, "Asylum in the EU for the Mastermind behind the Attacks at Istanbul Airport," Parliamentary Questions (E-005564-16), July 6, 2016, http://www.europarl.europa.eu/sides/getDoc.do?pubRef=-//EP//TEXT+WQ+E-2016–005564+0+DOC+XML+V0//EN&language=en.

40. UN Security Council, "Narrative Summaries of Reasons for Listing, QDi.365, Akhmed Rajapovich Chataev," October 2, 2015, https://www.un.org/sc/suborg/en/sanctions/1267/aq_sanctions_list/summaries/individual/akhmed-rajapovich-chataev.

41. Ibid.

42. For more information, see Cerwyn Moore, "Foreign Bodies: Transnational Activism, the Insurgency in the North Caucasus and 'Beyond,' " *Terrorism and Political Violence* 27, no. 3 (May 2015), 395–415.

CHAPTER 6

The Revolutionary Armed Forces of Colombia (FARC): A Transnational Criminal-Insurgent-Terror Phenomenon

Max G. Manwaring

The traditional distinctions among crime, terrorism, subversion, and insurgency; popular militias, mercenary, and gang activity, and warfare are blurred. Underlying these ambiguities is the fact that most of these activities tend to be intrastate conflicts. These relatively small internal conflicts are likely to have different names, different base motives, and different levels of violence. Regardless of what these conflicts or what their organizers are called—terrorists, criminals, insurgents, *narco*-traffickers, or something else—they will likely use terror as a tactic or operational-level strategy to achieve their grand political-strategic objective of commercial enrichment and/or radical political-economic-social change.

Many political, military, and opinion leaders involved in the global security arena have been struggling with these "new" aspects of the *narco*-insurgent-terror phenomenon for years. They have been slow to understand how governments might ultimately control—or succumb to—the coercive terroristic threats inherent in contemporary unrestricted intranational and international conflict. To achieve this understanding, however, leaders and the informed public must know who and what they are dealing with. One can take an important step toward understanding the unconventional criminal-insurgent-terrorist wars in our midst by examining a case in point. That is, Colombia, 1930–2017.

Thus, the introductory "Contextual Background" part of this chapter provides a short reminder of Colombia's violent political history. It illustrates how it is that "the political structure and elites simply accommodate the continuing criminal violence, absorb it, while the population makes the necessary psychological adjustments, as if it were a normal condition, like rain."[1] This explains one level or another of virtually continuous conflict throughout Colombia's political history.

This kind of problem takes us to "The Basic Linkage between Colombia's Transnational Criminal Organizations (TCOs; also called "*Narcos*") and FARC Insurgents." This second part of the chapter demonstrates that although nonstate actors may differ in terms of names, motives, and modes of operation, they must eventually establish a level of political power that will guarantee freedom of movement and action. As noted, that freedom of action is necessary in order to achieve grand-strategic commercial, ideological, and/or political ends. That is, both Revolutionary Armed Forces of Colombia (FARC) and the *narcos* need to gain control of the Colombian government and state. This is the common denominator that brings TCOs and insurgents together, and into an interesting if not unlikely "marriage of convenience." In that alliance, organized criminal techniques and terror are used as tactical and operational-level activities to achieve strategic political objectives. Importantly, these efforts equate to insurgency or some other name for internal war.

The next part of this chapter outlines "The Transition of FARC from a Violent Revolutionary *foco* (an insurrectionalist armed enclave) to a More Benign 21st-Century Intrastate Political-Military Actor." It appears that FARC leadership has come to the conclusion that less belligerent political-psychological innovations are viable substitutes for Che Guavara's violent *foco* strategy for the conduct of contemporary internal war (insurgency), and for the creation of a 21st-century socialist state.[2] This new rhetoric and the seeming contradiction of traditional Marxist-Leninist-Maoist ideology, however, have not changed FARC's grand strategic-level objective of achieving a "true Bolivarian democracy," a "21st Century Socialist state," or something else that represents the same idea. The new rhetoric also takes us back to the *foco*. These armed enclaves (also called zones, ungoverned spaces, alternately governed territory, and malgoverned areas) are known to become quasi-states within the state and present a serious threat to the state. Whatever the rhetoric, and regardless of whether or not FARC fragments as a result of the 2016 Peace Accords, it appears that FARC will continue to be much more than a terrorist group that partners with organized crime.

Part four elaborates on "The *Narco*–FARC Nexus." The *narco*–FARC connection is not new. The FARC role as TCO partner and enforcer has been understood for a long time. What has not been well understood is that the nexus is not simply criminal-terrorist in nature. It is more. As noted, the intent of both parties in using a combination of criminal terror methods and insurgency war at the tactical and operational levels of conflict is to gain the political-military power necessary to achieve their common grand-strategic objective. At the least, that objective is to control (rather than govern) the Colombian government and the state. In either case, control or actual governance equates to an existential political, economic, and social threat to the Colombian state.[3]

All this takes us well beyond organized criminal trafficking in illegal drugs. This also takes us beyond seemingly mindless terrorist attacks on military and police facilities, institutions such as the Colombian Supreme Court, and kidnapping and assassination of specifically and randomly targeted people. Thus, we end this chapter with "A Cautionary Tale" and "Recommended Response."

A BIT OF CONTEXTUAL BACKGROUND

In the 1930s and 1940s, chronic political, economic, and social problems created by self-serving civilian and military oligarchies began to create yet another set of crises in the long list of internal conflicts in Colombian history. In 1930, Liberal reformists came to power and deprived Conservatives of the control of the central government and related patronage. The Liberals also initiated an ambitious social agenda that generated increasing civil violence between Conservative and Liberal partisans. The catalyst that ignited the 18-year period of internal conflict called *la violencia* (the violence) in April 1948 was the assassination of Liberal populist Jorge Eliécer Gaitán. That murder sparked a riot known as the *Bogotazo* that left much of the capital city destroyed and an estimated 2,000 dead. Although the government was able to dominate the rebels in Bogotá, it was not strong enough to control the violence that spread through the rest of the country. Rural violence became the norm as an estimated 20,000 armed Liberal and Conservative combatants settled old political scores. Over the period from 1948 to 1966, *la violencia* claimed the lives of another 200,000 to 250,000 Colombians.

During those years, the various Colombian governments dealt with this intrastate violence as a conventional war of attrition, and on an ad hoc basis. There was no strategic-level plan. There was no adequate or timely intelligence. There was no consensus among the political, economic, and military elites regarding how to deal with armed internal adversaries. Also, there was very little meaningful cooperation, coordination, or communication between the civil governments and the security forces. Then, over the next half-century up to the present, Colombia has suffered another estimated 200,000 political deaths, 5 million people displaced, and more than 25,000 people disappeared. All this has seriously retarded Colombia's political-socio-economic development and reminds us of Sun

Tzu's warning, 2,500 years ago, that there has never been a protracted war from which a country has benefited.[4]

THE BASIC LINKAGE BETWEEN COLOMBIA'S TCOs AND FARC INSURGENTS

In the unstable and insecure environment of virtually uncontrolled violence, rural poverty, political disarray, and central government weakness in Colombia, the illegal drug industry began to grow, prosper, and take on a criminal identity. That TCO prosperity, as early as 1982, provided resources that encouraged a mutually supportive "marriage-of-convenience" with FARC.[5] Later, as the various Colombian governments continued to prove less and less effective in exercising legitimate control of the national territory and the people in it, right-wing vigilante United Self-Defense Groups of Colombia (AUC) paramilitary groups emerged. By 2005, however, the AUC was demobilized. The resultant organizational fragmentation provides a model for hard-core FARC members should FARC break up as a result of the 2016 Peace Accords.

In that connection, various AUC units became increasingly autonomous, and a large number of demobilized members began to operate in an outsourcing mode as "subsidiaries," "pseudo-paramilitaries," or "gangs"—that is, *Bandas Criminals* (BACRIMs or criminal gangs) and *Grupos a las Margines de la Ley* (GAMLs or groups working at the margins of the law). These gangs do what criminal gangs all over the world do best. They generate more and more political-economic-social insecurity, instability, and violence over wider and wider sections of the map. As they evolve, they need more and more freedom of movement and action to secure their self-serving commercial-political strategic objectives. In turn, they destabilize more and more territory and the people who live there. This process has been known to act as a Leninist "midwife" to new social orders, quasi-states, criminal states, and new Democratic People's Republics.[6]

The thread that permits violent nonstate actors to develop, grow, and remain active in any given security arena is adequate freedom of movement and action over time. The equation that links TCOs to insurgents and gangs in Colombia—and elsewhere—turns on a combination of need, organizational infrastructure, sophisticated communications, and weaponry. For example, the criminal *narco* industry possesses cash and lines of transportation and communication. Insurgent and paramilitary organizations have followers, organization, and discipline. Traffickers need the power assets controlled by insurgents to help protect their own assets and protect their intranational and international freedom of movement and action. FARC, BACRIMs, and GAMLs are in constant need of logistical and communications support, weaponry, and money to protect their freedom of movement and action.[7]

All this protection equates to one level or another of violent conflict between one or more nonstate actors and a given state and/or between one or more nonstate actors versus one or more other nonstate actors. This takes us back to the fact that, in that compound-complex mix of violence, organized criminal techniques and terror are tactics that are used to achieve operational and strategic objectives of commercial enrichment and/or radical political-economic-social change.

THE TRANSITION OF FARC FROM A VIOLENT REVOLUTIONARY FOCO TO A MORE BENIGN 21ST-CENTURY INTRASTATE POLITICAL-MILITARY ACTOR

For over 50 years, FARC claimed to be what Che Guevara called a *foco* in search of a mass base. These insurgents developed a military organization designed to achieve the "armed colonization" of relatively small geographical areas (zones or *focos*) within the Colombian national territory. The intent was to "liberate and mobilize the disaffected and the dispossessed" population into an alternative society. That is, FARC attempted to develop a human and geographical base from which to violently do away with the state as it now exists in Colombia.[8] Kidnapping, extortion, intimidation, assassination, and other coercive terrorist tactics were so common as to go without comment except in the most extreme cases. That terroristic military-centric approach, however, proved to be not all that successful.

At a convention called by Venezuela's president Hugo Chavez in 2005, he distributed copies of Jorge Verstrynge's *La Guerra Periférica* (*Peripheral or Indirect War*) to the Venezuelan officer corps and several other officers invited from within the Latin American community—to include FARC. Verstrynge, a Spanish Marxist-Leninist scholar, called for the "revalidation of guerrilla war." A translation of this rhetoric explains that the concept of traditional insurgency war must be superseded by those of Sun Tzu's "indirect" war, Clausewitz's "war by other means," or Lenin's "war by all means." In that context, Verstrynge's term "revalidation" requires 21st century socialist insurgency to move away from Guevara's Maoist military-centric *foco* approach to compel rapid radical political change. Verstrynge argues that modern insurgencies must be based on the notion that human terrain is the primary center of gravity and must revert to softer and more subtle uses of multidimensional (hybrid) combinations of nonkinetic power that rely on words, images, ideas, dreams, coercion, and time. Over time, these tools of power can capture the will of the people and bring about the conditions that lead to relatively benign radical political, economic, and social change.[9]

Consequently, FARC leadership came to the conclusion that political-psychological innovations—including peace talks with the government and integration into the liberal democratic political process—are indeed viable substitutes for conventional insurgency war. Accordingly, the grand-strategic FARC objective as demonstrated in the 2016 Peace Accords is straightforward. That is, to participate in a constitutional convention that would reform Colombia's fundamental law and create a new 21st-Century Socialist state.[10] Additionally, FARC strategic-level objectives include (1) gaining de jure as well as de facto legitimacy in the eyes of the Colombian people and the international community, (2) gaining legitimate access to the traditional Colombian political process, and (3) gaining de facto (if not de jure) control over the 80 or more zones where FARC has been active over the past several years.[11]

Thus, FARC has made its ideology and language appropriate to Verstrynge's 21st century insurgency strategy and Lenin's "war by all means." This portends the evolution of new war-making criminal insurgencies and new unrestricted variations on the ways and means of exerting FARC political-military power in Colombia.[12]

THE NARCO–FARC NEXUS

Colombian TCOs operate as a consortium that functions in much the same way as virtually any multinational *Fortune* 500 company. The consortium is organized to achieve super efficiency and maximum profit. It has at its disposal a very efficient flat organizational structure, the latest in high-tech communications equipment and systems, and the usual chief executive officers, public affairs officers, negotiators, project managers, security managers, and enforcers. Products are made, sold, and shipped; bankers and financial planners handle the monetary issues; and lawyers deal with legal problems. Decisions are made, communicated, and executed (pun intended) quickly. Consequently, these TCOs can ignore or supersede slow moving bureaucratic decisions and actions of the Colombian and other governments in the Americas, Europe, and elsewhere with which they deal.[13]

In this context, it is important to keep in mind that Colombia's TCO consortium has at its disposal a large and very potent enforcer organization; that is, FARC. As examples of *narco*-FARC political-military power in Colombia over the past few years, we see that (1) FARC negotiated an end to aerial and manual eradication of coca crops; (2) coca cultivation and production skyrocketed; (3) FARC income from illegal drug trafficking increased significantly; (4) FARC activities expanded to include illegal mining and lumbering; (5) FARC created autonomous "zones" in approximately 80 to 160 municipalities that the government calls "risk areas," "alternatively governed areas," or "ungoverned" territories; (6) FARC increased predatory activities—such as extortion—as indirect forms of terrorism intended to achieve a minimum level of control of the human terrain in as much of Colombia as possible;[14] and (7) FARC expanded its various activities to include cooperation with other transnational criminal-insurgent-terrorist organizations such as the Mexican Zetas and the Iranian Hezbollah.[15]

Clearly, the *narco*-FARC connection is not new, and it is not confined to Colombia. It must also be remembered that the common grand-strategic objective is—at the very least—to take control of the government and the state. That common objective may or may not change, but this "marriage of convenience" has lasted for a long time and appears to be getting along just fine. The logic is simple. Taking control of territory and the people in it is of common benefit to the TCOs and FARC. If all else fails, one or more parties to the alliance may be able to use tactical-level "armed propaganda" (extortion, assassination, and other terrorist tactics), operational-level peace talks, and/or the strategic-level democratic process to take control of territory one piece at a time over time and "out politic" the Colombian government. That kind of persuasion and coercion must inevitably result in an epochal transition from traditional values to the values of the transnational criminal-insurgent-terrorist phenomenon.

The question, then, is not whether FARC terrorist activities are organized crime. The question is whether or not FARC terrorist activities are insurgent tactics, operational and grand strategy, and/or organized crime. The answer is that FARC activities are tactical; they are operational-level strategy; they are grand strategic-level activity; and they are organized crime. These are the empirical realities of power operating in Colombia and elsewhere around the world. Accordingly, some close observers of the global terrorist-insurgent-criminal phenomenon assert that the coerced change of values in targeted societies might well lead to a "New Dark Age."[16]

A CAUTIONARY TALE

The historical record around the world and over time reveals several reasons to worry about the fate of FARC and Colombia in the post-2016 period. Whether or not FARC fragments or remains a singular entity as a result of the 2016 Peace Accords, the following concerns apply.

First, it is hard to credit the notion that (1) anyone who has been studying, teaching, and practicing Maoist Marxism-Leninism for 20 to 50 or more years would passively give up that political philosophy for liberal democracy; (2) anyone who had been involved in Che Guevara's military-centric *foco* approach to taking down a targeted government would give up the fight against that government without having been defeated in detail; (3) anyone who has been receiving all or more money he/she wants for his/her political, military, and/or personal needs would give up that level of income for standard Colombian wages; and (4) on the other hand, there is the problem of possible retribution by victims of violent FARC behavior over the past several years. All that puts the quality of the negotiated 2016 Peace Accords into question and reminds one of *la violencia*, 1948–1966.[17]

Second, we return one more time to the common denominator that brings the transnational criminal-insurgent phenomenon together. That is, the primary and common objective of insurgents, drug cartels, private armies, and other violent nonstate actors is to attain the level of freedom of movement and action to operate with impunity and maximize the possibilities for achieving operational and strategic objectives. Operational-level objectives would include the achievement of short- and mid-term policy goals and establish acceptance, credibility and de facto legitimacy within the local, national, and international communities. In turn, freedom of movement and action takes us to the definition of war. That is, the strategic grand-political motive—whether specifically political, commercial, or ideological—is to impose one's will on one's adversary. Rephrased slightly, these activities also define insurgency—that is, coercing radical change of a given political, economic, and social system in order to neutralize it, control it, or depose it, that is, compelling one actor to accede to another actor's strategic-level policy objectives.[18] This is a great deal more than simple terrorism or organized criminal activity. Qiao and Wang and revolutionary theorist Abraham Guillen warn us that even though contemporary war and insurgency might be less bloody than conventional conflict, any other kind of coercion is no less grievous. "It is a struggle without clemency that exacts the highest political tension."[19]

Third, as the ability to wage war devolves from traditional hierarchical nation-state organizations to Internet-worked transnational and national nonstate actors, we can see the evolution of new war-making criminal entities such as BACRIMs (criminal gangs) and GAMLs (groups working at the margins of the law). We can also see new unrestricted ways and means of conducting contemporary conflict.[20] The traditional distinctions among crime, terrorism, subversion, and insurgency; popular militia, mercenary, and gang activity; and conventional warfare, however, are blurred. In these kinds of conflict, there are virtually no enforceable rules. In these conflicts there are normally no formal declaration of termination of conflict, no easily identifiable enemy military formations to attack and destroy, and no specific territory to take and hold. There are no legal niceties such as mutually recognized laws of war and Geneva Conventions to help control a given situation, no guarantee that an agreement between contending parties will be honored, and no commonly accepted rules of engagement intended to constrain any state or nonstate actor. Additionally, there is no physical or human territory that cannot be bypassed or used; no national boundaries or laws that cannot be ignored or used; no method or means that cannot be disregarded or used; no battlefield (dimension of conflict) that cannot be ignored or used; and no national, transnational, nor nonstate actor or international organization that cannot be ignored or used in some combination. This is one set of reasons why Qiao and Wang titled their seminal book on contemporary conflict *Unrestricted Warfare*.[21]

Fourth, John Sullivan has identified an important shift in state form that is generated by various violent and nonviolent disruption, destabilization, and conflict processes. Under these conditions, nation-state form evolves from nation-state to market state and from market state to criminal quasi-state status. Sullivan warns us that resultant quasi-states (*focos*, zones, risk areas, alternately governed spaces, or malgoverned spaces) operating within the traditional nation-state are known to promulgate their own policy and laws—and impose their criminal values on societies and parts of societies all around the globe. At the same time, these quasi-states "create a bazaar of violence where criminal entrepreneurs fuel the convergence of crime and war."[22] Ambassador David C. Jordan argues that this disruption and destabilization is a prime mover toward narco-socialism and criminal states.[23]

Fifth, and last, the cautionary notes outlined so far represent a quintuple threat to the authority, legitimacy, and stability of targeted governments. Generally, these threats include (1) undermining the ability of a government to perform its legitimizing functions; (2) diminishing a government's state-building capabilities; (3) isolating municipalities and other communities from the rest of the nation's society and replacing traditional state authority with alternative (criminal and/or insurgent) governance; (4) transforming politically isolated human terrain into virtual states or quasi-states within the state; and (5) and radically changing political, economic, and social state form into something very likely unpopular and unwanted.

Again, the TCO–FARC nexus is much more than an organized criminal-terrorist enterprise. It is the kind of transnational criminal-insurgent phenomenon that uses terrorism as a means to achieve its grand-strategic objective of commercial enrichment and/or radical political-economic-social change. It also fuels Sullivan's ambiguous "convergence of crime and war." And, in these terms, it is an existential threat to the contemporary political-economic-social structure of the Colombian state. This cautionary tale takes us to the problem of response.

RECOMMENDED RESPONSE

Empirical realities operating throughout the spectrum of conflict, and as they apply to Colombia, mandate a mix of hard (kinetic) and soft (nonkinetic) power assets that equate to what Professor Joseph Nye Jr. calls "smart power."[24] In this context, it must be remembered that the enemy may not be a recognizable military force or have the industrial and technical capability to undertake conventional conflict. The enemy may be an inanimate "root cause" (poverty and malgovernance are two examples) of instability, insecurity, or threat to personal and/or collective well-being.

In this "new" security environment, war is no longer an exclusive military-economic-diplomatic undertaking conducted by traditional nation-states. In short, the power to exploit poverty and malgovernance, make war, control war, and destroy states and societies is now within the reach of virtually anyone or any organization with a "cause."[25]

The Challenge

The basis for the development of "smart power" is a unified field theory (a strategic concept, a paradigm, a blueprint for action, or a theory of engagement) designed to direct policy, strategy, and power asset management toward the achievement of a grand geopolitical strategic objective. An example of such a theory would be Ambassador George Kennan's theory of containment of the Soviet Union that was published in 1947.[26] That campaign plan was the basis for developing subordinate operational-level and supporting tactical plans that would make direct contributions to the achievement of the desired geopolitical end state rather than respond to ad hoc operational and tactical "mission creep."[27]

The Task

As noted in the previous section, the logic of the smart power philosophy calls for more than a military or other singular ad hoc solution. At the same time, all this is not only a moral-humanitarian concern. Evidence over time and space also calls for a security paradigm that moves through an all-inclusive upward circular process of interdependent relationships from (1) a singular tactical-operational military and/or law enforcement approach to (2) a holistic smart power strategic-level political-diplomatic, socioeconomic, psychological-moral, and rule of law effort to (3) legitimizing political reform and a sustainable peace, and all this circles back to an enhanced level of personal and collective safety again, and again, and again.[28]

This challenge and task are nothing new, and not even close to radical. They are only the logical extensions of basic security and strategy and national and international hard and soft power asset management. By accepting this challenge and task, the United States, the West, and perhaps others in the global community can help replace conflict with cooperation, harvest the hope, and fulfill the promise that a new multidimensional smart power security paradigm offers.[29] Another word of caution, however. Universal strategic lessons learned over the past several years lead to the conclusion that nothing of the smart power option is quickly, easily, or cheaply accomplished. Nevertheless, these are better than the inconclusive, destructive, and murderous alternatives.

Options

U.S. and Colombian security practitioners tend to share a general intellectual and philosophical outlook—Realism and Liberalism. Realism is based on two key assumptions. The first is that the principle actor in international politics is the nation-state. The second assumption is that the state follows a rational decision-making process in seeking to secure its interests. Thus, nonstate actors have no role to play in the global security arena. It is traditional military, economic, and diplomatic (hard or kinetic power) that are the principle instruments of well-planned and carefully implemented nation-state statecraft. Liberalism is dedicated to the cause of peace and democracy. The cause of peace and democracy is served by helping nation-states take down malgoverning regimes. That kind of action—often with the help of military power—will theoretically create democracy and a legitimate nation-state.[30]

The reality of the situation, however, demonstrates the fact that no U.S. or Colombian decision maker has authorized or implemented anything like a "smart power" security plan since 1947 (Kennan's containment plan). The most obvious and well-used policy options have been/are simple "wish lists," "muddling-through" notions, and "ad-hoc-ery." These self-defining policy alternatives are not known for their sterling successes. These policy alternatives have been vague and open-ended with no clear path (ends, ways, and means) to any geostrategic definition of success or victory. Consequently, the problems associated with contemporary *intrastate* conflict rage relatively unchecked around much of the world and have devastated the lives of millions of human beings. At the same time, indirect and unmet needs lead people into greater personal and collective insecurity.

So, what are the options? Simply put, there are no viable policy options at present.

In Colombia, as an example, the promulgation of Plan Colombia in the year 2000 provided the basis for a coherent political-military project, but not much else.[31] The various governments dealt with the narco-FARC phenomenon as a military and/or law enforcement issue, and on a completely ad hoc basis. Moreover, this was done within an environment of mutual enmity between the civil governments and the armed forces. The various civil-military elites tended to do little more than watch, debate, and wrangle about what—if anything—to do about the supposedly "new and unknown" narco-FARC phenomenon. At the same time, Colombia's most powerful ally, the United States, focused its money, training, and attention almost entirely on the counter-drug campaign. As a result, Colombia and the United States achieved a series of tactical "successes" in the coca fields, the laboratories, and the streets. Nevertheless, the narco-FARC actors remained strong and became even wealthier.[32]

More recently, the United States has encouraged Colombia to add a few "items" (a "wish list") to its planning for the present and the future. Only three items need be listed as examples. They would include (1) Colombian civil and supporting military operations that pertain to a populace-centric effort should be better balanced, better coordinated, and better resourced; (2) intelligence, psychological/information operations, and civil affairs activities must be given highest priority; and (3) all that is done must be intended to capture the imagination of the Colombian people, thereby winning a public opinion trial of moral rectitude (legitimacy).[33]

All this does not mean that the United States must be involved all over the world all the time. It does mean, however, that the United States must rethink and renew the concept of security and its priorities. Philosophical underpinnings (a smart power theory of engagement) must be devised for new policies to deal with more diverse threats—from unpredictable directions and by more diverse state and nonstate actors. Again, these are the strategic-level means by which, over time, the state and its external allies can make its internal enemies and their external allies irrelevant—or not.

CONCLUSIONS

A new and dangerous dynamic is at work around the world today. That dynamic involves the migration of political power (the authoritative allocation of values in a society)[34] from the traditional nation-state to unconventional nonstate actors. These actors promulgate their own rule of law and conduct their own type of war against various state and nonstate adversaries. This transnational criminal-insurgent-terrorist phenomenon is being ignored or, alternatively, is considered too hard to deal with. Yet, this phenomenon is an existential threat to the existence, stability, security, and well-being of Colombia, other nation-states, and their international neighbors.

NOTES

1. These and subsequent assertions are based on the author's field notes, Colombia, 2000–2015. These notes include interviews with over 300 junior and senior Colombian and U.S. civilian and military officials and are supplemented by consensus statements based on more recent interviews and observations.

2. Ernesto "Che" Guevara, *Guerrilla Warfare* (New York: Monthly Review Press, 1961); Ernesto Che Guevara, *Obras Completas* (Buenos Aires: Cepe, 1973).

3. Robert J. Bunker and John P. Sullivan, "Cartel Evolution: Potentials and Consequences," *Transnational Organized Crime* 4, no. 2 (Summer 1998), 55–78; John Rapley, "The New Middle Ages," *Foreign Affairs* (May/June 2006), 93–103; John P. Sullivan, "Maras Morphing: Revisiting Third Generation Gangs," *Global Crime* 7, no. 3–4 (August–November 2009), 493–494; "War's Human Cost," *UNHCR Global Trends*, 2015 (New York: UNHCR, 2016); Robert J. Bunker and Pamela Ligouri Bunker, "The Modern State in Epochal Transition: The Significance of Irregular Warfare," *Small Wars & Insurgencies* 27, no. 2 (2016), 325–344. Also see, Carl von Clausewitz, *On War*, edited and translated by Michael Howard and Peter Paret, Orig. pub. 1832 (Princeton, NJ: Princeton University Press, 1976), 72–93.

4. Sun Tzu, *The Art of War*, translated by Samuel B. Griffith (Oxford: Oxford University Press, 1963), 73. Also see, Vernon Lee Fluherty, *Dance of the Millions: Military Rule and Social Revolution in Colombia, 1930–1956* (Pittsburgh, PA: University of Pittsburgh Press, 1957); Luis Alberto Restrepo, *Violence in Colombia* (Wilmington, DE: SR Books, 1992); Hall Klepack, "Colombia: Why Doesn't the War End?" *Jane's*

Intelligence Review (January 2000), 41–45; Angel Rabassa and Peter Chalk, *Colombian Labyrinth: The Synergy of Drugs and Insurgency and Its Implications for Regional Stability* (Santa Monica, CA: Rand, 2001).

5. In 1982, a decision was made at the Seventh Conference of the FARC to develop links with the Colombian illegal drug industry that would provide the money and arms necessary to create a "true Bolivarian democracy." Rabassa and Chalk, *Colombian Labyrinth*. Also see, "An Interview with FARC Commander Simon Trinidad," *NACLA Report on the Americas* (September/October 2000); Alfred Molano, "The Evolution of FARC: A Guerrilla Group's Long History," *NACLA Report on the Americas* (September/October 2000); Jane's Information Group, "FARC: Finance Comes Full Circle for Bartering Revolutionaries," January 19, 2001; "FARC Inc.," *Semana*, January 30, 2005, www.semana2.terra.com.co/opencms/Semana/articulo,html?id+84464.

6. Carlos Pinzón, Colombian minister of defense, presentation entitled, "Colombia's Strategic Overview: From National Security to Public Safety," given at the U.S. National Defense University in Washington, DC, April 24, 2013. Also see V. I. Lenin, "The State and Revolution," in *The Lenin Anthology*, ed. Robert C. Tucker (New York: W.W. Norton, 1975), 324.

7. Ibid. Also see, "Survey of Colombia," *Economist*, April 21–27, 2001; Douglas Porch, "Uribe's Second Mandate," *Strategic Insights* 5, no. 2 (February 2006), www.ccc.nps.navy.mil.

8. Nothing in this or other assertions regarding FARC should be considered the author's opinion. Anyone may check FARC doctrine or other information at http://farc-ep.col. Also see, Ernesto "Che" Guevara, *Guerrilla Warfare*, 1961; Ernesto "Che" Guevara, *"Che" Guevara on Revolution: A Documentary Overview* (Miami, FL: University of Miami Press, 1969).

9. Jorge Verstrynge Rojas, *La Guerra Periférica y el Islam Revolucionario*, Special Edition for the Army of the Bolivarian Republic of Venezuela, IDRFAN, Enlace Circular Militar (Madrid, Spain: El Viejo Topo, May 2005); Guevara, *"Che" Guevara on Revolution: A Documentary Overview*; Also see, Tzu, *The Art of War*; V.I. Lenin, "Report on War and Peace," in *The Lenin Anthology*, ed. Robert C. Tucker (New York: W.W. Norton, 1975); Carl von Clausewitz, *On War*.

10. Interviews with former insurgent and, later, mayor of Bogotá, Gustavo Petro, reported in *Revista DEF* (Argentina), December 2012; and former insurgent and, then, governor of the Colombian Department of Nariño, in *Revista DEF* (Argentina), December 2012, published in January 2013, 98–102. Also note that "New 21st Century Socialist State is the new name for the old 'true Bolivarian democracy.'"

11. For a good discussion of these points, see, General Carlos A. Ospina, Thomas A. Marks, and David H. Ucko, "Colombia and the War-to-Peace Transition," *Military Review* (July–August 2016), 40–52.

12. For discussions of these points, see, Ospina, Marks, and Ucko, "Colombia and the War-to-Peace Transition"; Nick Miroff, "The Frightening Issue That Could Destroy Colombia's Peace Deal," *Washington Post*, January 3, 2017, https://www.washingtonpost.com/world/the_americas/the-frightening-issue-that-could-destroy-colombias-peace-deal/2017/01/02/3e0a7fec-c304-11e6-92e8-c07f4f671da4_story.html.

13. Carlos Pinzón, "Colombia's Strategic Overview: From National Security to Public Safety." Also see, Edwin Mora, "House Report: Hezbollah Trafficking

Drugs, 'Virtually Unopposed' in Latin America," December 21, 2016, http://www.breitbart.com/national-security/2016/12/21/congressional-task-force-hezbollah-drug-trafficking-latin-america/.

14. Carlos Pinzón, "Colombia's Strategic Overview: From National Security to Public Safety"; Ospina, Marks, and Ucko, "Colombia and the War-to-Peace Transition"; Mira Galanova, "Is Colombia Going from War to Peace to Genocide?" *Colombia Report*, March 6, 2017, https://colombiareports.com/colombia-going-war-peace-genocide/.

15. Mora, "House Report: Hezbollah Trafficking Drugs."

16. Phil Williams, *From the New Middle Ages to a New Dark Age: The Decline of the State and U.S. Strategy* (Carlisle, PA: Strategic Studies Institute, U.S. Army War College, June 2008); and Rapley, "The New Middle Ages."

17. Ospina, Marks, and Ucko, "Colombia and the War-to-Peace Transition"; Miroff, "The Frightening Issue That Could Destroy Colombia's Peace Deal"; Fluherty, *Dance of the Millions*; Restrepo, *Violence in Colombia*.

18. See, Clausewitz, *On War*. Also see, *U.S. Army/Marine Corps Counterinsurgency Field Manual* (Chicago: University of Chicago Press, 2007); *Field Manual 100–20*, "Military Operations—Low Intensity Conflict," HQDA, Washington, DC, 2014.

19. Qiao Liang and Wang Xiangsui, *Unrestricted Warfare* (Beijing: PLA Literature and Arts Publishing House, 1999); Abraham Guillen, *Philosophy of the Urban Guerrilla: The Revolutionary Writings of Abraham Guillen* (New York: Morrow, 1973), 278–279.

20. Adriaan Alsema, "Peace with FARC Marked 'New Phase of Armed Conflict' in Colombia," *Colombia Reports*, March 16, 2017, https://colombiareports.com/peace-farc-marked-new-phase-armed-conflict-colombia-report/.

21. Qiao and Wang, *Unrestricted Warfare*.

22. John P. Sullivan, "Terrorism, Crime, and Private Armies," *Low Intensity Conflict & Law Enforcement* 11, no. 2–3 (Winter 2002), 239–253; John P. Sullivan and Robert J. Bunker, "Rethinking Insurgency, Criminality, Spirituality, and Societal Welfare in the Americas," *Small Wars & Insurgencies* 22, no. 5 (December 2011), 742–760.

23. David C. Jordan, *Drug Politics: Dirty Money and Democracies* (Norman, OK: University of Oklahoma Press, 1999), 142–157.

24. Joseph S. Nye Jr., "Restoring American Leadership through Smart Power," *Global Strategic Assessment* (Washington, DC: National Defense University, Institute for National Strategic Studies, 2009), 474–476. Also see, General Rupert Smith (UK, Ret.), *The Utility of Force: The Art of War in the Modern World* (New York: Knopf, 2007).

25. Smith, *The Utility of Force*. Also see, Lee Feinstein and Ann Marie Slaughter, "A Duty to Prevent," *Foreign Affairs* (January/February 2004), 147–148; and Amatai Etzione, "Changing the Rules," *Foreign Affairs* (November/December, 2011), 173.

26. George F. Kennan, "The Sources of Soviet Conduct," *Foreign Affairs* (July 1947), 566–582.

27. Author interview with General John R. Galvin (USA, Ret.), August 6, 1997, Boston, MA. The complete interview is included in the Spring 1998 *Special Issue of Small Wars & Insurgencies*, no. 1, 9.

28. All this goes back to Tzu, *The Art of War*; Clausewitz, *On War*; Vo Nguyen Giap, *People's War, People's Army: The Vietcong Insurrection Manual for Underdeveloped Countries*, 1962 (NP: Tannenburg, 2015); Boutros-Boutros Ghali, *Agenda for*

Peace: Preventive Diplomacy, Peacemaking and Peace-keeping, report of the secretary-general pursuant to the statement adopted by the summit meeting of the Security Council on January 31, 1992, June 17, 1992; *Milennium Report*, 2001; OAS *Declaration on Security*, 2003. Also see Feinstein and Slaugher, "A Duty to Prevent," 147–148; Etzione, "Changing the Rules," 173; and Stephen Krasner, "An Orienting Principle for Foreign Policy: Responsible Sovereignty," *Policy Review*, no. 163 (Palo Alto, CA: Hoover Institution, Stanford University, October 1, 2010).

29. Albert Camus, *The Rebel* (New York: Vintage, 1956), 302.

30. Graham T. Allison, "Conceptual Models and the Cuban Missile Crisis," *American Political Science Review* 63, no. 3 (September 1969), 689–718.

31. Author observations. From the mid-1990s through the mid-2000s, the author was in a position from which to observe the political-military situation in Colombia. Additionally, these and subsequent assertions are based on the author's field notes, Colombia, 2000–2015.

32. Ibid.

33. Ibid., and the unclassified "Consultative Team Report," written for the Commander of the U.S. Southern Command (USSOUTHCOM), September 17, 2012.

34. Ibid. Also see: David Easton, *The Political System: An Inquiry into the State of Political Science* (New York: Knopf, 1963), 99, 128–129.

CHAPTER 7

Boko Haram and al-Shabaab: Adaptable Criminal Financing amid Expanded Terror

Omar S. Mahmood

Islamic-inspired terrorist organizations have thrived in parts of Africa over the past decade, marking the continent as a new frontier in the global battle against terrorism. Two of the most prominent organizations, Boko Haram and al-Shabaab, have had their operations underpinned through successful criminal financing efforts, in part to make up for declining popular support. Through similar but distinct avenues, both have made ingenious use of the local environment in which they operate, enhanced by aspects of territorial control and a reliance on the local civilian populace.

BOKO HARAM'S FINANCIAL RISE AND FALL

Boko Haram is a terrorist organization that emerged out of the preaching of Nigerian founder Muhammad Yusuf in the mid-2000s.[1] Following a similar ideological approach of Salafi-jihadist movements in the mold of Al-Qaida, Yusuf combined these influences with locally rooted rhetoric that criticized the dismantling of precolonial Islamic empires, illegitimacy of the resulting secular postcolonial Nigerian state, and prominence of Western-style education systems over more traditional forms of Islamic schooling.

Now present in northeast Nigeria and the Lake Chad Basin, which includes parts of neighboring Cameroon, Chad, and Niger, the organization's astonishing rise in a just few years earned it notoriety as the deadliest terror group in the world in 2014. Boko Haram also achieved significant but fleeting financial success, named by *Forbes* as the 10th richest terrorist organization the same year with a value of $25 million.[2] By early 2017, however, this situation had reversed, with UN envoy Jeffrey Feltman noting the group is "plagued by financial difficulties."[3] While not as dominant as before, the movement's continued strength in rural areas has nonetheless allowed it to maintain control over a few key revenue streams.

The question of how Boko Haram was able to rise to such a prominent status so quickly, but then ultimately squandered much of it, will be a primary underlying theme of this section through an examination of the group's criminal activities.

Early Days

The criminal aspects of Boko Haram's financing have taken a myriad of different avenues, shifting over time in reaction to external developments. Initially during the days of Muhammad Yusuf, the group built a "state within a state," in Maiduguri, and was largely self-sufficient through membership dues and small enterprises like selling water or renting motorcycles.[4] Some of these profits were reportedly channeled to the purchase of weaponry in advance of a likely confrontation with the Nigerian state, indicating that linkages with criminal elements in the arms trafficking space had already begun.[5]

KEY MOMENTS IN BOKO HARAM'S HISTORY

- July 2009—Crackdown by Nigerian security forces kills nearly 1,000 group members, including founder Muhammad Yusuf.
- September 2010—Boko Haram reemerges as a terrorist organization under new leader Abubakar Shekau and expands activity to include central Nigeria.
- May 2013—Civilian vigilantes opposed to Boko Haram emerge in urban areas; the militants flee to the countryside and transform into a rural movement.
- July 2014—Boko Haram embarks on territorial control for the first time; predatory attacks on civilians increase in response to support for the vigilantes.
- March 2015—Shekau pledges allegiance to the Islamic State; regional efforts to degrade the group gather pace, resulting in the loss of territorial control and bringing an end to Boko Haram's short-lived governance project.
- August 2016—Boko Haram splits into two factions: one led by Shekau and the other backed by the Islamic State and headed by Abu Musab al-Barnawi.

The movement emerged as a terrorist entity under new leader Abubakar Shekau in 2010, regrouping following a violent crackdown on its members in 2009. To fund these new operations, criminal financing took on an increased importance.

Robbery

Simply stealing cash and other goods has been a predominant theme characterizing Boko Haram's criminal behavior. Initially, the robbing of banks in northeast Nigeria was a primary activity. This aligned with other objectives, as Boko Haram members attacked police stations simultaneously in small towns, fulfilling a strategic objective to confront Nigerian security forces and also a practical one to limit response while the group carted away cash. This theme of combining violence with strategic looting has been an important one in the movement's financial history.

Particularly prominent during the movement's reemergence and expansion in 2011–2012, earnings from bank robberies are estimated to be as high as $6 million.[6] In 2011 alone, 30 of the 100 banks attacked in Nigeria were attributed to Boko Haram.[7] Nonetheless, reported bank robberies declined over time, while others may not have been specifically linked to the group but rather criminal elements whose activities were lumped together under the Boko Haram moniker. While the reasons for this decline are uncertain, it is clear that this criminal activity was a boon to the sect during its reemergence.

During its initial foray into territorial control in 2014, banks that fell under its sway were again raided for cash. For example, after taking control of the town of Mubi in northern Adamawa state, N100 million (approximately $500,000) was taken from a local bank, emphasizing how territorial control can enhance group financing.[8]

In addition to robbing banks, Boko Haram also robbed other sources. A spate of attacks in 2011–2012 targeted government vehicles transporting local salaries, as the group took advantage of an environment in which payments were still physically transported in cash to recipients. In a July 2011 incident, militants made away with N21.5 million ($140,000) in Borno State, while another attack in neighboring Yobe in July 2012 garnered N35 million ($215,000)—an indication of the sums available.[9]

Extortion

Closely tied to the blatant act of stealing is the practice of extortion. This has taken a variety of forms and targets, continuing throughout the movement's history. Protection money has been a large aspect of this, with unconfirmed but persistent allegations that the governors of Kano and Bauchi State even paid Boko Haram to avoid attacks.[10] Local businessmen and other citizens have also been intimidated, often through SMS text.[11]

The threat of violence has forced many to comply, but the individualized and undocumented nature of this activity makes it impossible to quantify. What is clear, however, is that extortion and intimidation are ongoing, with noncompliance subject to the punishment of death. For example, in March 2017 a herder near Lake Chad was slaughtered by militants after he refused protection money demands.[12]

Kidnapping

Perhaps the most lucrative criminal activity in which Boko Haram became involved is kidnapping for ransom (KFR). The highest profile cases dealt with foreign (often Western) nationals, but much KFR activity centers around local civilians as well.

Despite a previous abhorrence of the activity, by 2013 Boko Haram began to see KFRs as a lucrative opportunity.[13] Five prominent incidents outlined in Table 7.1, along with reported ransom payments totaling an approximate $25 million, likely dwarfed all other income streams. The incidents occurred in neighboring Cameroon, as the lack of daily Boko Haram violence at the time rendered it a location that was not yet off limits to foreign nationals. Ultimately, however, this activity proved unsustainable, as Boko Haram's subsequent incursions into the border regions of Cameroon, Chad, and Niger led to travel restrictions, reducing the available pool of potential hostages.

In this sense, KFRs served as a temporary, albeit highly lucrative, activity and directly preceded the group's zenith, marked by large-scale territorial control in mid-2014 to early 2015. The windfalls from this activity likely contributed to this strength, but the inability to maintain similar levels of financial support meant it was only a temporary increase, forcing the group to readjust to financing levels similar to the pre-KFR period once this stream dried up. The influx of foreign nationals in northeast Nigeria involved in humanitarian relief and other assistance programs since 2015, however, could provide an outlet to resurrect this activity.[14]

Local Kidnappings

The abduction of local civilians is another hallmark of Boko Haram, most infamously demonstrated by the kidnapping of 219 schoolgirls from the town of Chibok in April 2014. Yet the abduction of ordinary citizens is often conducted without financial motive, but rather to indoctrinate them into the movement or fulfill other roles (e.g., targeting females as sexual partners under the guise of forced marriage). Nonetheless, those who could pay for their freedom were released at times, while others were specifically targeted because of their wealth in cases much less heralded in the international media.

Table 7.1
Successful Boko Haram KFR Operations[1]

Date	Location	Hostages	Ransom	Notes
February 19, 2013	Near Waza, Cameroon	French family of 7, including 4 children	Estimated between $3 and $7 million[2]	Released after two months in April 2013
November 13, 2013	Koza, Cameroon	French priest	$12.5 million[3]	Released in December 2013
April 4, 2014	Tchéré, Cameroon	2 Italian priests, 1 Canadian nun	Unknown	Released in May 2014
May 16, 2014	Near Waza, Cameroon	10 Chinese construction workers	$2.6 million[4]	Released along with Kolofata victims (below) in October 2014
July 27, 2014	Kolofata, Cameroon	Prominent members of Kolofata	$3.1 million[5]	Hostages included wife of Cameroon vice president and local traditional leader

1. Boko Haram also obtained the release of some detained group members in exchange for the hostages.

2. "Nigeria's Boko Haram 'Got $3m Ransom' to Free Hostages," BBC, April 27, 2013, http://www.bbc.com/news/world-africa-22320077; "Confronting Boko Haram in Cameroon," *International Crisis Group*, November 16, 2016, 16.

3. Yuh Timchia, "Boko Haram 'Was Paid' $12.5m to Release French Priest," *Africa Review*, January 7, 2014, http://www.africareview.com/News/Boko-Haram-paid-millions-to-release-French-priest-/-/979180/2137672/-/j1qvxf/-/index.html?relative=true.

4. "Confronting Boko Haram in Cameroon," *International Crisis Group*, November 16, 2016, 16.

5. Ibid.

For example, in 2013, Shettima Ali Monguno, a respected former civil servant who served as a former oil minister, was kidnapped from his home in Maiduguri. Eventually released for N50 million (over $300,000), his case is symbolic of this activity.[15] While other wealthy Nigerians have reportedly been released for as much as $1 million per hostage (likely a high estimate), a proliferation of smaller-scale activity has resulted in releases for amounts as small as $4,000.[16]

Impact of Territorial Control

The advent of territorial control in mid-2014 enhanced several avenues of financing while opening up others. For example, the group released abducted civilians from its notorious jails in return for financial gain.[17] In addition, taxation became an aspect of group financing, as militants demanded funds at checkpoints and from local businesses—a form of extortion.[18] Additional extortion based on the threat of retributive violence against a civilian populace often viewed as the enemy, such as protection to not burn down local farms, also occurred.[19] While Boko Haram did not control territory in 2017 as it did in 2014, its presence and strength in rural areas ensure it continues to benefit in certain schemes, such as through the intimidation of local populations, or its involvement in local commodity trading.

Local Commodities

Following Boko Haram's transformation into a more rural outfit in 2013, the group placed an emphasis on stealing basic supplies such as foodstuffs, medicines, and other material goods rather than cash to ensure survival in rural hideouts. The group also supplemented the lack of cash by becoming involved in local commodity trading and smuggling, often characterized by a cross-border element.

Initial reports of the movement's involvement in cattle rustling emerged in late 2014, coinciding with the advent of territorial control. During the group's predominately urban lifestyle prior to 2013, the stealing and herding of large amounts of cattle would have been difficult. After it gained control of large swathes of territory, this practice became commonplace, as Boko Haram profited by transporting cattle through areas where it faced little to no resistance.

This has occurred primarily via stealing cattle in northern Cameroon, at times during attacks and at times as an end in itself, and then transporting the livestock across the border to middlemen in Borno State, who sell them in local Nigerian markets at reduced prices.[20] Alternatively, the group also utilizes circuitous routes to local markets in order to disguise the origin of the cattle.[21] This became such a frequent practice that the Nigerian military even temporarily shut down cattle markets while the Borno State government also banned cattle imports in an attempt to prevent Boko Haram from profiting from the trade.[22] One credible estimate from late 2016 put the total financial accumulation in this realm at $3.4 million, though others have been significantly higher.[23]

Similar involvement has occurred in the pepper trade in Niger, which authorities also temporarily banned in 2015.[24] Around the shores of Lake Chad, Boko Haram has likewise become involved in the sale of fish, following a similar pattern by seizing quantities of fish and passing them along to consenting middlemen who sell them in local markets. In Borno, the transportation of fish has been outlawed in response, with the military seeking to control the trade to ensure Boko Haram does not profit.[25]

These activities demonstrate Boko Haram's "live off the land" approach to sustaining group finances and also the predicament for local authorities to counter this in a manner that is not injurious to civilian livelihoods dependent on such trades. The restrictions imposed may indeed curtail financing to the Islamist sect and also serve as a double shock for civilians who have been preyed upon by Boko Haram for their livelihoods, only for such activities to subsequently become restricted. Given the backdrop of a major humanitarian emergency unfolding in the Lake Chad Basin region, with up to 7 million suffering from crisis levels of food insecurity, such limiting responses take on a magnified impact.

Summary

Criminal activity has been a key part of Boko Haram's ability to finance itself since its reemergence in 2010, as it shifted its financial model from one based on organizational income generation to one based on criminal financing, evidenced by the activities noted in Table 7.2.[26] The success of certain measures allowed the group to build a substantial war chest in a short period of time. Nonetheless, the reduction of kidnapping operations and removal from areas of territorial control reduced overall income streams. Where Boko Haram has been successful is in inserting itself and extorting local trades, namely, livestock, dried fish, and pepper.[27] Nonetheless, while this activity has helped the group sustain its operations, it is a far cry from the height of the organization's financial prowess between 2013 and 2014. One possible manifestation of this decline may be a rash of surrenders in late 2016 and early 2017, in which former members complained about a lack of supplies, among other concerns.[28]

In addition, Boko Haram's predatory activity and targeting of the local population have reduced its overall ability to prey upon them for supplies. For example, Boko Haram attacks under Shekau frequently have a punitive aspect to them, with militants burning down houses and local supplies or killing farmers in their fields.[29] Combined with the flight of over 2 million people displaced mainly from Boko Haram areas of influence and an ongoing humanitarian disaster, the ability to prey upon the local population has been reduced, in turn disadvantaging the movement itself.

This underlines a key vulnerability in Boko Haram's criminal activities—they are largely dependent on having a local population from which to extract concessions.[30] The failure of Boko Haram to develop alternative funding schemes beyond its limited involvement in KFRs stands in contrast to al-Shabaab, the subject of the remainder of this chapter. While al-Shabaab plunders from the local population as well, its strategic location along the longest coastline in mainland Africa, combined with its proximity to key global markets, has allowed the movement to survive in the wake of reduced public support and loss of key areas of territorial control.

Table 7.2
Major Boko Haram Criminal Activity, by Year

Year/Activity	Bank Robbery	Stealing/Extortion	KFR (foreigners)	KFR (locals)	Taxes (control)	Cattle Rustling	Fish and Pepper
2011	█	█					
2012	█	█	█				
2013	█	█	█	█			
2014		█	█	█	█	█	
2015		█		█	█	█	█
2016		█	█	█	█	█	█
2017		█	█	█	█	█	█

Note: The black areas of the table indicate the years in which the criminal activity was a main source of revenue for the group, while the white portions indicate periods when it was not significant.

AL-SHABAAB'S SUCCESSFUL ADJUSTMENTS

Steeped in a similar Salafi-jihadist ideology as Boko Haram, al-Shabaab is the latest and most violent manifestation of Islamism in Somalia, with many movements emerging in the vacuum created by the collapse of central government rule in 1991. Initially serving as the militant youth wing of the Islamic Courts Union (ICU), al-Shabaab rose to prominence following the Ethiopian invasion of Somalia in late 2006 and has occupied large swathes of southern and central Somalia in the decade since, serving less as a pure terrorist organization and more as a governing entity. While many key areas of control tied to revenue streams, such as the capital Mogadishu and port cities of Kismayo and Barawe, have since fallen out of al-Shabaab's hands, the movement remains a strong force in the country, in large part due to its ability to consistently adjust to local conditions.

As an indication of this success, the UN Monitoring Group on Somalia and Eritrea, which has extensively investigated the group, "conservatively" estimated al-Shabaab's annual revenues to be between $70 and $100 million in 2011.[31] In comparison, the Transitional Federal Government (TFG) in Somalia operated in the first half of 2011 on a budget of approximately $50 million, only 30 percent of which was generated locally.[32]

Al-Shabaab's criminal enterprises are diverse and have altered over time—space limitations prevent consideration of each and every avenue,

KEY EVENTS IN AL-SHABAAB'S HISTORY

- 2006–2008—Emerges out of the Islamic Courts Union (ICU) and serves as the leading movement combating the Ethiopian invasion of Somalia; exerts control in South-Central Somalia.

- January 2009—Ethiopian forces withdraw, while political reconciliation includes many Islamists in a new Transitional Federal Government (TFG) for Somalia; both aspects diminish al-Shabaab's popularity, but the movement takes on additional territorial control.

- August 2011—Al-Shabaab withdraws from Mogadishu; a poor response to the 2011 famine further erodes public support.

- October 2011—Kenya invades Somalia, followed shortly after by Ethiopia again; both interventions push al-Shabaab from key areas of control.

- February 2012—Al-Shabaab officially merges with Al-Qaida, formalizing a relationship after years of courtship.

- September 2012—Al-Shabaab withdraws from the key port of Kismayo but maintains a stranglehold on rural areas surrounding the city.

- October 2014—Al-Shabaab withdraws from its last major port stronghold in Barawe but continues to control significant swathes of rural territory.

or its expanding reach beyond Somalia. Rather, a focus on a few principal streams will be discussed, which illustrate the movement's ability to generate financing.

Diaspora Funding

Al-Shabaab rose to prominence primarily as an outlet to combat the unpopular invasion of Somalia by Ethiopia, viewed as a Christian nation with a long history of aggression, and its initial financial fortunes played upon this popularity. Donations flowed from the disperse Somali diaspora, a community whose global position had been enhanced by the preceding two decades of strife. Monetary transfers often occurred via the informal *hawala* system, confounding efforts by law enforcement personnel to monitor them. The group combined traditional measures with more modern innovations, holding fund-raising forums online, often linked to specific campaigns. For example, one in August 2009 raised $40,000 specifically for fighters in the Bakool, Bay, Gedo, and Hiraan regions.[33] The presence of large Somali communities both in the West, where most of the money originated, and the Middle East, where much of it transited before arriving in Somalia, underlined the global structure of this network.

Actions to regulate this activity have resulted in temporary shutdowns of remittance companies, a detriment to a Somali populace heavily dependent on this lifeline, and another example of a restrictive measure aimed at countering terrorist financing, but with wider implications.[34] Nonetheless, as al-Shabaab's popularity began to wane (see the previous box), this level of financing was also affected. While not completely drying up, the movement was forced to seek out alternative forms of funding—a task to which it proved quite able.[35]

Taxation and Extortion

Taxation and extortion have been key means of generating income. Taxation occurs through a variety of forms and, while collected at a regional level, quickly became centralized within al-Shabaab, demonstrating the movement's penchant for bureaucracy. Al-Shabaab has even published literature outlining its taxation policy, in addition to providing receipts at checkpoints valid throughout al-Shabaab territory to eliminate double taxation. In this sense, while al-Shabaab taxation has generated significant local resentment, it has also been held up as a model compared to the more haphazard and corrupt processes undertaken by various regional militias and the federal government.[36]

Organizations operating in areas of al-Shabaab control have been required to pay for that privilege, with some of the most notable cases involving aid agencies. For example, a September 2010 directive regulating aid access demanded a $10,000 initial fee, a $10,000 one-time registration fee, and $6,000 every six months thereafter, in addition to a 10 percent duty on all vehicles and 20 percent of supplies distributed per organization.[37] By 2011, however, al-Shabaab banned aid agencies, viewing the primarily Western organizations both as a moralizing influence antithetical to al-Shabaab's ideology and as an espionage risk likely to report on group movements.[38] While that would prove a disastrous decision in terms of response to an ongoing drought, it also signaled that the group's financial balance sheet was healthy enough to withstand the loss of this source of income generation.[39]

Smaller local businesses were also required to pay taxes, with al-Shabaab determining the amount.[40] As late as 2015, some businesses in Mogadishu reportedly still paid taxes to al-Shabaab rather than the government, four years after the group's departure from the city. This was an indication of al-Shabaab's continued ability to project power vis-à-vis the fledgling Somalia Federal Government (SFG) even in areas it does not actively control.[41]

Individuals are also subject to taxation, which al-Shabaab justifies on religious grounds, demanding *zakat* and *sadaqh*. *Zakat* is a religious obligation typically set at 2.5 percent of an individual's annual profit, but al-Shabaab expropriated this practice, insisting it was a credible-enough religious authority to undertake collection. *Sadaqh* refers to voluntary donations, which al-Shabaab violated by demanding a specific amount.[42] Both raised legitimacy concerns and have sparked clashes between local civilians refusing to part with their income or possessions, leading to seizure by force.[43] Nonetheless, the practice is so widespread and lucrative that al-Shabaab has claimed it made $9 million in 2014 through *zakat* payments alone.[44]

Other taxes on economic production and trade, such as on farm production, livestock, and consumer goods, have contributed to al-Shabaab's war chest. The UN Monitoring Group remarked that taxing farmland production earned the group $9.5 million in 2016, and its role in helping compensate for losses elsewhere should not be overlooked.[45]

Control of Economic Resources

The emphasis on territorial occupation has also opened up financing streams for additional taxes, namely, via the control of various economic resources. Earnings from Somali seaports, markets, or checkpoints along major roads have garnered al-Shabaab millions of dollars. Acting as a semi-government entity, the example of the port of Kismayo is instructive in this regard.

Al-Shabaab captured Kismayo, southern Somalia's most important port in 2008, and ruled it in alliance with another Islamist group, Hizbul Islam. Estimates during this time hover around $5.6 million per year earned from port operations alone.[46] In 2009, al-Shabaab wrested sole control of

Kismayo after a clash with Hizbul Islam. Estimated profits rose, aided by the illegal exportation of charcoal (see later in this chapter), to $35 to $50 million per year, a substantial increase from a few years prior.[47]

Kenyan troops invaded southern Somalia and seized the port of Kismayo by September 2012. The hope was the fall of the port would be a major disruption to al-Shabaab finances, in turn weakening the group. The loss of Kismayo did indeed affect al-Shabaab, with many of the proceeds from the lucrative port now flowing to the Kenyan Defence Forces (KDF) and their locally supported Ras Kamboni militia. Yet al-Shabaab was still able to profit by shifting activity to other ports still under its control, and continuing to tax trade entering and leaving Kismayo by road, given its presence along key routes.[48] This is an indication that while the control of the port itself is important, such a focus was not enough by itself to degrade group financing.

Markets and checkpoints along roads have served as other sources of income derived from territorial control of key economic sectors. For example, in 2011 al-Shabaab earned $30 to $60 million per year controlling the major markets of Bakaara in Mogadishu and Suuq Baad.[49] Al-Shabaab's presence on the road between Mogadishu and Beledweyne also generated an estimated $3 million in roadside taxes in 2015, while a similar system around the city of Jowhar generated $9 million in 2013.[50]

Nonetheless, while al-Shabaab has profited from control of key economic resources, it has also demonstrated an ability to adjust upon losing that control. Al-Shabaab's strength in the rural countryside allows it to exert control over trade routes and even blockade certain cities to hinder nascent government efforts to establish control. The presence around the port of Kismayo or the continued collection of taxes in Mogadishu despite the organization's flight from the city years earlier are clear examples of this.

Charcoal and Sugar Trades

While taxation and extortion have been important means of criminal financing throughout al-Shabaab's history, perhaps the most important illicit revenue stream has been the group's involvement in certain commodities, taking advantage of Somalia's natural environment, local corruption, and proximity to external markets.

The charcoal trade has been one of the single highest income streams for al-Shabaab. Southern Somalia contains acacia trees, valued primarily in the Middle East for their sweet smell when manufactured into charcoal. Al-Shabaab's control of large swathes of southern Somalia by 2011, combined with the establishment of business relationships with major charcoal producers and exporters, led to a burgeoning illicit trade. Generating $15 million in 2011, this increased to $25 million in 2012 and paradoxically resulted in even greater earnings in 2013 and 2014, despite al-Shabaab's loss of Kismayo. This occurred given al-Shabaab's ability to project power along other aspects of the value chain, such as transport routes and production areas, in addition to possession of alternative ports, such as Barawe (controlled until October 2014).[51]

After the seizure of Kismayo, this trade involved implicit collaboration between the KDF, al-Shabaab, and the emerging Jubbaland administration in Kismayo, as all profited from a trade that transited through areas of control under the sway of all forces.[52] The profits at stake were too great to consider halting activities, resulting in, at a minimum, the tacit collusion between al-Shabaab and two entities ostensibly aimed at combating its existence. Nonetheless by 2015, Jubbaland had effectively cut al-Shabaab out, to the point where the organization began to actively obstruct the trade.[53]

When profits from charcoal began to decline, al-Shabaab shifted to the smuggling of imported sugar to Kenya, again relying on tacit, or even explicit, collusion with security officials in return for high profits. Al-Shabaab took advantage of market economics, by overseeing the importation of duty-free sugar to Somalia, in turn making a profit by facilitating its continued journey to Kenya, where high sugar tariffs result in an annual domestic consumption deficit of approximately 200,000 tons.[54] Earning $400,000 to $800,000 per year through this activity in 2011, this rose as charcoal revenues fell to become the single-most important earner for al-Shabaab by 2016, garnering between $12 and $18 million per year.[55]

Al-Shabaab taxes sugar trucks approximately $1,000 outside of Kismayo, one of a handful of extortion payments made to various entities on their journey from Somali ports to Kenyan markets.[56] Allegedly this has involved officials high up in Kenyan political and security circles who are ostensibly aware of al-Shabaab's role in generating revenue off this smuggling network. The example demonstrates al-Shabaab's ability to leverage market economics and its strategic location while taking advantage of the blatant corruption of local officials.

Summary

Al-Shabaab's criminal financing has shown a distinct ability to adjust, especially to the loss of control over key economic sectors.[57] The organization's strength in rural areas has ensured continued influence over certain trades, while the combination of market economics, corruption, and a strategic location also facilitates income generation, depicted in Table 7.3.

Al-Shabaab activity has also been reliant on predatory activity with regard to the local population, but such aspects have not been as destructive as Boko Haram's behavior, as the group has diversified into other streams that do not require civilian acquiescence. Nonetheless, this remains an important aspect, underlining two of the main determinants of successful financing efforts—civilian support and territorial control.

Table 7.3
Major Al-Shabaab Criminal Activities, by Year

Year/Activity	Diaspora Funding	Religiously Justified Taxation (individual)	Taxation (businesses and organizations)	Taxation (economic activity and trade)	Charcoal	Sugar
2007	■	■	■	■		
2008	■	■	■	■		
2009	■	■	■	■		
2010		■	■	■		
2011		■	■	■	■	■
2012		■	■	■	■	■
2013		■	■	■	■	■
2014		■	■	■	■	■
2015		■	■	■		■
2016		■	■	■		■
2017		■	■	■	■	■

Another key aspect of al-Shabaab's criminal financing is that the group largely emerged in a vacuum given the absence of central government control in Somalia. In this sense, al-Shabaab has served more as a governing entity and a direct counter to the emergent but fledgling SFG, whose survival has been dependent on African Union peacekeepers. Thus, al-Shabaab's financing has been intertwined with governance and has resulted in the provision of services back to the population it claims to serve, rather than completely channeled toward terrorist operations.[58] In this sense, al-Shabaab is less of a terrorist entity, but rather a governing organization that engages in terrorist violence, with resulting implications for efforts to counter its financial base.[59]

CONCLUSION AND POLICY OPTIONS

Both Boko Haram and al-Shabaab initially enjoyed a degree of initial popularity within the local communities in which they operated. Such measures tied into both groups' financial fortunes, relying on voluntary membership and donations. Both, however, had their popularity wane through a combination of expanded extremist activity, draconian religious practices, and larger shifts in their operating environment.

This transition led to more criminal activity, a clash between ideals professed by the movements, and the reality of emerging moneymaking schemes. Boko Haram's previous abhorrence for kidnapping stands in stark contrast to the high profits it gained from the tactic. Al-Shabaab, in turn, may have misapplied religious injunctions regarding *zakat* and *sadaqh*, while defector Zakariya Ahmed Hersi, a one-time high up official in al-Shabaab's intelligence wing, complained afterward about the organization's entrance into organized crime.[60] This points to the difficulties in balancing a strict ideological commitment with the need to generate funding. Such aspects may be an opportunity for governments to exploit, reducing support for the movements by highlighting their waywardness and descent into common criminality.

Thereafter, both groups continued to rely on the local population to maintain operations, but in a less voluntary manner. Nonetheless, measures to combat this activity have in turn restricted local livelihoods, be it via the ban on the cattle trade in northeast Nigeria, or remittance company shutdowns in Somalia. There is a need to balance measures that curtail terrorist group financing with the impact on the local population, lest the restrictions inflame tensions and ultimately result in additional support for the militant groups. Furthermore, better civilian protection and insulation from the wrath of such groups may help reduce support, especially in cases of duress or intimidation. In this sense, civilian protection should be a key priority as both groups possess the ability to project power into areas of government control, with ensuing ramifications for terrorist financing.

In addition to civilian acquiescence, the largest other determinant of financial success has been territorial control, and especially of key economic resources. But as both cases have demonstrated, the approach of securing the urban at the expense of the rural does not go far enough in isolating key economic sectors from militant influence. The ability to exert leverage in any and all aspects of a commodity supply chain results in group windfalls. While it is difficult for overstretched security forces to secure thinly populated rural areas, it is important to consider aspects linked to economic supply chains. It is also critical to focus on more measured approaches that prioritize sustainable rural control rather than just isolated pockets of urban territory. A corollary aspect is the importance of enhanced border security, as both groups have demonstrated an ability to take advantage of cross-border activity to profit.

Al-Shabaab and Boko Haram have been innovative and adaptable when it comes to generating financing. Al-Shabaab has demonstrated more prowess in this regard but is also aided by a more suitable environment. Boko Haram under Shekau has made some strategic miscalculations in terms of its relationship with the civilian populace, which in turn has affected its status. Nonetheless, it is not certain that declining financial fortunes from previous highs in either group will be irreversible or permanent—both will constantly seek to get involved in new criminal activities, which may result in more durable solutions going forward, thus requiring continued vigilance and proactive counter actions.

NOTES

1. Boko Haram is more accurately referred to as *Jama'atu Ahlis Sunna Lidda'awati wal Jihad* prior to its March 2015 pledge to the Islamic State and *Wilayat Gharb Afriqiyya* or West Africa Province afterward.

2. Itai Zehorai, "The World's 10 Richest Terrorist Organizations," *Forbes International*, December 12, 2014, https://www.forbes.com/sites/forbesinternational/2014/12/12/the-worlds-10-richest-terrorist-organizations/#69ded7a14f8a.

3. "Boko Haram Is Broke, UN Envoy Tells Security Council," *Premium Times*, February 8, 2017, http://www.premiumtimesng.com/news/more-news/222907-boko-haram-broke-un-envoy-tells-security-council.html.

4. Andrew Walker, "What Is Boko Haram?" *United States Institute of Peace*, 2012.

5. Nick Tattersall, "Interview—Nigerian Sect Planned Bomb Attack during Ramadan," Reuters, August 4, 2009, http://in.reuters.com/article/idINIndia-41523920090804.

6. Terrence McCoy, "This Is How Boko Haram Funds Its Evil," *Washington Post*, June 6, 2014, https://www.washingtonpost.com/news/morning-mix/wp/2014/06/06/this-is-how-boko-haram-funds-its-evil.

7. "Nigerian Bank Raids Reach 100 This Year," *Bloomberg*, December 9, 2011, http://www.bloomberg.com/news/2011-12-09/nigeria-bank-raids-reach-100-this-year-on-boko-haram-attacks.html.

8. Senator Iroegbu, "How 30 Boko Haram Insurgents Overran 1,000 Troops in Mubi," *This Day*, December 29, 2014, http://allafrica.com/stories/201412292057.html.

9. "Robbers Kill 3 Soldiers, Snatch LG Salary," *PM News*, August 2, 2012, https://www.pmnewsnigeria.com/2012/08/02/robbers-kill-3-soldiers-snatch-lg-salary/; Daniel Kanu, "Boko Haram Kills Four, Steals N21.5 Million LG Salaries in Borno," *Daily Independent*, July 4, 2011, http://allafrica.com/stories/201107050865.html.

10. Emmanuel Aziken, AbdulSalam Muhammad, Victoria Ojeme, and Ndahi Marama, "We're on Northern Govs' Payroll—Boko Haram," *Vanguard*, January 24, 2012, http://www.vanguardngr.com/2012/01/we-re-on-northern-govspayroll-boko-haram/.

11. Hamza Idris, "Boko Haram Extorts Money through Threat SMS," *Daily Trust*, October 27, 2012, https://www.facebook.com/dailytrust/posts/372102422871135.

12. "Boko Haram Kidnaps 22 Girls, Women in Borno," AFP, April 1, 2017, http://www.vanguardngr.com/2017/04/boko-haram-kidnap-22-girls-women-borno/.

13. The offshoot group Ansaru conducted four foreign national KFRs between 2011 and 2013, but Boko Haram publicly disavowed the tactic. All but one of Ansaru's victims were killed rather than ransomed off, indicating that the primary motivation was likely ideological in nature, centering around the propaganda value of holding foreign nationals as hostages, rather than seeking financial windfalls; "Boko Haram Denies Abducting Europeans Killed in Failed Rescue Bid," AFP, March 9, 2012, http://www.vanguardngr.com/2012/03/b-r-e-a-k-i-n-g-n-e-w-s-boko-haram-deny-abducting-europeans-killed-failed-rescue-bid/.

14. The U.K. and U.S. embassies in Nigeria issued a warning in May 2017 that militants were actively seeking to kidnap foreign nationals in the Bama area, along the Cameroonian border; "Boko Haram Planning Foreign Kidnaps in NE Nigeria," *Vanguard*, May 6, 2017, http://www.vanguardngr.com/2017/05/boko-haram-planning-foreign-kidnaps-ne-nigeria/.

15. Ola' Audu, "How Boko Haram Turned to Kidnapping to Raise Funds in Borno," *Premium Times*, May 20, 2013, http://www.premiumtimesng.com/news/135082-how-boko-haram-turned-to-kidnapping-to-raise-funds-in-borno.html.

16. Nonetheless, recent negotiations with the Nigerian government have centered around prisoner swaps, rather than ransom payments. This is likely an indication of both Boko Haram's decimated ranks after sustained military operations since 2015, and the government's desire to avoid funneling cash that could help resurrect the movement. This was pertinently demonstrated by the release of 103 of the Chibok schoolgirls during two rounds of negotiation in October 2016 and May 2017, in which Boko Haram accepted just the release of detained commanders, further symbolizing its declining ability to secure revenues through KFR operations; Moki Kindzeka, "Freed Boko Haram Hostages Recount Their Ordeals," *Deutsche Welle*, March 25, 2016, http://allafrica.com/stories/201603260012.html.

17. "Boko Haram Rules Bama with Force, Jails Residents, Collect Fees for Bail—Escapees," *Leadership*, October 22, 2014, http://babsol.com.ng/boko-haram-rules-bama-with-force-jail-residents-collect-fees-for-bail-escapees/.

18. Monica Mark, "This Is How Boko Haram Is Trying to Turn Captives into Suicide Bombers," *Buzz Feed*, February 16, 2016, https://www.buzzfeed.com/monicamark/this-is-how-boko-haram-is-trying-to-turn-captives-into-suici

19. "How Boko Haram Is Killing off Farms," *IRIN*, December 17, 2015, http://www.irinnews.org/analysis/2015/12/17.

20. Philip Obaji Jr., "How Boko Haram Makes Its Cash from Stolen Cattle," *Ventures Africa*, January 5, 2017, http://venturesafrica.com/boko-haram-makes-cash-from-stolen-cattle/.

21. "Terrorism Financing in West and Central Africa," Financial Action Task Force, October 2016, 12–13.

22. "Borno Govt. Criminalizes Cattle Import to Check Terror Funding," Channels Television, March 4, 2016, http://www.channelstv.com/2016/03/04/borno-govt-criminalizes-cattle-import-to-check-terror-funding/.

23. For example, a Financial Action Task Force (FATF) report investigating criminal financing in West Africa noted that a single incident involving 20,000 heads of cattle in Jigawa State of Nigeria in July 2016 may have garnered up to $10 million, in addition to another approximately $14 million from a series of incidents in northern Cameroon. These estimates, however, are on the high end of the spectrum. "Infographie—Comment Boko Haram a Changé le Cameroun," *Jeune Afrique*, November 16, 2016, http://www.jeuneafrique.com/374617/politique/infographies-boko-haram-a-change-cameroun/; "Terrorism Financing in West and Central Africa," Financial Action Task Force.

24. "Niger: les Habitants de Diffa Souffrent des Restrictions," *RFI*, July 13, 2015, http://www.rfi.fr/afrique/20150713-reportage-niger-habitants-diffa-souffrent-restrictions/.

25. Apochi Suleiman and Onyema Nwachukwu, "Military Bans Fish-Smuggling in North-East, Patrols Waterways in Niger Delta," Press Release Nigeria, May 5, 2017, https://prnigeria.com/security/military-fish-smuggling-waterways/.

26. In addition to the discussed sources, Boko Haram has received limited funding in its history from external groups, including from some Islamic charity organizations linked to extremist organizations. Ad hoc support from Al-Qaida and Al-Qaida in the Islamic Maghreb (AQIM) has perhaps been the most important, but much from the latter in particular came in the form of training as well, rather than direct financial remuneration. Little evidence of this type of funding has emerged since the March 2015 pledge to the Islamic State; Phil Stewart and Lesley Wroughton, "How Boko Haram Is Beating U.S. Efforts to Choke Its Financing," Reuters, July 1, 2014, http://af.reuters.com/article/topNews/idAFKBN0F63BE20140701?sp=true; "The Financing of Terrorism in Central Africa," Groupe D'Action Contre le Blanchiment D'Argent en Afrique Centrale (GABAC), April 2017, 26.

27. In addition, little concrete evidence has connected Boko Haram to the drug trade, despite persistent rumors. The movement has been associated with Tramadol, a pain reliever that is often abused in the region. But this has likely been for internal consumption to drug its own members and suicide bombers, rather than as a trafficking-based element. Rather, the distance from major drug trafficking routes across parts of the Sahel around Mali, and the shrinking area of territorial control, renders any serious profit from this activity unlikely; "200 kg de Drouge Destinés à Boko Haram Saisis Par le Douane Camerounaise," *Africa News*, June 18, 2017, http://fr.africanews.com/2017/06/18/200-kg-de-drogue-destines-a-boko-haram-saisis-par-la-douane-camerounaise/.

28. "Troops Rescue 88, Kill 3 Insurgents in Bama, Borno," *PM News*, August 16, 2016, https://www.pmnewsnigeria.com/2016/08/16/troops-rescue-88-kill-3-insurgents-in-bama-borno/; "MNJTF: Over 1,300 Boko Haram Members Surrendered in January," *Channels Television*, February 24, 2017, http://www.channelstv.com/2017/02/24/mnjft-1300-boko-haram-members-surrendered-january/.

29. This short-sighted strategy was driven by Shekau's extreme views in which he considered the entire local population to be enemy combatants, primarily due to their support for civilian vigilante organizations.

30. The split into two major factions in August 2016 may also lead to confrontation over supply routes and funding streams, but little activity in this regard has been witnessed thus far. Rather, it appears both factions are continuing to loot basic supplies from the local population and remain involved in the fish and cattle trades. To date, the split has not resulted in new revenue streams nor drastically altered the means of income generation compared to those prior to the division of the movement, although there are indications that the Barnawi faction may be more successful in securing civilian acquiescence for basic supplies.

31. Letter dated July 18, 2011, from the Chairman of the Security Council Committee Pursuant to Resolutions 751 (1992) and 1907 (2009) Concerning Somalia and Eritrea Addressed to the President of the Security Council, S/2011/433, 27.

32. Abdirazak Fartaag, "Audit Investigative Financial Report—2011," Transitional Federal Government, February 20, 2012, 4. http://fartaagconsulting.com/publications.html.

33. UN Security Council letter dated March 10, 2010, from the Chairman of the Security Council Committee Pursuant to Resolutions 751 (1992) and 1907 (2009) Concerning Somalia and Eritrea Addressed to the President of the Security Council, S/2010/91, 30.

34. For example, in 2015 the Somali diaspora remitted home an estimated $1.4 billion, making up 23 percent of total GDP; "World Bank Makes Progress to Support Remittance Flows to Somalia," The World Bank, June 10, 2016, http://www.worldbank.org/en/news/press-release/2016/06/10/world-bank-makes-progress-to-support-remittance-flows-to-somalia.

35. While reduced, some level of support continued to flow from Somali business communities, especially those based in the Gulf. For example, money was raised in Qatar in 2012 for a campaign of al-Shabaab assassinations targeting security officers and politicians in Mogadishu; similar activity was reported to emanate from communities in Saudi Arabia and the United Arab Emirates; Letter dated July 12, 2013, from the Chair of the Security Council Committee Pursuant to Resolutions 751 (1992) and 1907 (2009) Concerning Somalia and Eritrea Addressed to the President of the Security Council, S/2013/413, 58–59.

36. Al-Shabaab maintains a Ministry of Finance (*Maktabatu Maaliya*), an indication of its organization in this regard; Tom Keatinge, "The Role of Finance in Defeating al-Shabaab," Royal United Services Institute, December 2014, 9.

37. Report of the Monitoring Group on Somalia and Eritrea, July 18, 2011, S/2011/433, 61; Ashley Jackson and Abdi Aynte, "Talking to the Other Side: Humanitarian Negotiations with Al-Shabaab in Somalia," *Overseas Development Institute*, December 2013.

38. "Al Shabaab Rebels Ban Some Aid Groups in Somalia," Reuters, November 28, 2011, http://www.reuters.com/article/us-somalia-aid-idUSTRE7AR0N720111128.

39. It is unclear the degree to which aid agencies actually paid these fees, however, as few have admitted doing so. Nonetheless, in some cases concerned local staff paid on their behalf.

40. Letter dated October 7, 2016, from the Chair of the Security Council Committee Pursuant to Resolutions 751 (1992) and 1907 (2009) Concerning Somalia and Eritrea Addressed to the President of the Security Council, October 31, 2016, S/2016/919, 27.

41. For example, hotel owners in Mogadishu have been requested to pay up to $5,000 or risk attack; the owner of Naso Hablod Hotel stated that he refused demands from al-Shabaab tax collectors prior to an attack on his business in June 2016. As late as July 2017, the Puntland government also noted that local traders were still paying taxes to al-Shabaab; Letter Dated October 9, 2015, from the Chair of the Security Council Committee Pursuant to Resolutions 751 (1992) and 1907 (2009) Concerning Somalia and Eritrea Addressed to the President of the Security Council, S/2015/801, October 19, 2015, 29; Report of the Monitoring Group on Somalia and Eritrea, October 31, 2016, S/2016/919, 70; "Puntland President Blames Local Traders for Supporting Al Shabaab," *Baydhabo Online*, July 15, 2017, http://baydhabo.com/2017/07/15/puntland-president-blames-local-traders-for-supporting-al-shabaab/.

42. "It Will Be a Long War," International Crisis Group, June 26, 2014, 16.

43. An example of this occurred in the Galmudug region in November 2016, when local residents refused to part with livestock under the guise of *zakat*, resulting in a clash with al-Shabaab militants. Many village leaders were killed, who had complained they could not afford the *zakat* demands due to an ongoing drought; Abdi Sheikh and Feisal Omar, "Insurgents Behead Somali Village Elders over Islamic Tax," Reuters, November 30, 2016, http://af.reuters.com/article/topNews/idAFKBN13P19I?feedType=RSS&feedName=topNews&sp=true.

44. "Somalia's Shabaab Claims to Collect $9mn in Zakat," *World Bulletin*, December 16, 2014, http://www.worldbulletin.net/al-shabaab/150941/somalias-shabaab-claims-to-collect-9mn-in-zakat.

45. Report of the Monitoring Group on Somalia and Eritrea, October 31, 2016, S/2016/919, 27.

46. Letter Dated December 10, 2008, from the Chairman of the Security Council Committee Established Pursuant to Resolution 751 (1992) Concerning Somalia Addressed to the President of the Security Council, S/2008/769, 46.

47. Report of the Monitoring Group on Somalia and Eritrea, July 18, 2011, S/2011/433, 28.

48. Letter Dated October 10, 2014, from The Chair of the Security Council Committee Pursuant To Resolutions 751 (1992) and 1907 (2009) Concerning Somalia and Eritrea Addressed to the President of the Security Council, S/2014/726, 11.

49. Report of the Monitoring Group on Somalia and Eritrea, July 18, 2011, S/2011/433, 28; Keatinge, "The Role of Finance in Defeating al-Shabaab."

50. Report of the Monitoring Group on Somalia and Eritrea, October 31, 2016, S/2016/919, 71; Report of the Monitoring Group on Somalia and Eritrea, July 12, 2013, S/2013/413, 56.

51. Letter Dated July 11, 2012, from the Chair of the Security Council Committee Pursuant To Resolutions 751 (1992) and 1907 (2009) Concerning Somalia and Eritrea Addressed to the President of the Security Council, July 13, 2012,

S/2012/544, 47; Report of the Monitoring Group on Somalia and Eritrea, October 13, 2014, S/2014/726, 11.

52. Report of the Monitoring Group on Somalia and Eritrea, July 12, 2013, S/2013/413, 427.

53. Nonetheless, some elements associated with al-Shabaab may continue to be involved in the trade; "Al Shabaab Releases 173 Prisoners from Its Own Jails," Shabelle Media Network, February 11, 2017, http://allafrica.com/stories/201702110201.html.

54. "Black and White: Kenya's Criminal Racket in Somalia," Journalists for Justice, November 2015, 19. http://www.jfjustice.net/.

55. Report of the Monitoring Group on Somalia and Eritrea, July 18, 2011, S/2011/433, 83; Report of the Monitoring Group on Somalia and Eritrea, October 31, 2016, S/2016/919, 27.

56. Report of the Monitoring Group on Somalia and Eritrea, October 19, 2015, S/2015/801, 30.

57. Other notable areas, but limited compared to the aspects discussed, include state sponsorship from Eritrea in the mid- to late 2000s, occasional support from external extremist organizations like Al-Qaida, experience with KFRs (both foreign nationals and local civilians—the most famous case of the former generated $5.1 million for a pair of Spanish nationals in 2013; the latter is an ongoing activity), and the tenuous, at best, connections to piracy and the ivory trade. Rukmini Callimachi, "Paying Ransoms, Europe Bankrolls Qaeda Terror," New York Times, July 29, 2014, http://www.nytimes.com/2014/07/30/world/africa/ransoming-citizens-europe-becomes-al-qaedas-patron.html.

58. For example, during the 2016–2017 drought, al-Shabaab unveiled its own drought committee and began distributing supplies to the needy through its charity wing.

59. In comparison, Boko Haram's period of territorial control and governance resulted in little actual service provision to the local population, but rather was more predatory in nature.

60. Andrew Harding, "Somali Defector: Why I Left al-Shabaab," BBC, May 20, 2015, http://www.bbc.com/news/world-africa-32791713.

CHAPTER 8

The Haqqani Network: Gangster Jihadists

Kimberley L. Thachuk

The Haqqani Network (HQN) arguably is one of the better examples of a terrorist criminal enterprise in South Asia. Designated a terrorist group by the United States in 2012, it is notorious for numerous audacious and brutal terrorist assaults, including suicide bombings.[1] Less well known is HQN's extensive criminal empire which makes it as much a mafia organization as an affiliate of the Taliban. Yet its financial motivations often are obscured by its terrorist assaults causing it to defy a simplistic categorization as an insurgent, terrorist, or even mafia group.

Indeed, the range and extent of HQN's criminal enterprises suggest its venal opportunism often surpasses its militancy. Yet, "[t]hese activities are conveniently cloaked in a jihadi guise and the group either distances itself from this type of activity, especially when it involves locals, or justifies it as necessary to sustain its holy war against Western invaders."[2] Such a virulent mixture of pecuniary and ideological motivations has dual consequences in a conflict environment such as Afghanistan: not only does crime fund much of HQN's terrorist activity, but it affords the group a high degree of resiliency and mobility.[3] Despite such adaptability, its tenure would have been short-lived were it not for corrupt and complicit Afghan and Pakistani officials. Indeed, as with other criminal-business oligarchs in both countries, HQN's profits allow it to secure impunity through the subornation of officials, fraud, and the exploitation of lax regulations. In turn, such impunity translates to extensive safe havens and oftentimes operational support from state leaders and security forces. Hence, HQN's pragmatic strategy has enabled it not only to survive for decades but also to evolve and become a terrorist criminal enterprise with international reach.

BACKGROUND

Since at least the Soviet invasion in 1979, Afghanistan's chronic conflict and successive weak and corruption-riddled governments provided "multiple opportunities and few constraints on organized crime growth and activity."[4] Not only did a war economy develop that enabled nimble strongmen to reap great profits, but when Kabul attempted to exert influence in remote regions through patronage politics, criminal fiefdoms emerged. As fighters traversed the same remote ratlines as smugglers, HQN founder and powerful warlord Jalaluddin Haqqani likely saw the significant opportunities for enrichment. Thus, HQN soon became "the Sopranos of the Afghanistan war."[5] The huge profits produced vicious gangland violence, including suicide bombings, as battles ensued between rival criminal-insurgents for territorial control of lucrative criminal industries, including extortion, smuggling, and kidnapping. For traditional organized crime, conflict usually is bad for business as excessive time and expense are devoted to protecting operations and personnel. Yet, groups like HQN navigate conflict environments readily, largely because the violence allows them to engineer the conditions that maximize profits and eliminate competitors. Indeed, "[m]en serve and die for these warlords for money, not tribal, ethnic, or political loyalty."[6]

To fight the Soviets, HQN received financial support and matériel from the U.S. and Saudi governments. Training was received from the Pakistani Directorate of Inter-Services Intelligence (ISI) through which many sources of foreign funding, including money from the Persian Gulf states, were also channeled.[7] This assistance relieved the Haqqani leadership of the burden of funding its insurgency and allowed it to expand into more lucrative criminal activities. Early in the war, Jalaluddin pledged his militia to the radical mujahedeen faction Hizb-e Islami Gulbuddin but later allied with the Taliban as it took over Kabul. In so doing, he joined the ranks of numerous insurgents whose early alliances with drug traffickers were both opportunistic and tactical.[8] His loyalty was rewarded with the sinecure Minister of Border and Tribal Affairs (1995–1999). This post became critical to the fortunes of HQN, ceding it control over all licit and illicit trade entering and leaving Afghanistan.

Yet, HQN's credibility and status both regionally and internationally already were high as a result of Jalaluddin's early alliance with Osama bin Laden. In 1986, bin Laden constructed the "lion's den" cave in the Haqqani-controlled Jaji in Paktia Province where Arab foreign fighters trained.[9] This accommodation gratified sympathetic partners and funders, which was particularly valuable for HQN when it expanded its criminal enterprises internationally.

HQN's primary zone of influence lies in the mountainous Afghan provinces Khost, Paktia, and Paktika (collectively called Loya Paktia), but in recent years it expanded operations to a number of other provinces and into Pakistan. Although its leadership numbers less than a dozen men, they command an extended clan of several hundred members.[10] Strong familial and economic linkages among tribesmen provide a fluctuating 5,000 to 15,000 affiliates, "including the Taliban, criminal gangs, warlords, and corrupt state actors, [who] have adapted to the complex threat environment."[11] Key to the group's success are its clan-based ties that straddle the 2,430 Afghanistan–Pakistan border or Durand Line. Since being contrived by the British Empire in 1896, it has been ignored by local Pashtun tribesmen who live on both sides of it and cross it at will. Thus, HQN also is welcomed in Pakistan's Federally Administered Tribal Areas (FATA), which "has become more a home to absconded criminals, gangs, [and] non-state actors . . . who have systematically eliminated and replaced the respected 'Masharaan'or tribal elders."[12] HQN's main base was a madrassa compound,[13] Manba Ulom, outside Miramshah in the town of Danda Darpa Khel in Pakistan's North Waziristan. When Jalaluddin relocated there in 1974, it became his de facto state replete with taxation, policing, and regulation and served for decades as a base of operations for HQN criminal and insurgent activities.[14]

In 2014 when Jalaluddin died, his son, Sirajuddin, succeeded him. Sirajuddin was appointed the Taliban's second-in-command, as the Afghan insurgency is decentralized and fractious, and its "leadership [was] desperate to keep the Haqqani organization's fighting forces onside."[15] His pragmatic entrepreneurial approach likely led him to accept this position as much to safeguard HQN from attacks by rival criminal groups as it was to align with the Taliban. Indeed, much of the group's criminal success results from Sirajuddin's willingness to adapt his organization to the politics of a region that requires a strong profile of ideological purity as "his criminality feeds his ideology, and his ideology feeds his criminality."[16]

Despite strong rhetoric indicating dedication to ideological purpose, HQN's criminal ventures net funds exceeding its operational requirements by tens of millions of dollars. It has reinvested these profits and diversified into a nimble transnational criminal enterprise that extends directly to China, Iran, and the Persian Gulf, and indirectly to Europe and possibly Latin America.[17] Its multifarious organized crimes include bank robbery, extortion of licit and illicit enterprises including smuggled natural resources, kidnapping for ransom, trafficking in weapons and precursor chemicals, and even a stolen-car racket facilitated by its ownership of automobile dealerships in many of Pakistan's large cities, and possibly the United Arab Emirates (UAE). HQN's accomplices range from innocuous businessmen such as fabric and clothing traders from Paktia, who also operate electronics and auto parts shops in Ghazni City that launder HQN criminal profits, to government officials, to front men with sufficient business and political clout to win U.S. government contracts.[18]

The proceeds from HQN's criminality also are exchanged for weapons or laundered in cities such as Karachi and Peshawar and then divided among fighters and the leadership or sent via Haqqani-owned hawalas to Dubai, which serves as a key regional financial hub for organized crime and corrupt leaders.[19] Oddly, despite the ease with which hawalas transfer money, UAE authorities have intercepted HQN bagmen arriving with suitcases containing millions of dollars.[20] In addition to other locales, there the HQN leadership owns luxury real estate as well as front businesses, including construction firms and a transport company. The money also pays for lavish criminal lifestyles on both sides of the Durand Line, as well as more mundane items such as food, gasoline, and medical supplies.[21]

Integral to most contemporary transnational mafia organizations is the ability to blend licit and illicit enterprises. This enables organized crime not only to obscure criminal proceeds but also to diversify funding streams quickly and covertly. HQN has invested in a number of licit businesses making its illicit profits difficult to track, were regional authorities so inclined. However, corrupt officials on both sides of the Durand Line are easily suborned by HQN and provide it impunity and safe havens, thereby enabling it to become "a little economic empire with countless transnational ramifications."[22]

The majority of HQN's licit businesses are in Afghanistan, Pakistan, and the Persian Gulf. These enterprises presumably launder the proceeds of and serve as fronts for illicit transactions and operations, yet they cannot be discounted for their own earning potential. They include a jihadist market in Waziristan, which may be leased to HQN by the Pakistani government,[23] hawalas, used car and parts dealerships in Pakistan and possibly the UAE (Sharjah), lumberyards, textile and appliance shops, and import-export offices. HQN's syndicate even extends "bizarrely" to the sale of honey in the Persian Gulf and sugar smuggled to Afghanistan via Pakistan.[24]

Sirajuddin reportedly owns at least one construction company, Pakistan-based Saadullah Khan and Brothers (SKB) Engineering and Construction, which is also involved in trading and mining with operations (or at least offices) in Afghanistan, Bangladesh, India, Saudi Arabia, Sudan, Turkmenistan, the United States (Virginia), the UAE, and Yemen.[25] In 2011, its front man, Haji Khalil Zadran, helped it win a $15 million U.S. Agency for International Development (USAID) contract to build a road between Gardez and Khost.[26]

HQN also maintains warehouses and a cargo transport company that moves up to 200 semitrailers per day between Khost and North Waziristan.[27] Ownership of warehouses and freight companies is one of the hallmarks of sophisticated organized crime; contraband can be stored and smuggled using company assets without raising suspicion. Moving money efficiently is another attribute of established mafias. Although HQN owns numerous hawalas in both Afghanistan and Pakistan, it also uses banks. One of its companies, Afghanistan-based Fazal Karim Maidanwal operated by Abdul Baqi Bari, aide to now-deceased Haqqani fund-raiser Badruddin, sent large sums of money to HQN in Miramshah, Pakistan. Some or all of the $60 million distributed between 32 bank accounts, frozen in 2009 by the Pakistani government, either belonged to or was intended for HQN.[28] Finally, to maintain a reputation of ideological fervor, HQN advertises its battlefield exploits in its magazine *Manba' al-Jihadi* (*Fountainhead of Jihad*) where bank addresses and deposit information for accepting donations are advertised.[29] Such publicity is normally shunned by more evolved organized crime, as it attracts the attention of law enforcement, but HQN clearly enjoys significant impunity.

Despite this public face, the actual whereabouts of the HQN leadership often is steeped in mystery due to its near-constant movement between Afghanistan and Pakistan. In part, this may explain why repeated efforts by the U.S. government to pressure Islamabad to drive it out of Pakistan are mixed. As of late December 2016, the group enjoyed safe haven in Pakistan as well as a largely unfettered ability to travel to Afghanistan.[30] U.S. officials attribute this to the support HQN receives from the ISI, claiming it is "an arm of Pakistan's main intelligence agency."[31] Some of HQN's proxy role in Afghanistan likely is a geopolitical gambit by Pakistan to block India's ambitions there.[32] Yet, other parts of the relationship can only be explained as corruption and collusion; the ISI protects HQN in Pakistan, including facilitating the importation of precursor chemicals and issuing HQN members fake passports.[33]

EXTORTION

Control of the routes between mainly Loya Paktia and North Waziristan (but also other HQN-controlled border regions) largely through extorting convoys of both licit and illicit cargo is a lucrative income-generator for HQN.[34] The group began its extortion rackets by extracting protection money from drug convoys but soon added the "taxation" of between 10 and 20 percent of the value of cargos on trucks laden with timber and stone on the Gardez-Khost-Kabul road.[35] With the 2001 U.S. invasion, the stakes became still higher as it charged NATO for protection of supply trucks and construction projects, such as the $232 million Gardez-Khost road, routinely signaling its rates were increasing by attacking both.[36] HQN also extorts between 10 and 20 percent of any funds dispersed to local contractors by foreign aid for development projects.[37] Former Haqqani commander Maulavi Sardar Zadran claimed this extortion to be "the most important source of funding for the Haqqanis . . . [they] know that the contractors make thousands and millions of dollars, so these contractors are very good sources of income for them."[38]

HQN predation on local businesses extends to farmers, mobile telephone operators, water and electrical utilities, and mining companies.[39] "They are asking money or goods from shopkeepers . . . District elders and contractors are paying money to Afghan workers, but sometimes half of the money will go to Haqqani's people."[40] Even ordinary travelers are taxed to use the roads.

The most lucrative HQN protection monopoly is on the drug trade. HQN does not trade in opium directly. Not only is Loya Paktia inhospitable to poppy cultivation, but HQN reportedly does not want to fight other Taliban factions over drug spoils.[41] It thus adapted its strategy to profit, albeit in a parasitic manner, from Afghan narcotics trafficking. Not only does it extort convoys smuggling approximately 150 tons of heroin and 80 tons of opium annually through its territory,[42] it also taxes the mobile drug labs punctuating the border, charging producers between $50 and $70 per kilo or in-kind trade.[43]

HQN is also geographically well positioned to take advantage of the lucrative smuggling of Afghan mineral wealth, gems, and natural resources flowing via its territory to Pakistan and beyond.[44] In 2010, the United States estimated mineral deposits in Afghanistan could be worth $1 trillion.[45] Yet were it not for the corruption stretching to Kabul that encourages the outright theft of natural resources, "Afghanistan could become the 'Saudi Arabia of lithium.'"[46] Moreover, such riches lead to battles between militant factions and brutal predation upon thousands of artisanal miners. Ghazni's salt basins contain some of the world's largest deposits while its unmined gold and copper are worth approximately US$30 billion. Ghazni, Kunar, and Logar are chromite and gold-rich. Khost has chromite, copper, jade, lead, and mercury, and Nangarhar is rich in talc. About 500 illegally mined loads of talc per day, worth $46 million per month, are smuggled to Pakistan by "a strong network of militants, local mafia, and some civil and military officials in the country."[47] As an example of what HQN likely extorts from all of these smugglers, it charges a percentage of the 1,000 tons per day of chromite valued between $280 and $700 per ton trafficked through its territory to just two Pakistani plants.[48]

In 2011, 90 to 99 percent of all Afghan-mined gemstones worth an estimated $200 million were illegally smuggled out of the country with the help of corrupt Afghan officials.[49] Many trafficked stones are sorted, cut, and polished at the Namak Mandi Market in Peshawar and then sent to India, the United Kingdom, and the United States where rubies are worth approximately US$43,923 and blue sapphires US$12,100.[50] HQN taxes these smuggling operations between 10 and 25 percent of the gems' value while simultaneously charging smugglers for protection.[51]

Thousands of acres of forest have been illegally logged in Loya Paktia, including 2 million cubic meters of precious deodar cedar. In southeastern Khost alone, approximately 65 percent of the forests have been illicitly felled.[52] The wood is moved openly by donkey train or floated down rivers to Pakistan, suggesting the collusion of Afghan officials. In Pakistan, the "timber mafia" transports the wood to markets in centers such as Peshawar, which sell illicitly harvested pine, oak, and wild olive destined for Dubai and Ras al-Khaimah.[53]

HQN charges 20 percent of the value of each timber shipment moved through its territory. In Nangarhar, $4,000-to $6,000 per load is extorted as minerals, gems, and opium often are hidden under the logs, indicating HQN maintains considerable oversight of the illicit activities in this region, which adjoins Loya Paktia.[54] The group also appears to regulate the timber and other smuggling using "a formalized, yet unofficial system for the accounting of money, loans, and security."[55] This prearranged parallel agreement is stamped onto the wood (timber brand) pronouncing the smugglers immunized from paying additional fees to corrupt officials, rival criminals, and insurgents.

ARMS AND PRECURSORS

Between 1978 and 1989, China, Egypt, Israel, and the United States transferred thousands of small arms to the Afghan mujahedeen via the Pakistani ISI, including 400,000 Kalashnikovs and ammunition purchased from Warsaw Pact countries.[56] This arms pipeline continues to transfer weapons to Afghanistan from states previously or still involved in conflict and subject to UN arms embargos.[57] The trade constitutes an important source of HQN firepower and, more important, yields illicit profits.[58]

Often colluding with police, convoys of between 20 and 50 people disguise themselves as "cloth traders, laborers, [and] aid workers," hiding weapons on vehicles (including police cars) and pack animals transporting building materials, produce, flour, livestock, and cigarettes.[59] To avoid official border posts, smugglers use 111 mountain passes, trails, and dirt roads to cross the Durand Line at illegal, unmanned locations.[60] When hauling heavy machine guns that require larger vehicles, main border stations such as Ghulam Khan in Khost are used. These pose few obstacles as corrupt officials routinely accept small bribes to facilitate successful crossings without inspections.[61] Significant matériel is smuggled to Khost; in the Sabari District, Kalishnikovs cost $1,000 and are sold everywhere from arms bazaars to jewelry stores.[62]

In Pakistan, significant illicit matériel is manufactured in Darra Adam Khel and Landi Kotal, both west of Peshawar. There, skilled gunsmiths replicate light weapons ranging from revolvers to antiaircraft guns, often from scrap metal or degraded arms. Considered the regional center of illicit weapons, Darra produces approximately 20,000 weapons annually and "100 AK-47s per day at a cost of less than $150 per weapon," netting the town about $2 million per year.[63] They are sold from 100 shops mainly to Afghan customers. The remainder are sent to smugglers' bazaars like Karkhanai Bazaar and Bara Market in Peshawar where HQN buys large numbers of weapons. Over the years significant matériel has been seized by security forces on both sides of the border. Often, weapons are found in caves and other secretive locations, but just as often they are openly displayed.[64]

HQN purchases most of its weapons in Pakistan with illegally mined Afghan gems, narcotics, or timber.[65] Namak Mandi gem market in Peshawar is notorious for such transactions.[66] There, U.S.-made M-4 rifles fitted with night-vision equipment, silencers, and lights sold by Afghan deserters sell for $12,000 and pistols fitted with silencers sell for between $800 and $900.[67] Moreover, arms are exchanged for heroin, which nets greater profits than the sale of only one of these commodities. "Each time the weapons are exchanged for heroin, both sides get a profit from both arms and heroin . . . I know people who have luxury palaces in Dubai and other Arab countries thanks to this trade."[68]

The smuggling of precursor chemicals used to process opium into morphine base and heroin is a significant criminal enterprise for HQN. By supplying labs with these chemicals, once again the group demonstrates its adaptability as a criminal organization. As with its protection schemes on drug production and trafficking, such indirect participation enables it to adroitly sidestep conflict with other militant factions and exploit a necessary and lucrative niche opportunity within the Afghan narcotics industry.

Banned in Afghanistan, approximately 1.3 million liters of acetic anhydride is trafficked into the country annually, primarily via Iran and Pakistan from China, Dubai, India, Japan, and South Korea.[69] At source, a liter of acetic anhydride costs about $1, yet by the time it reaches Afghanistan, it costs $350 per liter, which translates to a $200 to $350 million profit per year.[70] In this enterprise HQN once again demonstrates its nimble criminal strategy. It likely uses several of its licit businesses to obscure consignments; seizures indicate chemicals often are mislabeled as motor oil and disinfectant.[71]

As a result of their flammable and large quantities, the precursors cross the border on container trucks using main roads rather than labyrinthine goat paths. This means HQN uses official posts that necessitate the compliance of corrupt officials. For instance, at the Kharlachi border facility, southwest of Parachinar where the road crosses into Paktia, "unofficial trade" likely exceeds the $27.66 million in official trade. There, dilapidated facilities lack electricity and inspection docks, and truckers complain of the number of bribes they pay.[72] Farther south at the Ghulam Khan post, hundreds of trucks traveling between Miramshah and Khost stop only to pay officers to smuggle loads through unchecked.[73]

KIDNAPPING

Kidnapping is a highly coordinated and thriving income-generator and enables oft-unpaid lower-level HQN fighters to operate independent criminal schemes. They usually collude with local organized gangs who identify and kidnap victims whom they transfer to middlemen with whom HQN then haggles to "buy." A variety of victims have been kidnapped in Afghanistan and Pakistan, including Afghan and U.S. soldiers, journalists, foreign-aid workers, local government officials, and ordinary citizens.[74] This industry is heavily reliant on the complicity of corrupt officials not only to ensure the kidnappers enjoy impunity but that they and their victims also remain undiscovered, despite their use of easily discoverable safe houses inside major towns and cities.

Significant media attention for the kidnappings of journalists Sean Langman and David Rohde, Afghan diplomat Haji Khaliq Farahi, and U.S. soldier Bowe Bergdahl assisted HQN to increase ransoms into the millions of dollars.[75] Badruddin Haqqani controlled these kidnappings, demanding approximately $20 million for Rohde, Afghan journalist Tahir Luddin, and Asad Mangal, their driver.[76] They were abducted outside Kabul and transferred to North Waziristan where they were held for seven months before escaping.[77] Although HQN lieutenant Sangeen Zadran, shadow governor of Paktika, took credit for capturing Bergdahl, the soldier was first kidnapped by local tribesmen in Paktika and then sold to a timber merchant who smuggled him to Pakistan. He was then moved between Miramshah and remote forested locations for five years until he was released in a prisoner exchange for five Taliban Guantanamo detainees, one of whom was a member of HQN.

POLICY CHALLENGES

HQN's pragmatic and nimble strategies have not only enabled it to survive in the Afghan conflict environment for decades but also ensured its expansion into a range of lucrative criminal enterprises. The group's successful adoption of crime for profit demonstrates that uncoupling organized crime from terrorism in an era when state sponsorship for terrorists has abated is unrealistic. Indeed, conceiving of HQN as being solely ideologically motivated only perpetuates the use of inadequate strategies to combat it. Clearly HQN should be viewed as a terrorist criminal enterprise whose members are as motivated by profit as by ideology.

Narratives matter when it comes to a reputation dependent on ideological purity. Although the lure of untold riches may be an irresistible draw for many of HQN's recruits, if not its leadership, the role jihadi rhetoric plays cannot be ignored. Indeed, HQN's greatest vulnerability may lie in this apparent incongruence. Because of it, HQN must hide its pursuit of criminal profits behind ideological appeals; it cannot openly display such intemperance in a region that prides itself on the moral rectitude of its insurgencies. Thus, by exposing HQN members as criminals, there is an opportunity to dilute local citizen support/passive acceptance for the group, which, along with the ability to make money and maintain impunity, is one of the more pernicious enablers of terrorist groups.[78] In addition to using traditional counterterrorist tactics, countering HQN openly as a terrorist criminal enterprise using the knowledge and tools honed by decades of international cooperation in combating mafias may be an effective method for at once diminishing its income as well as its popular support.

Of course, any strategy to combat the HQN will need to counter graft and corruption in both Afghanistan and Pakistan. Indeed, HQN's successful criminal strategies would not endure were it not for corrupt and complicit officials on both sides of the Durand Line. As is the case with other terrorist and criminal-business oligarchs in both countries, HQN's profits allow it to suborn public servants who reward it with impunity, safe havens, and even operational support. Perhaps more than any other factor, corruption has allowed HQN to successfully navigate readily and survive successfully for numerous decades as a terrorist criminal enterprise in this conflict environment.

NOTES

1. Some of these attacks include Kabul's Serena Hotel in 2008, killing 8; government buildings in Kabul in 2010, killing 5 and wounding 70; Kabul's Intercontinental Hotel in 2011, killing 13; the U.S. Embassy and the International Security Assistance Force (ISAF) Headquarters in Kabul in 2011, killing 16; on four Afghan cities in 2012, killing 15.

2. Gretchen Peters, *Haqqani Network Financing: The Evolution of an Industry* (West Point, NY: Combating Terrorism Center, July 2012), 39.

3. Jeffrey Dressler, "Combating the Haqqani Terrorist Network," Testimony to the House Committee on Foreign Affairs, Subcommittee on Terrorism, Nonproliferation and Trade (Washington, DC, September 13, 2012), 1.

4. *Addiction, Crime, and Insurgency: The Transnational Threat of Afghan Opium* (Vienna: UNODC, 2009), 102.

5. Mark Mazetti, Scott Shane, and Alissa J. Rubin, "Brutal Haqqani Clan Bedevils U.S. in Afghanistan," *New York Times*, September 24, 2011, http://www .nytimes.com/2011/09/25/world/asia/brutal-haqqani-clan-bedevils-united-states-in-afghanistan.html.

6. Michael Bhatia and Mark Sedra, *Afghanistan, Arms and Conflict* (New York: Routledge, 2008), 84.

7. Gretchen Peters, *How Opium Profits the Taliban* (Washington, DC: U.S. Institute of Peace, August 2009), 7.

8. Pierre-Arnoud Chouvy, "Drugs and the Financing of Terrorism," *Terrorism Monitor* 2, no. 20 (May 9, 2005), https://jamestown.org/program/drugs-and-the-financing-of-terrorism/; *Afghanistan's Narco-War: Breaking the Link between Drug Traffickers and Insurgents* (Washington, DC: Report to the Committee on Foreign Relations, U.S. Senate, August 10, 2009), 9.

9. Ambreen Agha, "Haqqani Network: Desperate Measures," *South Asia Intelligence Review* 10, no. 18 (November 7, 2011), http://www.satp.org/satporgtp/sair/Archives/sair10/10_18.htm.

10. Don Rassler and Vahid Brown, *The Haqqani Nexus and the Evolution of al-Qa'ida* (West Point, NY: Combatting Terrorism Center Harmony Project, July 14, 2011).

11. Hayder Mili and Jacob Townsend, "Tribal Dynamics of the Afghanistan and Pakistan Insurgencies," *CTC Sentinel*, August 15, 2009.

12. *Examining the Dimensions, Scale and Dynamics of the Illegal Economy: A Study of Pakistan in the Region* (Pakistan: UNODC, December 2011), 21.

13. This may have been HQN's first madrassa. From there at least 80 more were established and became important sources for recruiting operatives as well as more pious funders especially in the Persian Gulf states. As of 2008, its command center in Afghanistan was located in the village of Zambar in Khost.

14. Anand Gopal, Mansur Khan Mahsud, and Brian Fishman, "Inside the Haqqani Network," *Foreign Policy*, June 3, 2010; Noor ul Haq, Rashid Ahmed Khan, and Maqsudul Hasan Nuri, "Federally Administered Tribal Areas (FATA): Pakistan's Post-9/11 Politico-Strategic Response," *IPRI Paper* 10 (March 2005), 30.

15. "Afghanistan's Elusive Peace," *Northern Express*, August 7, 2015, https://www.northernexpress.com/news/opinion/article-7085-afghanistans-elusive-peace/.

16. Yochi Dreazen, "The Taliban's New Number 2 Is a 'Mix of Tony Soprano and Che Guevera,' " *Foreign Policy*, July 31, 2015.

17. Marvin G. Weinbaum and Meher Babbar, "The Tenacious, Toxic Haqqani Network," *MEI Policy Focus*, September 23, 2016, 8; UN Security Council Committee Pursuant to Resolutions 1267 (1999) and 1989 (2011), *Khalil Ahmed Haqqani*.

18. Matthew P. Dearing and Cynthia Braden, "Robber Barons Rising: The Potential for Resource Conflict in Ghazni, Afghanistan," *Stability: International Journal of Security & Development* 3, no. 1 (2014), 7.

19. Edwina Thompson, "The Nexus of Drug Trafficking and Hawala in Afghanistan," in *Afghanistan's Drug Industry: Structure, Functioning, Dynamics & Implications for Counter-Narcotics Policy*, ed. William Byrd and Doris Buddenberg (New York: UNODC/World Bank, 2007), 177–179.

20. *Afghanistan's Narco-War: Breaking the Link between Drug Traffickers and Insurgents* (Washington, DC: Report to the Committee on Foreign Relations, U.S. Senate, August 10, 2009), 29–30.

21. "Nasiruddin Haqqani: Senior Militant Shot Dead in Pakistan," *BBC News Asia*, November 11, 2013, http://www.bbc.com/news/world-asia-24898804. Nasiruddin reportedly was well educated, dressed in expensive clothes, rode in luxury cars, and owned three homes in and around Islamabad.

22. Christophe Jaffrelot, *The Pakistan Paradox: Instability and Resilience* (London: Random House, 2015), 258.

23. Abubakar Siddique, *The Pashtun Question: The Unresolved Key to the Future of Pakistan and Afghanistan* (London: Hurst & Co., 2014), 83.

24. "Taliban Expert Views: Money from Honey," BBC News Asia, September 22, 2015, http://www.bbc.com/news/world-asia-34283774; "Taliban-Linked Traders Found Involved in Illegal Sugar Sale," *Dawn*, March 11, 2006, https://www.dawn.com/news/182554.

25. Other construction companies linked to HQN, including Afghan German Construction, Arvin Kam Construction, German Afghan and Khalil Construction,

Green Land Star Construction, Haji Khalil Construction, Khalil Construction, Onyx Construction, and Zurmat Construction, were debarred by the Special Inspector General for Afghanistan Reconstruction in September 2012.

26. Jessica Donati and Mirwais Harroni, "Afghan Businessman Accused of Channeling Aid Money to Insurgency," Reuters, October 22, 2013, http://www.reuters.com/article/us-afghanistan-funding-haqqanis-idUSBRE99L09F20131022; According to USAID, the contract was canceled when the link to HQN was discovered, although by then Zadran had already received approximately $125 million in reconstruction funds.

27. Gretchen Peters, "Traffickers and Truckers: Illicit Afghan and Pakistani Power Structures with a Shadowy but Influential Role," in *Impunity: Countering Illicit Power in War and Transition*, ed. Michelle Hughes and Michael Miklaucic (Washington, DC: NDU Center for Complex Operations, 2015), 125–149.

28. Muhammad Amir Rana, "Financial Sources of Pakistani Militant and Religious Organizations," Pak Institute for Peace Studies, July–September 2009, 5.

29. Peters, *Haqqani Network Financing*, 15.

30. "Taliban, Haqqani Network Retain Safe Havens in Pakistan, Says Pentagon," *Hindustan Times*, December 17, 2016, http://www.hindustantimes.com/world-news/taliban-haqqani-network-retain-safe-havens-in-pakistan-says-pentagon/story-dS7huJ1OhMuVhUMEyKv9qI.html.

31. "Pakistan's ISI and Military Supporting Insurgents in Paktia: Officials," *TOLOnews*, July 15, 2015, http://www.tolonews.com/afghanistan/pakistans-isi-and-military-supporting-insurgents-paktia-officials.

32. Mazetti, Shane, and Rubin, "Brutal Haqqani Clan Bedevils U.S. in Afghanistan."

33. "Mullen Launches Diatribe against ISI," *Dawn*, April 21, 2011, https://www.dawn.com/news/622579; Mariam Mufti, *Religion and Militancy in Afghanistan and Pakistan: A Literature Review* (Washington, DC: Center for Strategic and International Studies, June 2012), 64. The ISI allegedly paid HQN $200,000 to attack CIA Camp Chapman in December 2009 in which seven American agents and three others were killed. See, for example, "Pakistan's ISI paid $200,000 to Haqqani Network in 2009 to Attack CIA Camp in Afghanistan," *Firstpost*, April 14, 2016, http://www.firstpost.com/world/pakistans-isi-paid-200000-to-haqqani-network-in-2009-to-attack-cia-camp-in-afghanistan-2730172.html.

34. "The Funding Methods of FATA's Terrorists and Insurgents," *CTC Sentinel*, Vol 1, Issue 6, May 2008.

35. Don Rassler and Vahid Brown, *Fountainhead of Jihad*, 144–145.

36. Gretchen Peters, *Crime and Insurgency in the Tribal Areas of Afghanistan and Pakistan* (West Point, NY: United States Military Academy, 2010), 37.

37. UN Security Council Letter dated September 4, 2012, from the Chair of the Security Council Committee Pursuant to Resolution 1988 (2011) Addressed to the President of the Security Council S/2012/683, 15.

38. Mazetti, Shane, and Rubin, "Brutal Haqqani Clan Bedevils U.S. in Afghanistan."

39. UN Security Council Letter dated September 4, 2012, 13.

40. Nahal Toosi, "Haqqani Network Challenges US-Pakistan Relations," *Seattle Times*, January 29, 2009, http://www.deseretnews.com/article/705354843/Haqqani-network-challenges-US-Pakistan-relations.html.

41. Peters, *How Opium Profits the Taliban*, 20.

42. *Addiction, Crime, and Insurgency*, 121.

43. Gretchen Peters, *Seeds of Terror: How Heroin Is Bankrolling the Taliban and al Qaeda* (New York: Thomas Dunne Books, 2009), 82.

44. Farhad Naibkhel, "Bootie of Natural Riches: Insurgents Earns $46m from Illegal Mining to Continue War in Afghanistan," *Afghanistan Times*, February 1, 2017, http://afghanistantimes.af/bootie-of-natural-riches-insurgents-earns-46m-from-illegal-mining-to-continue-war-in-afghanistan-survey/.

45. Matthew DuPee, "Afghanistan's Conflict Minerals: The Crime-State-Insurgent Nexus," *CTC Sentinel*, February 16, 2012.

46. James Risen, "U.S. Identifies Vast Mineral Riches in Afghanistan," *New York Times*, June 13, 2010, http://www.nytimes.com/2010/06/14/world/asia/14minerals.html; see, for example, UN Environmental Program, *Natural Resource Management and Peacebuilding in Afghanistan* (Nairobi: UNEP, 2013).

47. Noor Zahid, "Report: Militant Groups in Afghanistan Get Rich off Mineral Smuggling," *Voice of America*, February 1, 2017, https://www.voanews.com/a/militant-groups-in-afghanistan-get-rich-off-mineral-smuggling-report-says/3702327.html.

48. *Chromite Extraction in Kunar: Factor of [In]stability* (Kabul: Integrity Watch Afghanistan, 2013), 15.

49. "Illegal Mining in Afghanistan at an All-time High," *TOLOnews*, July 17, 2013, http://www.tolonews.com/afghanistan/illegal-mining-afghanistan-all-time-high.

50. Adnan R. Khan, "The Dangerous World of Pakistan's Gem Trade," *Macleans*, May 24, 2014, http://www.macleans.ca/news/world/pakistans-blood-stones/; "Afghanistan's Fabulous Ruby Mines Plundered by Thieves," BBC News Asia, May 26, 2012, http://www.bbc.com/news/world-asia-18070571; "Jagdalak Rubies End Up in Peshawar," *Pajhwok Afghan News Mines Special Page*, n.d., http://mines.pajhwok.com/content/jagdalak-rubies-end-peshawar.

51. UN Security Council Report S/2013/656 Letter dated November 10, 2013, from the Chair of the Security Council Committee Established Pursuant to Resolution 1988 (2011) Addressed to the President of the Security Council, 14.

52. Hedayatullah Khostai, "Khost Forests Shrink, Thanks to Illegal Logging," *Pajhwok Afghan News*, December 8, 2011, http://www.pajhwok.com/en/2011/12/08/khost-forests-shrink-thanks-illegal-logging.

53. Harry R. Bader, Clint Hanna, Clint Douglas, and John D. Fox, "Illegal Timber Exploitation and Counterinsurgency Operations in Kunar Province of Afghanistan: A Case Study Describing the Nexus among Insurgents, Criminal Cartels, and Communities within the Forest Sector," *Journal of Sustainable Forestry* 32, no. 4 (April 2013), 17; Syed Irfan Ashraf, "Militancy & Black Economy," *Dawn*, March 22, 2009, https://www.dawn.com/news/843075.

54. Dearing and Braden, "Robber Barons Rising," 7.

55. Bader, Hanna, Douglas, and Fox, "Illegal Timber Exploitation and Counterinsurgency Operations in Kunar Province of Afghanistan," 19.

56. Paul Holtom, *United Nations Arms Embargoes: Their Impact on Arms Flows and Target Behaviour Case Study: The Taliban, 2000–2006* (Stockholm: Stockholm International Peace Research Institute 2007), 5; By 1997, the United Nations estimates that 10 million small arms were unaccounted for in Afghanistan.

57. United Nations, Report of the Monitoring Group Established Pursuant to Security Council Resolution 1363 (2001) and Extended by Resolution 1390 (2002), UN Document S/2002/541, May 15, 2002, 9.

58. Small Arms Survey notes that it is difficult to know what matériel crosses the Af–Pak border. Assessments of the quantities and types of arms trafficked require extrapolation from seized arms caches. See, *Small Arms Survey 2012: Moving Targets* (Geneva: Small Arms Survey), 316.

59. Aqab Malik, "Darra Adam Khel: 'Home Grown' Weapons," *ASPJ Africa & Francophonie*, 1st Quarter, 2016, 86; Musa Khan Jalalzai, "Afghanistan's Kidnapping and Arms Smuggling Industry," *Daily Outlook Afghanistan*, June 21, 2011, http://outlookafghanistan.net/topics.php?post_id=970.

60. Thomas H. Johnson and M. Chris Mason, "No Sign until the Burst of Fire: Understanding the Pakistan-Afghanistan Frontier," *International Security* 32, no. 4 (March 1, 2008), 44.

61. *Afghan Narcotrafficking: The State of Afghanistan's Borders* (Washington, DC: East-West Institute, April 2015).

62. Helal Ershad, "Afghanistan: Khost Residents Armed to the Teeth," *Institute for War & Peace Reporting*, February 22, 2012.

63. Salman Siddiqui, "The Weapons Trail—Part 1: Where Do 20M Illegal Arms Come From?" *The Express Tribune*, May 17, 2012, https://tribune.com.pk/story/380032/the-weapons-trai-part-1-where-do-20m-illegal-arms-come-from/.

64. Jamie Tarabay, "Afghanistan's Gun Problem: Too Many Weapons, Not Enough Oversight," *Al Jazeera*, July 28, 2014, http://america.aljazeera.com/articles/2014/7/28/afghanistan-s-gunproblemtoomanyweaponsnotenoughoversight.html.

65. Kerry Lynn Nankivell, "Afghanistan at a Crossroads: Transnational Challenges and the New Afghan State," in *Issues for Engagement: Asian Perspectives on Transnational Security Challenges* (Hawaii: Asia-Pacific Center for Security Studies, February 2012).

66. Khan, "The Dangerous World of Pakistan's Gem Trade"; "A Town Near Peshawar Where Guns Sell Cheaper Than Smartphones," Geo TV, July 29, 2016, https://www.geo.tv/latest/110338-A-town-near-Peshawar-where-guns-sell-cheaper-than-smartphones.

67. Aamir Latif, "Flood of US Weapons in Afghanistan and Pakistan Fueling Militant Groups, Experts Say," *GlobalPost*, June 22, 2011, https://www.pri.org/stories/2011-06-22/flood-us-weapons-afghanistan-and-pakistan-fueling-militant-groups-experts-say.

68. Sayed Yaqub Ibrahimi, "Turning Afghan Heroin into Kalashnikovs," Institute for War & Peace Reporting, June 30, 2008.

69. *The Global Afghan Opium Trade: A Threat Assessment* (Vienna: UNODC), 9; seven liters of acetic anhydride converts opium into approximately one kilogram of heroin.

70. *Examining the Dimensions, Scale and Dynamics of the Illegal Economy*, 44.

71. "South Korean Police Arrest Taliban-linked Drug Ring," *Taipei Times*, July 5, 2008, http://www.taipeitimes.com/News/world/archives/2008/07/05/2003416563.

72. Zulfiqar Ali, "Kharlachi—A Hub of Cross Border Trade but an Eyesore Too," *Dawn*, June 30, 2015, https://www.dawn.com/news/1191382.

73. Ahmad Shah, "Smuggling Threatens Legal Economy in Afghan Southeast," *IWPR*, March 19, 2014, https://iwpr.net/global-voices/smuggling-threatens-legal-economy-afghan-southeast.

74. Dressler, "Combating the Haqqani Terrorist Network," 24.

75. UN Report S/2014/402 Letter dated June 9, 2014, from the Chair of the Security Council Committee Established Pursuant to Resolution 1988 (2011) Addressed to the President of the Security Council, 18.

76. David Rohde, "You Have Atomic Bombs, but We Have Suicide Bombers," *Pittsburgh Post Gazette*, October 20, 2009, http://www.post-gazette.com/news/world/2009/10/20/You-Have-Atomic-Bombs-but-We-Have-Suicide-Bombers/stories/200910200192.

77. David Rohde, "Held by the Taliban," *New York Times*, October 17, 2009, http://www.nytimes.com/2009/10/18/world/asia/18hostage.html?pagewanted=all&_r=0.

78. See, for example, Kimberley L. Thachuk, "Countering Terrorist Support Structures," *Defence Against Terrorism Review* 1, no. 1 (Spring 2008), 13–28.

CHAPTER 9

The Evolution of the PKK into a Criminal Enterprise

Mahmut Cengiz and Süleyman Özeren

INTRODUCTION

The need for money to carry out their activities has caused some terrorist organizations to transform into terrorist criminal enterprises. Recently, terror groups around the world have engaged in criminal activity ranging from smuggling and trafficking to extortion and counterfeiting. Corruption within the terrorist groups themselves and the inability of law enforcement agencies to thwart financing sources of terrorist activities have enabled terrorist groups to diversify their financial resources. A prime example is the Kurdish Worker's Party (Partiya Karkerên Kurdistanê-PKK) based in northern Iraq and Turkey.

Turkey has been grappling with terrorism for decades. A considerable number of terrorist groups categorized as leftist, revolutionary, separatist, and religious have operated in the country. Among these terrorist groups, the PKK occupies a special place in terms of its long-lasting activities and bloody attacks. Motivated by a leftist and separatist ideology and facilitated by endemic corruption, the PKK has been funded and financed by various revenue streams. This chapter, after analyzing the nature of the PKK terrorist network, focuses on how the PKK operates like a criminal enterprise by categorizing its revenue generated from various kinds of smuggling, drug trafficking, and corruption. Policy recommendations are given at the end of the chapter.

HISTORICAL AND IDEOLOGICAL BACKGROUND

The PKK was established by Abdullah Öcalan and his friends in 1978 to create an independent Kurdistan based on Marxist-Leninist ideology.

In the 1970s, the group started to target tribal leaders and emerged as the dominant entity among other separatist groups. The PKK used brutal tactics to silence and overpower rival groups within the separatist movement. Security agencies did not pay attention to the PKK until August 15, 1984, when the towns of Eruh and Semdinli in southeastern Turkey were attacked—making the Kurdish people in Turkey one of the first groups the PKK brutally targeted. "More importantly, more than 40,000 people were killed hitherto because of the PKK's attacks and military's operations, leaving in turn indelible wounds in the collective imagination of both Turks and Kurds in the country."[1]

Published in 1978, the manifesto of the Kurdistan revolution explains the purpose of the PKK and proclaims the Marxist-Leninist ideology as the fundamental principle of the organization.[2] While the Marxist ideology represents the ideological structure of the PKK, the principle of "national self-determination" will be the most important ideological argument for the PKK in future periods. The ultimate goal of the PKK was defined as the realization of an "independent united democratic Kurdistan," which had been constantly emphasized throughout the 1980s.[3]

In terms of organizational strategy, three periods predominated between 1984 and 1999. From 1984 to 1989, the PKK mainly attacked civilians, including Kurds, teachers, clerics, and government officials. Between 1990 and 1995, however, the PKK moved into another phase, which it defined as the "guerrilla stage."[4] From 1995 to 1999, the PKK targeted large cities, including Ankara, Diyarbakir, and Istanbul. These attacks aimed to galvanize ethnic clashes between Turks and Kurds.

The New PKK?

After the capture of Öcalan in February 1999, the organization increased its violent actions. In September 1999, it proclaimed its version of a cease-fire. Moreover, after Öcalan's capture, the PKK underwent several organizational restructurings and transformations. For example, several changes were made to the organization's name and its overall goal. These changes were made to facilitate the existence of the PKK in the new environment in Turkey and the region. Accordingly, in 2002 it changed its name to the Kurdistan Freedom and Democracy Congress (KADEK) and proclaimed adherence to nonviolence in support of Kurdish rights.[5] In 2003, the "PKK sought to engineer another political face-lift, renaming the group Kongra-Gel (KGK) and brandishing its 'peaceful' intentions, while continuing to commit attacks and refuse disarmament."[6]

The PKK, in its 10th Congress on June 1, 2004, proclaimed that it ended its six-year unilateral cease-fire and returned to what it called an active legitimate self-defense.[7] The PKK used this term when it carried out a terrorist attack against security forces, in particular during the periods when attempts were made to resolve the conflict and find a solution to the

Kurdish issue. During these periods, the PKK claimed it would pursue the creation of a "democratic republic," a stance that might be considered a major step back from its ultimate purpose of establishing the "independent united democratic Kurdistan."[8]

In 2007, the PKK took another step toward expanding its organizational structure to the extent that it included all of the elements in Europe, Iran, Iraq, Syria, and Turkey. While one aspect of this move was a survival strategy, it also was an indication of the PKK's ability to adapt to the changing environment in the national and international arenas. This move included the establishment of the KCK organization (Koma Ciwaken Kurdistan/ Kurdistan Communities Union). The KCK is an umbrella organization that calls for "the creation of an alternative state system, with the PKK as one part of its structure."[9] The KCK structure represents an interesting chapter in the history and evolution of the PKK. This new structure actually is the end product of an ongoing transformation and restructuring of the organization. The KCK agreement anticipates what Öcalan calls "democratic autonomy" in Turkey, and it reflects the ideology of democratic confederalism for Greater Kurdistan,[10] including Iran, Iraq, Syria, and Turkey. The KCK structure included both political entities and military wings and groups such as the Kurdistan Freedom Hawks (TAK), an offshoot of the PKK. The TAK has claimed responsibility for several terrorist attacks[11] in recent years in large Turkish cities, including Istanbul and Ankara. "In short, since the establishment of the KCK in 2007 the group has been following a dual strategy, according to which it has carried out politicization activities and armed actions simultaneously."[12] The PKK and Öcalan used resolution processes in 2009 and 2012 to 2015 to gain more ground on several fronts, including social, political, psychological, and international. According to an International Crisis Group report on December 2014, "The PKK has been able to build up its strength in south-eastern towns and acquire unprecedented international and domestic legitimacy."[13]

Regional Developments and the PKK

The PKK will not disarm until it proclaims an independent Kurdistan. Furthermore, the Syrian conflict and the turmoil in Iraq have provided the PKK with opportunities for recruitment, logistics, and international recognition. Currently, the PKK has an advantage that it has never had before. The emergence of the Islamic State in Syria and Iraq or Da'esh paved the way for the Syrian Kurdish Democratic Union Party (PYD), an offshoot of the PKK in Syria. The conflict in Syria not only opened a window of opportunity for the PYD to become a legitimate group in Syria, but it also allowed the PYD to emerge as an ally for the United States in its fight against Da'esh. Similarly, the turmoil resulting from the emergence of Da'esh as a power in Iraq allowed the PKK to expand its area of control in the locales where previously it had no concrete influence. In short, the Syrian conflict enabled the PKK to become a regional player in Iraq and Syria, which created pressure on Turkey.

CRIMINAL INTERESTS OF THE PKK

The PKK has various revenue streams, ranging from extortion and fraud to ongoing trafficking and smuggling rackets along the eastern and southeastern borders of Turkey, leading to the organization's involvement in global-level transnational smuggling and trafficking. The PKK has undergone a transformation with respect to the financing of its activities. The main financial sources of the PKK in its early years were donations and extortion.[14] In the 1990s, the PKK collected £2.5 million (approximately $3.6 million) each year, mostly from Kurdish people in the United Kingdom.[15] In the late 1990s, the PKK collected money from 8,000 Kurdish people living in Romania. It should be noted that the PKK used Romania as a hub to transfer explosives and weapons bought from European countries and Russia.[16] Regular payments and donations are still important sources of income for the PKK, with its militants continuing to collect extortion money in the eastern and southeastern parts of Turkey[17] and in European countries where it has collected €30 million (approximately $35 million) in a year.[18]

Recently, the PKK has become actively involved in smuggling operations from Iran, Iraq, and Syria into Turkey. For example, the organization has taxed human smugglers, drug traffickers, and oil smugglers at border crossings. At eight so-called customs points on the Iranian side of the Turkish border, the PKK receives taxes from smugglers. For example, the tax is $3 per horse or mule from tobacco smugglers and $800 to $1,000 per person smuggled who wants to enter Turkey and $10,000 per person smuggled who wants to go Europe.[19]

The PKK's involvement in global human smuggling and trafficking generates a significant amount of revenue, as migrants in areas controlled by the PKK must pay to cross the territory.[20] Using transnational crime networks, the PKK engages in the smuggling of immigrants to Western European countries through Romania.[21] In addition, the PKK takes an active role in the smuggling of people from Middle Eastern countries. In past years, the PKK prepared false documents for refugees and provided logistical support to Kurdish refugees who attempted to migrate to European countries.[22]

Different forms of counterfeiting have also been exploited by terrorist organizations because of the lower risk and higher profit.[23] Global terrorist organizations tend to generate income by engaging in activities such as document forgery and fraud related to banking transactions, credit cards, identity cards, and passports.[24] In term of forgery, the PKK specializes in identity and passport forgery and documents needed in human smuggling.[25] In a case recorded in 2016, the Turkish police arrested 38 human smugglers affiliated with the PKK and seized fake materials used to prepare counterfeit passports and travel documents. These smugglers earned $10,000 from each immigrant.[26] Furthermore, ongoing conflict in Syria has presented the PKK with opportunities for the transfer of refugees. The PKK is one of the main criminal organizations responsible for the smuggling of refugees. For example, the group smuggled around 100,000 Syrians and earned $300 million from human smuggling between 2011 and 2015.[27]

Cigarette smuggling is another revenue source for the PKK. It was determined in a case study that the PKK gained a significant amount of revenue from two cigarette factories opened illegally in northern Iraq. The organization received taxes from these factories and became involved in the trafficking of the cigarettes. Moreover, the PKK became part of the cigarette trafficking networks that started in Puerto Rico.[28] Inside Turkey, the PKK is one of the beneficiaries of cigarette smuggling.[29] The organization taxes Kurdish smugglers $100 per mule, and each mule can carry 3,000 packages of cigarettes. The PKK earned $500 million from taxing cigarette smugglers in 2015.[30] Tax losses arising from cigarette smuggling reached 520 million Turkish lira (TL; approximately $170 million) in 2015. With 80 percent of the cigarettes in Turkey having entered the country along its eastern and southeastern borders—areas where PKK militants are dominant—it is clear that such smuggling is a huge revenue source for the PKK.[31]

The PKK is also involved in money laundering of its revenue. Two investigations by European police have revealed the powerful money-laundering capacity of the PKK. Scotland Yard and the Belgian police cooperated in an operation in 1996 called Sputnik. The operation included activities in Luxembourg and Germany and investigated allegations that the PKK had laundered gains from drugs and weapons smuggling through an account for MED TV, an international Kurdish satellite television station. At the end of the operation, the police confiscated almost $11 million from the account of MED TV and concluded that the money belonged to the PKK. The PKK had laundered the money using a total of 15 companies. In another operation conducted in 2002, the Belgian and French police determined that a company connected to the PKK (the Kurdish Foundation Trust) prepared false documents and laundered money. During the investigation, it was revealed that revenues obtained from sympathizers or militants were transferred to the PKK.[32]

PKK and Drug Trafficking

Given its geographical location on global drug routes, Turkey has a high potential for drug trafficking. A significant part of this potential is under the control of the PKK and other terrorist organizations.[33] In 2008, an investigation by the U.S. Treasury and Drug Enforcement Administration (DEA) led to the designation of the PKK as a significant foreign drug narcotics trafficker under the U.S. Kingpin Act.[34]

The PKK's involvement in drug trafficking goes back decades. For example, the PKK gained revenue of around $300 million annually from drug trafficking in the 1990s.[35] Police seizures in Turkey show that the PKK is active in every stage of drug trafficking and that the organization receives taxes from drug traffickers and controls the cannabis fields in the southeastern region of Turkey. Furthermore, the PKK is active in the distribution of drugs in European countries.[36] For instance, French police statistics show that 65 to 70 percent of the heroin market is under the control of Turkish criminal groups, and around half of this percentage is controlled by the PKK.[37]

The PKK has had linkages to drug trafficking in Turkey since the 1980s. Police seizures verified the PKK's involvement in 377 cases of drug trafficking between 1984 and 2012. In these cases, 1,232 traffickers were arrested. The drugs seized were 4.584 kg of heroin, 36.5 tons of cannabis, around 6 million cannabis plants, 4.305 kg morphine base, 27.630 liters of acetic anhydride, 22 kg of opium gum, 710 kg of cocaine, and around 350,000 tablets of synthetic drugs.[38]

Another important source of income for the PKK is taxes paid by the traffickers. Taxation was common in the 1980s, with the PKK stipulating that traffickers share 10 percent of their income with the terrorist organization. In the 2000s, traffickers passing across borders were required to pay the PKK based on the number of kilograms of drugs the traffickers were carrying. Traffickers in drug cases related to the PKK have said that the PKK controlled borderlands on the Iranian side of the Turkish border and that it was impossible to cross the border without making payments to the PKK. If the traffickers refused to pay the PKK, their passage was prohibited. The only exception was traffickers who were connected to the terrorist organization.[39]

Police operations between 2011 and 2014 in southeastern Turkey show a major financial source of the PKK—namely, income derived from the cultivation of cannabis plantations. According to the findings of the police operations, the PKK controlled cultivation of cannabis in rural areas of Bingol and Diyarbakir Provinces and organized the production of marijuana. The PKK then sold the drugs in metropolitan cities of Turkey. Being involved in every stage of cannabis trafficking—from cultivation to selling—allows the PKK to maximize its income.[40]

Police cases substantiate the ongoing linkage of the PKK to drug trafficking. The first case involved drugs seized by the Diyarbakir police in 2010. When police searched the oil tank of a truck, they found 65 kg of marijuana and 64 kg of explosives. The investigation revealed that three suspects were linked to the PKK and that the explosives belonged to the terrorist organization. The second drug case connected to the PKK also was in Diyarbakir. In an operation conducted in 2010, 25 kg of marijuana was seized from a trafficker who was a PKK militant. The findings of these two operations showed that the traffickers were capable of making bombs and deploying them in major cities for the PKK. The third case was in Kayseri Province, which is situated on one of the alternative drug-trafficking routes in Turkey. The police seized 450 kg of marijuana from a PKK-affiliated trafficker. The fourth case, in 2012, verified the connection of the PKK to cannabis fields. The police arrested nine traffickers in possession of 500,000 cannabis plants, four tons of marijuana, and two weapons. Two of nine traffickers said that they were taxed monthly by the PKK. The fifth and last case reaffirmed the PKK's linkage to drug trafficking. The police seized five tons of marijuana that belonged to the PKK in Van city.[41]

Financing of the PKK through Corruption

The reciprocal relationship among organized crime, terrorism, and corruption has been discussed at length in recent years, including the observation that terrorists and organized crime groups are more active in countries where corruption is endemic. This relationship, however, is about more than just reciprocity. Terrorists, organized crime groups, and corruption are entangled and have common features. In other words, one can expect to see the features of organized crime and corruption in acts of terrorism.[42] One example is the PKK. In the 1980s and 1990s, the PKK was focused solely on terrorism; however, the PKK now has characteristics associated with organized crime and engages in smuggling and trafficking activity. Recently, the linkage of the PKK to corruption has also been detected.

Terrorist financing in Turkey typically brings to mind smuggling cases, and as mentioned earlier, smuggling is an important source of income for the PKK. For the most part, however, the flow of money to the PKK through corruption has been ignored. Interviews with members of law enforcement agencies working in southeastern Turkey in 2012 provided detailed information about how the PKK is financed by corruption. Some of the findings obtained in the interviews are as follows:[43]

- The PKK generates income from sympathizers who work in municipalities and belong to a political party affiliated with the PKK. These sympathizers take bribes from contractors in return for giving building permits. After taking a certain amount of bribery money for themselves, the sympathizers transfer the rest of it to the PKK.

- These municipalities transfer some money from corruption obtained in tenders. The officials in the municipality are corrupt, and, after taking some of the money from the tenders for their own use, they send the remainder to the terrorist organization.

- Tenders made by these municipalities are deliberately given to companies that are linked to the PKK. In a road construction tender held in 2012, a company linked to the PKK won the contract after giving the lowest bid. A police operation revealed that the municipality and the company had made an agreement before the bidding started. Also, the company used municipal facilities and vehicles in violation of the bidding law.

- Nepotism is common in the PKK. The relatives of PKK militants who lost their lives in terrorist incidents were unlawfully employed by municipalities as directed by the PKK-affiliated political party.

- The amount of money from corruption that is transferred to the PKK from a small city is around 5 million TL (approximately $1.7 million), while the amount from a metropolitan city is 15 million TL (approximately $4.8 million). The funds come primarily from bribery money obtained from tenders.

- Police operations against violations of tender laws have prompted company managers who commit the crime of rigging tenders to be more vigilant. The police operations revealed that these people never use cell phones because such devices can be tapped; instead, they typically meet face-to-face in shopping centers.

- Corruption revenue in municipalities directed by the PKK is transferred to the terrorist organization through the PKK-affiliated member of the Finance Committee Board of the KCK. Then, the money goes abroad as cash to the center of PKK operations in northern Iraq.

Policy Recommendations

The PKK is both a terrorist organization and a criminal enterprise, making it necessary for countries interested in fighting terrorism and crime to develop policies at the national, regional, and global levels.

Turkey successfully fought criminal groups and terrorist organizations until December 2013 when corruption scandals[44] involving ministers, high-level bureaucrats, and the son of President Recep Tayyip Erdogan erupted. After these scandals, even though the investigations were conducted by the Istanbul Financial Investigation Unit, the Erdogan government in retaliation against the police fired the entire antiterror police force. During this period, Turkish law enforcement lost its decades-long institutional memory and knowledge about crime and terrorism. Therefore, Turkey should create policies that curb corruption and aid in the fight against terrorism and crime. Turkey also should acknowledge the importance of institutionalizing its fight against terrorism and refuse to allow anyone to cover up corruption scandals in the government or to destroy the entire system used to fight terrorism and crime.

Although the PKK has operated in and gained revenue from its activities along Turkey's borders with Iran, Iraq, and Syria, law enforcement cooperation between Turkey and these countries has been nonexistent since the PKK launched its terrorist activities. Turkey's new policy model should include ways to cooperate with these countries.

The conflict in Syria created rather awkward alliances making countering the financing of terrorism in the Middle East more complex than ever. The United States, for example, established a partnership with the PYD and its military wing, YPG, in its fight against Da'esh. The United States provides the PYD with military equipment, logistics, and financial aid. The arrangement is problematic because it will be difficult to ensure that the PKK does not gain access to this military and financial aid. The United States should create oversight mechanisms to monitor the distribution and use of its military and financial aid. To ensure transparency, an independent committee should be assembled. Nongovernmental organizations should oversee the process of distributing the aid and how the aid will be used.

CONCLUSION

The PKK, which is motivated by Marxist ideology, has been Turkey's deadliest terrorist organization with active operations in northern Europe, Iraq, and Turkey itself. Similar to other terrorist organizations in the world, the PKK has been funded and financed by various revenue streams. Its main sources are extortion, taxation, drug trafficking, cigarette smuggling, and human smuggling, though the PKK also generates revenue from counterfeiting. Drug trafficking is the PKK's leading criminal activity and involves taxing drug traffickers operating along Turkey's eastern and southeastern borders. Recently, the PKK has taken an active role in the smuggling of Syrians to European countries. It should be noted that corruption not only helps the PKK to generate revenue, but it also presents opportunities for PKK-affiliated municipalities to funnel bribery money to the terrorist organization. The PKK's extensive criminal interests have made it a terrorist criminal enterprise.

With respect to policy implications, the PKK benefits from the vacuum created by the Turkish government and the governments of neighboring states. Turkey's destruction of its own security force in the wake of graft scandals and its inability to effectively cooperate with countries where the PKK operates create a favorable environment for the PKK to generate revenue from criminal activities. It is mandatory for Turkey to fill these gaps and develop an effective policy model.

NOTES

1. Suleyman Ozeren, Murat Sever, Kamil Yilmaz, and M. Alper Sozer, "Whom Do They Recruit? Profiling and Recruitment in the PKK/KCK," *Studies in Conflict & Terrorism* 37, no. 4 (2014), 326.

2. Abdullah Öcalan, *Manifesto Kürdistan Devriminin Yolu* (Almanya: Weşanen Serxwebun Yayınları 1978).

3. Abdullah Öcalan, *Kürdistan Ulusal Kurtuluş Problemi ve Çözüm Yolu* (Almanya: Weşanen Serxwebun Yayınları, 1982).

4. İhsan Bal, "PKK Terör Örgütü Tarihsel Süreç ve 28 Mart Diyarbakır Olayları Analizi," *Uluslararası Hukuk ve Politika* 2, no. 8 (2007), 75–89.

5. Globalsecurity.org, http://www.globalsecurity.org/military/world/para/pkk.htm.

6. "Kongra-Gel (KGK) / Kurdistan People's Congress / PKK," TRAC Terrorism Research and Analysis Consortium, https://www.trackingterrorism.org/group/kongra-gel-kgk-kurdistan-people's-congress-pkk.

7. Süleyman Özeren ve Oğuzhan Başıbüyük, "Kendi Dilinden KCK: Sivil Siyaset mi, Yeniden PKK mı?" in *Terörizm Paradoksu ve Türkiye*, ed. Süleyman Özeren ve Murat Sever (Ankara: Karınca Yayınları, 2011), 93–126.

8. Burhan Semiz, "PKK'da Değişen Ne?" in *Terörizm Paradoksu ve Türkiye*, ed. Süleyman Özeren ve Murat Sever, 58.

9. Ozeren, Sever, Yilmaz, and Sozer, "Whom Do They Recruit?" 327.

10. KCK Sözleşmesi, http://rojbas3.wordpress.com/kck-sozlesmesi/.

11. Tuvan Gumrukcu, Daren Butler, and David Dolan, "Offshoot of Kurdish Militant PKK Claims Istanbul Soccer Attacks," Reuters, December 11, 2016, http://www.reuters.com/article/us-turkey-blast-claim-idUSKBN1400T3.

12. Ozeren, Sever, Yilmaz, and Sozer, "Whom Do They Recruit?" 327.

13. "Turkey and the PKK: Saving the Peace Process," International Crisis Group, November 6, 2014, https://www.ecoi.net/file_upload/1002_1415293444_234-turkey-and-the-pkk-saving-the-peace-process.pdf.

14. Mitchel Roth and Murat Sever, "The Kurdish Workers Party PKK as Criminal Syndicate: Funding Terrorism through Organized Crime: A Case Study," *Studies in Conflict and Terrorism* 30 (2007), 901–920.

15. N. B. Criss, "The Nature of PKK Terrorism in Turkey," *Studies in Conflict and Terrorism* 18 (1995), 17–37.

16. Enis Berberoglu, "Romanya'da PKK'ya 8 bin kişi haraç ödüyor," *Hurriyet*, July 28, 1998, http://www.hurriyet.com.tr/romanyada-pkkya-8-bin-kisi-harac-oduyor-39031165.

17. "PKK'nın haraç timleri sokakta," *Yeni Safak*, July 28, 2016, http://www.yenisafak.com/gundem/pkknin-harac-timleri-sokakta-2500639.

18. "Pkk, Uyuşturucu, Kaçakçılık Ve Haraçtan Besleniyor," *Milliyet*, December 28, 2016, http://www.milliyet.com.tr/pkk-uyusturucu-kacakcilik-ve-haractan-diyarbakir-yerelhaber-1740334/.

19. "Terörün Ekonomisi: Sınır İllerinde Kaçakçılık ve Terörün Finansmanı Raporu," *UTSAM* (Ankara: Polis Akademisi Yayınları, 2009).

20. S. Janssens and J. Arsovska, "People Carriers: Human Trafficking Networks Thrive in Turkey," *Jane's Intelligence Review* (December 2008), 44–47.

21. M. Gheordunescu, "Terrorism and Organized Crime: The Romanian Perspective," in *The Future of Terrorism*, ed. M. Taylor and J. Morgan (London: Frank Cass Publishers, 2000).

22. S. E. Cornell, "The Interaction of Drug Smuggling, Human Trafficking, and Terrorism," in *Human Trafficking and Human Security*, ed. A. Jonsson (New York: Routledge, 2009), 48–66.

23. Louise Shelley, "The Diverse Facilitators of Counterfeiting: A Regional Perspective," *Journal of International Affairs* 66, no. 1 (2012), 19–37.

24. F. S. Perri and R. G. Brody, "The Dark Triad: Organized Crime, Terror & Fraud," *Journal of Money Laundering Control* 14, no. 1 (2011), 44–59.

25. Mahmut Cengiz, *Turkiye'de Organize Suc Gercegi ve Terorun Finansmani* (Ankara: Seckin Yayinevi, 2015), 171.

26. "İstanbul'da insan kaçakçılığı operasyonu," CNN Turk, December 26, 2016, http://www.cnnturk.com/video/turkiye/istanbulda-insan-kacakciligi-oper asyonu.

27. "PKK, göçmenlerin yılda 300 milyon $'ını çalıyor!" *Sabah Gazetesi*, May 29, 2015, http://www.sabah.com.tr/gundem/2015/09/05/pkk-gocmenlerin-yilda-300-milyon-ini-caliyor.

28. Sharon Melzer and Louise Shelley, "Nexus of Organized Crime and Terrorism: Two Case Studies in Cigarette Smuggling," *International Journal of Comparative and Applied Criminal Justice* 32, no. 1 (Spring, 2008), 43–63.

29. "PKK'nın en büyük gelir kaynağı kaçak sigara," *Haberturk*, September 26, 2015, http://www.haberturk.com/gundem/haber/1132720-pkknin-en-buyuk-ge lir-kaynagi-kacak-sigara.

30. "PKK'nın kaçak sigara gelirine ağır darbe!" *Yenicag*, May 11, 2015, http://www.yenicaggazetesi.com.tr/pkknin-kacak-sigara-gelirine-agir-darbe-114113h.htm.

31. *2014 Turkish Report of Anti-Smuggling and Organized Crime* (Ankara: KOM Daire Baskanligi), 53.

32. Roth and Sever, "The Kurdish Workers Party PKK as Criminal Syndicate."

33. *2012 Turkish Report of Anti-Smuggling and Organized Crime*, 82.

34. "Treasury Sanctions Supporters of the Kurdistan Workers Party (PKK) Tied to Drug Trafficking in Europe," U.S. Department of the Treasury, February 1, 2012, https://www.treasury.gov/press-center/press-releases/Pages/tg1406.aspx.

35. Mark Galeotti, "Turkish Organized Crime: Where State, Crime, and Rebellion Conspire," *Transnational Organized Crime* 4, no. 1 (Spring, 1998), 25–42.

36. *2012 Turkish Report of Anti-Smuggling and Organized Crime*, 82.

37. Mahmut Cengiz, *Turkish Organized Crime from Local to Global* (Saarbrücken, Germany: VDM Publishing, 2011), 79.

38. *2013 Turkish Report of Anti-Smuggling and Organized Crime* (Ankara: KOM Daire Baskanligi), 4.

39. *2012 Turkish Report of Anti-Smuggling and Organized Crime*, 83.

40. Cengiz, *Turkiye'de Organize Suc Gercegi ve Terorun Finansmani*, 174.

41. *2012 Turkish Report of Anti-Smuggling and Organized Crime*, 83–84.

42. Louise Shelley, *Dirty Entanglements Crime Corruption and Terrorism* (New York: Cambridge Press, 2014).

43. Cengiz, *Turkiye'de Organize Suc Gercegi ve Terorun Finansmani*, 175–176.

44. The police conducted operations on December 17 and 25, 2013. In the first operation, the Iranian facilitator, Reza Zarrab, who was in charge of breaking the U.S. embargo on Iran, circulated and laundered Iranian money in return for giving bribes to Turkish politicians, bureaucrats, and particularly to the family members of President Recep Tayyip Erdogan. Zarrab was arrested in Miami on March 19, 2016, on similar charges and indicted by the U.S. Southern District Court. The Federal Bureau of Investigation (FBI) launched an investigation about Zarrab in 2012. In the second operation on December 25, the son of Erdogan and several Saudi businessmen were charged with being part of an international bribery scandal.

CHAPTER 10

Hezbollah: The Continuing Expansion of a Robust Criminal Enterprise

Rhea D. Siers

INTRODUCTION

This chapter explores existing criminal involvement by Hezbollah as well as the growing pressure on it to diversify and increase the profitability of its criminal enterprises. Recent law enforcement actions provide significant insights into Hezbollah's use of criminal enterprises, primarily in drug smuggling and money laundering. As its need for capital continues to grow, how will Hezbollah expand? Will it focus solely on existing primary conduits such as the drug trade or will it seek to utilize newer criminal enterprises such as cybercrime?

The involvement of Hezbollah (translation: "Party of God" or "Party of Allah") in worldwide criminal activities has been widely discussed since the group's official founding in 1985. Hezbollah's criminal involvement ranges from drug smuggling to extortion. For many years, these activities were designed to supplement Hezbollah's support from the Iranian government. The other sources of Hezbollah funding are business enterprises (including front companies), Lebanese government sources such as municipal funding, and charities.

Hezbollah, already dependent on criminal proceeds, needs to maintain and expand its criminally gained income for several reasons. First, the potential changes in assistance received from its Iranian government and Islamic Revolutionary Guard Corps (IRGC) benefactors could dent its income (although there is no reason to assume a significant cut in Iranian aid, which is estimated at between $100 and $400 million).[1] Second, the group faces a rise in expenses for Hezbollah because of its involvement in Syria, specifically support for families and survivors of Hezbollah fighters back in Lebanon. Third, it must fund its continued robust program of social services for the Shia communities in Lebanon. Finally, it must expand due to the impact of U.S. sanctions and global law enforcement targeting banks and financial institutions designated as having ties to Hezbollah.

There has been speculation for several years that Hezbollah is suffering from reduced revenues. Recent media reports stated that Hezbollah is actually close to bankruptcy due to the Syrian war as well as the diversion of its cash to the personal accounts of Hezbollah's leaders, such as Sheikh Hassan Nasrallah, the secretary general of the organization. In its investigation of Hezbollah finances, *Die Welt* noted that Sheikh Nasrallah's son used Hezbollah-funneled cash to open a chain of coffee houses in Beirut and that Nasrallah himself is personally worth $250 million.[2]

It is difficult to confirm the validity of these claims, given that the Hezbollah leadership rarely discusses this issue publicly. In response to U.S. sanctions in 2016, Nasrallah claimed that all of Hezbollah's money for its activities was derived from Iran, claiming that "as long as Iran has money, we have money."[3] Magnus Ranstorp notes that Iran had cut funding to Hezbollah due to declining oil revenues and that this in turn resulted in Hezbollah "cutting back on social services, firing employees and experiencing problems paying suppliers."[4] In an unusual public effort, Hezbollah launched a public funding campaign, entitled "Equip a Mujahid," on social media.[5] Even if these dire financial predictions are exaggerated, the winding down of the civil war in Syria necessitates that Hezbollah reassert its influence in Lebanon. Thus, the group will need an infusion of capital to underwrite its "social projects" and other political activities to repair its tarnished image in the Arab world and to maintain the operational skills gained as Iran's foot soldiers in Syria.[6]

Hezbollah has been active in the drug trade from the beginning of its existence, using its presence and influence in Lebanon's Bekaa Valley to both grow poppies and cannabis and, as Ganor and Wernli note, "establish one of the world's largest concentrations of laboratories for the processing of hashish, heroin and cocaine" smuggled into Lebanon from both the Middle East and South America.[7]

Some of this expansion necessitates building upon Hezbollah's existing markets, such as its extensive drug-smuggling network. For example, Hezbollah participates in the manufacture and sale of Captagon, an amphetamine popular with jihadists that has recently seen a dramatic increase in distribution.[8] This expansion is built upon by its already existing involvement in the drug trade.

THE HEZBOLLAH CRIMINAL ENTERPRISE

The existing Hezbollah organized criminal enterprise has a global structure stretching from the Middle East to Europe to the Americas and diverse connections to other criminal organizations and intermediary organizations. Celina Realuyo has described Hezbollah as "the best organized and most business-savvy terrorist organization that relies on global facilitators engaged in narcotics, arms and counterfeit trafficking and money laundering."[9] Matthew Levitt, one of the first to identify the Hezbollah terror-crime nexus, states unequivocally that Hezbollah operates as a "Transnational Criminal Organization (TCO)" pursuant to U.S. law (Executive Order 13581),[10] a conclusion that has been supported by U.S. and international law enforcement and intelligence.[11]

Previously, there was a lack of definitive information as to whether all elements of the criminal infrastructure supporting Hezbollah were directly controlled by Hezbollah leadership or in fact consisted of a looser construct of Hezbollah members and supporters funneling the proceeds from a wide range of criminal activity into Hezbollah's coffers.[12] Now it is apparent that both constructs exist simultaneously in the Hezbollah-related criminal enterprise and that "Hezbollah has morphed from being a terrorist organization . . . to becoming a transnational criminal terrorist resistance organization fueled by a large and global illicit financial and business apparatus," according to recent Congressional testimony.[13] Christian Leuprecht, Olivier Walther, David Skillcorn, and Hillary Ryde-Collins conducted a social network analysis on two Hezbollah-connected criminal groups in the United States, both involved in very lucrative cigarette smuggling in the 1990s. They found that the groups were based on kinship and expanded accordingly—not an unusual construct among such Middle East terror and criminal groups.[14] Dependent on ethnic and familial ties, these groups recruited from within a narrow circle, outside of the purview of the Hezbollah organization itself.

However, joint U.S. and European law enforcement investigations resulted in important findings regarding the direct involvement of Hezbollah's operational or terrorist wing in criminal and money-laundering activity and its direct connections to other transnational criminal organizations such as the drug cartels in the Western Hemisphere.[15] Later in this chapter, we will explore how these investigations and subsequent criminal proceedings provided detailed information of how Hezbollah collects the proceeds from criminal activity worldwide.

Hezbollah has a diverse criminal business enterprise. According to Leuprecht, Walther, Skillcorn, and Ryde-Collins, Hezbollah is engaged in "drug and arms trafficking, human trafficking, cigarette smuggling, trading diamonds, counterfeiting goods and medications, laundering money, credit card and identity theft, and passport fraud, sham marriages, and intellectual property crime."[16] Hezbollah is involved in the full gamut of criminal activity but some are enabling functions, such as passport and credit fraud and others, such as drug smuggling, are pivotal because of high profits. By examining its activities in one of its regional hubs, we can better understand the value of certain criminal activities to the Hezbollah organization as a whole.

HEZBOLLAH IN THE TRI-BORDER AREA

There has been considerable discussion of the Hezbollah presence in South America, specifically in the crime center of the Tri-Border Area (TBA) of Argentina, Brazil, and Paraguay where the Iguazu and Paraná rivers converge. While much has been made of this activity, factual information is somewhat limited. The former commander of the U.S. Southern Command, General John F. Kelly, testified before the Senate Armed Services Committee that "unfortunately, our limited intelligence capabilities make it difficult to fully assess the amount of terror financing generated in Latin America, or understand the scope of possible criminal-terrorist collaboration."[17] However, the Iranian presence in South America, which includes its diplomatic facilities, provided Hezbollah with an operational foothold through its sponsorship by Iran's IRGC. Meanwhile, the Lebanese Diaspora in Argentina and Brazil is the largest outside of Lebanon, numbering approximately 8 million.[18] On the terror side, Hezbollah claimed credit for the bombing of the Israeli Embassy in Buenos Aires in 1992 and was believed to have worked with Iran in the bombing of Argentina's largest Jewish community organization, Asociación Mutual Israelita Argentina (AMIA), in 1994.[19] The question that persists is whether crime connected to Hezbollah utilized any of the existing formal IRGC-Hezbollah operational network and/or if there is proof that the rampant criminal activity in the TBA could be linked to Hezbollah.

The key to assessing the connection between Hezbollah and criminal enterprise in the TBA appears to center on the activities of a known Hezbollah supporter, Assad Ahmad Barakat. In the 1990s, Hezbollah created a comfortable environment for its supporters in the TBA and, in return, benefited from "donations" of profits from these supporters and other petty criminals in the area. By mid-2000, a Library of Congress report estimates that approximately 460 Hezbollah operatives were present in the TBA.[20] Levitt notes that Barakat was Nasrallah's personal representative to the area, creating his own network for fund-raising centered in a shopping center known as "Galeria Page" in Ciudad del Este, Paraguay, that served as Hezbollah headquarters in the region.[21]

Paraguayan police raided Barakat's own small store in this shopping center and found "professional training materials for suicide bombers" as well as financial statements detailing transfers to the Middle East.[22] There is also speculation that Hezbollah has an extremely close relationship with the "Lebanese Mafia" active in the TBA, which engages in drug and arms smuggling, human trafficking, intellectual property theft, and money laundering; it is not entirely clear whether these are actually separate entities.[23] In May 2002, Ali Assi, a Lebanese citizen who ran a coffee shop in the Islamic Welfare Center in Ciudad del Este, was arrested at Beirut International Airport with 10 kilos of cocaine in his luggage.[24] Assi was closely connected to Barakat and Sobhi Mahmoud Fayad, a Hezbollah operative convicted of drug-smuggling offenses.[25] A number of additional arrests of Lebanese Mafia and Hezbollah operatives confirmed the TBA as a major transit point for the smuggling of cocaine and many of those arrested had connections with Barakat as well.[26] In the raid of Barakat's store, police found a letter from the Hezbollah organization "congratulating Barakat for financing activities in the Middle East."[27]

Barakat's activities were not limited to drug trafficking. The Paraguayan intelligence services believed that Barakat blackmailed Lebanese citizens to procure additional funds for Hezbollah.[28] Barakat was also connected to the piracy of software and other intellectual property; a series of raids by Paraguayan officials revealed pirated video game CDs and a lab in Ciudad del Este that was copying up to 20,000 CDs per day.[29] There were reports that Barakat was linked to the AMIA bombing and allegedly supplied matériel for the attack.[30] As a result, Barakat was named a "Specially Designated Global Terrorist" by the U.S. Treasury Department, and the Galeria Page shopping center was also sanctioned by the United States in 2006.[31]

There is no evidence that the drug trade and other criminal activity associated with Hezbollah in the TBA have stopped. In June 2017, Ali Issa Chamas, who had ties to Hezbollah through associates and family, was arrested in Paraguay at the Ciudad del Este airport with 39 kilos of cocaine that he intended to ship to associates in Houston. A Miami grand jury charged him with distribution of cocaine in the United States.[32]

LEBANESE CANADIAN BANK AND THE JOUMAA CRIME ORGANIZATION

While General Kelly's frustrations about a lack of intelligence on criminal activities by terrorist groups was understandable, several law enforcement and "follow the money" operations have filled in some of the intelligence gaps regarding Hezbollah's criminal activities. One of the key law enforcement operations that pierced the veil of Hezbollah's direct involvement in drug trafficking was the takedown of the Lebanese Canadian Bank (LCB) in 2011 by the U.S. Drug Enforcement Administration (DEA) and Treasury. A six-year global investigation exposed some of Hezbollah's connections to money laundering and drug trafficking in a network that spanned from "South America to Europe and the Middle East via West Africa." Several LBC senior officials were "recommended" by the Hezbollah organization to be hired by the bank.[33]

Investigators found that LBC managers assisted several clients in laundering drug proceeds through a scheme using the proceeds of used cars bought in the United States and sold in Africa, with a portion of the profits being funneled to Hezbollah.[34] Implicated account holders included Shiite businessmen in West Africa known to be Hezbollah supporters with a broad range of trade interests, which ranged from industrial diamonds to frozen chicken, according to the *New York Times*. It is believed that these were front companies for Hezbollah. The *New York Times* noted one arrangement in particular involving "the richest land deal in Lebanon's history," a $240 million purchase of 740 acres "overlooking the Mediterranean."[35]

Reports also connected various businessmen and Hezbollah operatives through their communications and emphasized the role of Ayman Joumaa who had been designated as a "drug kingpin" in January 2011. In a federal indictment in December 2011, Joumaa was linked not only to Hezbollah but also to the Zetas drug cartel in Mexico. Joumaa allegedly assisted Hezbollah in obtaining "financing" from LBC and also coordinated money laundering globally from the drug proceeds of his own criminal organization.[36] Levitt notes that the Joumaa and LBC trail also led investigators to Abdullah Safieddine, Hezbollah's representative to Iran and Nasrallah's cousin, clearly a senior and highly influential member of Hezbollah's inner circle.[37]

PROJECT CASSANDRA: TAKING DOWN HEZBOLLAH'S CRIMINAL LOCUS

Project Cassandra, a 2016 joint U.S.-European law enforcement operation, not only disrupted Hezbollah drug trafficking and money-laundering enterprises but also provided authoritative evidence linking the crime to Hezbollah's External Security Organization, specifically the Business Affairs Component (BAC), its financial arm.[38] The BAC was established by former operations chief Imad Mughniyeh, Hezbollah's planner for several terrorist attacks, including those at the Israeli Embassy and AMIA in Buenos Aires. Mughniyeh was killed in Damascus in 2008 and was believed to be assassinated by the Israeli intelligence service, their U.S. counterparts, or both.[39] Mughniyeh's direct connection to BAC is among the most compelling evidence that the terrorist operations wing of Hezbollah was benefiting directly from a broad range of crimes.

The DEA announced the results of Operation Cassandra, noting that it targeted not only Hezbollah's drug trade in the United States and Europe but also the "intricate network of money couriers" that move the proceeds back to the Middle East.[40] The DEA was quite clear about the attribution of the criminal activity, stating

> these drug trafficking and money laundering schemes utilized by the Business Affairs Component provide a revenue and weapons stream for an international terrorist organization responsible for devastating terror attacks around the world.[41]

The DEA also discussed the network of money couriers "who collect and transport millions of euros in drug proceeds from Europe to the

Middle East."[42] The money couriers, like others connected to several terrorist groups such as Al-Qaida, utilized the Hawala money remittance system to avoid attribution and a paper trail.[43]

Several known drug traffickers and money launderers, all known to funnel a portion of their profits to Hezbollah, were also indicted in Miami. One of the defendants in Miami was Mohammad Ahmad Ammar, a resident of Medellín, Colombia, who is believed to be a key money launderer for La Oficina, known as an "offshoot" of the Medellín Cartel.[44]

This law enforcement activity was quickly followed by the announcement of U.S. Treasury sanctions targeting Hezbollah and designating Hezbollah-affiliated money launderers Mohamad Noureddine and Madi Zaher El Dine as individuals associated with Hezbollah's "terrorism, criminal, commercial and procurement" activities pursuant to Executive Order (EO) 13224.[45] EO 13224 gives the U.S. government authority to disrupt financial assistance to terrorist organizations and individuals assisting those organizations. It allows for the blocking of assets of those groups and individuals; Hezbollah was part of the original designated list of terrorist organizations attached to EO 13224 in October 2001, and Hezbollah leader Nasrallah was named as a Specially Designated Terrorist pursuant to EO 12947 in January 1995.[46]

SEPARATING THE INSEPARABLE:
HEZBOLLAH "WINGS"

While Operation Cassandra was hailed as a triumph of multilateral cooperation in identifying and disrupting Hezbollah's criminal enterprise, efforts to analyze and act against those activities were limited by a compartmentalization problem in Europe. The United States has no issue designating Hezbollah, writ large, as a terrorist and criminal enterprise; however, European authorities suffer from what one author has described "the wing scam" in responding to terrorist groups, blacklisting only the "military wing" of Hezbollah.[47] The fact is that military and political leaders of Hezbollah are not necessarily distinct—take the example of Mughniyeh discussed earlier, who not only directed terrorist operations but also facilitated the movement of criminal proceeds and was heavily involved in political and executive activity of the entire Hezbollah organization. The leaders in Hezbollah's "Jihad Council" direct all of Hezbollah's activities, from political to military to financial.[48]

Charities allegedly funneling donations to Hezbollah or its related "social" charities do not provide any sort of transparency, according to the "Charity Navigator."[49] In fact, these charities have provided precisely the type of cover for money laundering so necessary for Hezbollah support. Levitt notes that several of these charities are no more than fronts for remittances, some of which are the result of criminal activity, including al-Aqsa International Foundation, banned by the United States for raising funds for both Hamas and Hezbollah but allowed to operate in Europe.[50] Levitt also cites the example of "The Martyr's Organization" that provides support to the families of suicide bombers. He notes that Paraguayan police found receipts from that alleged charity for donations amounting to more than $3.5 million from Sobhi Mahmoud Fayad in Ciudad Del Este.[51] As previously noted, Ciudad Del Este was a center for various Hezbollah-related criminal activities and Fayad was one of its prime operatives. Nasrallah himself has stated that Hezbollah is "inseparable" and that its three wings, military, security and political, are overlapping activities.[52]

The European Union (EU) designated only Hezbollah's military wing as "a terror entity" in 2013 to allow future discussions with the group's "political" wing. This designation occurred only after Hezbollah was linked to the attack on a bus of Israeli tourists in Bulgaria in 2012. Nevertheless, some considered this designation a step forward for the EU's attention to Hezbollah's criminal and money-laundering activity despite the difficulty in trying to "phrase language to punish only the armed wing of Hezbollah and not its other operations, which run schools, clinics, hospitals and charitable fund-raising activities."[53] Critics like Peter Marguiles note "the EU failure to impose sanctions on Hezbollah as a whole ignores that money is fungible and therefore the political wing of the group is able to subsidize the military wing, rendering the EU's current sanctions toothless."[54]

However, it is not known how much the political wing designation has impacted Europol and other European law enforcement services in their efforts to isolate the drug and money-laundering businesses connected to Hezbollah. It is known that information from U.S. law enforcement and intelligence sources was the catalyst for several multilateral operations, including Project Cassandra. The European law enforcement services, in turn, took effective measures against Hezbollah's criminal businesses. However, the "wings" confusion leaves a measure of ambiguity in policy regarding the imposition of wide-scale sanctions against the Hezbollah organization.

FUTURE CRIME AND POLICY FOCUS: HEZBOLLAH AND CYBERCRIME

Many transnational criminal organizations have utilized cyber capabilities initially to defend their operations against law enforcement and intelligence services but later to reap the substantial profits available through the use of ransomware and stolen identities. Will Hezbollah also head in this direction? The escalation of law enforcement operations and banking sanctions could force Hezbollah to move toward the very profitable cybercrime sector. Cybercrime would afford Hezbollah greater anonymity and protection for its criminal operatives and illicit enterprises.

To date, there have been no substantive indictments or publicly available investigations that directly cite Hezbollah for criminal activity in cyberspace. However, Hezbollah is already known to be one of Iran's "cyber proxies" and has benefited from a large influx of expertise and equipment from the IRGC to Hezbollah military and operational units.[55] In fact, most experts believe that Iran has used Hezbollah as an electronic or cyberwarfare test bed against Israel, including attacks against Israeli businesses and attempts against Israel's critical infrastructure.[56]

Additionally, it could operate cybercriminal enterprises from Lebanon and throughout the Lebanese Diaspora with limited exposure; not only is the Lebanese government reluctant and largely incapable of confronting Hezbollah's criminal operations, but it has also been reported that the IRGC is operating a "launching pad" for cyber operations from a Beirut neighborhood.[57] Hezbollah's existing connection to drug trafficking also necessitates its presence through intermediaries on the Dark Web, demanding separate, nonpublic access. The Dark Web is the epicenter of cybercrime, including ransomware and identity theft; it also provides easily utilized ransomware as a service.

Given the wide availability of ransomware, an already existing pool of skilled individuals, and lax cyber laws in Lebanon, cybercrime would be a lucrative diversification of Hezbollah's moneymaking activities. Law enforcement and intelligence services need to also focus on Hezbollah's cyber capabilities outside the military/operational arena.

INCISIVE POLICY AND LEGAL SOLUTIONS: HEZBOLLAH INTERNATIONAL FINANCING PREVENTION ACT

As this chapter discussed, the United States has been particularly proactive in using sanctions and terrorist designations of Hezbollah and its associated individuals and leadership in efforts to disrupt its criminal operations and funding. While these efforts have certainly impacted Hezbollah's operations and possibly its need for working capital, it is unrealistic to expect a complete shutdown of the Hezbollah criminal and terror enterprise. The reality is that Hezbollah benefits not only from Iran's state sponsorship but also from long-standing alliances of convenience with other criminal entities and a diaspora base to support its activities.

The Hezbollah International Financing Prevention Act (HIFPA) passed by Congress in December 2015 has sharpened the tools at the disposal of the U.S. Treasury Department. It facilitates the imposition of sanctions on foreign financial institutions that assist Hezbollah or its agents. The sanctions include the prohibition of a "payable-through" account in the United States by "a foreign financial institution that knowingly helps Hezbollah's activities."[58]

HIFPA has significantly ratcheted up the pressure on Hezbollah and its money-laundering conduits through several banks. It forced Lebanon's Central Bank to issue a circular ordering banks to close Hezbollah-linked accounts. According to Schenker and Bauer, this order resulted in the closing of hundreds of Hezbollah-associated accounts and is "threatening the militia's social support network and commercial interests" as well as its underground criminal enterprises.[59] The Lebanese Central Bank's reaction stems from fears that "Western banks have adopted no-tolerance policies with regards to foreign correspondents in the wake of large sanctions-related enforcement actions." Schenker and Bauer also note that "with 55 percent of Lebanese trade conducted in dollars, Lebanese banks would likely be unable to operate if cut off from dollar clearing whether as a result of an ultracautious New York bank or if 'made an example of' by U.S. officials."[60]

POLICY OPTIONS AND CONCLUSION

As a policy and operational tool, HIFPA may have already had a substantial impact on Hezbollah operations, as discussed in the first section of this chapter. The impact of these sanctions will need to be analyzed over time to assess their impact. HIFPA demands significant investigative and intelligence resources to buttress enforcement, so it serves a purpose of potentially strong financial sanctions and prioritizing intelligence collection efforts against the global Hezbollah enterprise.

The shadowy criminal enterprise connected to Hezbollah has been exposed through incisive law enforcement investigations and sanctions targeting the nodes in its financial network. Its connection to other transnational criminal organizations has been proven by pulling the threads in its money-laundering and smuggling operations. That exposure also demonstrates the utility of global policy and enforcement, including banks in Hezbollah's home base of Lebanon. These are positive steps in seeking to disrupt Hezbollah's ability to assert itself in Lebanon and beyond. But these efforts must be as agile as Hezbollah's terrorist and criminal capabilities, given Hezbollah's historic ability to adapt its strategy to changing conditions on the ground.

NOTES

1. "Hizbollah's Syria Conundrum," International Crisis Group, March 24, 2017, 19. https://www.crisisgroup.org/middle-east-north-africa/eastern-mediter ranean/lebanon/175-hizbollah-s-syria-conundrum.

2. "Hezbollah Nearly Bankrupt but Nasrallah Awash in Cash," *Times of Israel*, May 2, 2017, http://www.timesofisrael.com/hezbollah-nearly-bankrupt-but-nas rallah-awash-in-cash-report/.

3. "Hizbollah's Syria Conundrum," 19.

4. Magnus Ranstorp, *Hezbollah's Calculus after the Iran Nuclear Deal* (West Point, NY: Combating Terrorism Center, January 19, 2016), 11. https://ctc.usma.edu/posts/hezbollahs-calculus-after-the-iran-nuclear-deal.

5. "Hizbullah Launches Online Fundraising Campaign," Cyber & Jihad Lab, February 10, 2017, http://cjlab.memri.org/lab-projects/tracking-jihadi-terrorist-use-of-social-media/hizbullah-launches-online-fundraising-campaign/.

6. Abdul-Rahman Al-Masri and Alexander Corbeil, "Hezbollah Re-Ascendant in Lebanon," *Carnegieendowment.org*, August 17, 2017, http://carnegieendowment.org/sada/72856.

7. Boaz Ganor and Miri Halperin Wernli, "The Infiltration of Terrorist Organizations into the Pharmaceutical Industry: Hezbollah as a Case Study," *Studies in Conflict and Terrorism* 36, June 13, 2013, 699–712.

8. Chavala Madlena Radwan Mortada, "Syria's Speed Freaks, Jihad Junkies, and Captagon Cartels," *Foreign Policy*, November 24, 2015, http://foreignpolicy.com/2015/11/19/syria-isis-captagon-lebanon-assad/.

9. Celina B. Realuyo, *The Future Evolution of Transnational Criminal Organizations and the Threat to US National Security* (Washington, DC: National Defense University, July 2015). http://chds.dodlive.mil/files/2015/06/pub-OP-realuyo2.pdf.

10. See, Executive Order No. 13581, 3 CFR (2017).

11. Matthew Levitt, "Why the CIA Killed Imad Mughniyeh," *Politico Magazine*, February 9, 2015, http://www.politico.com/magazine/story/2015/02/mughniyeh-assassination-cia-115049.

12. Matthew Levitt, *Hezbollah's Criminal Networks: Useful Idiots, Henchmen, and Organized Criminal Facilitators* (Washington, DC: Center for Complex Operations, October 25, 2016). http://cco.ndu.edu/BCWWO/Article/980812/7-hezbollahs-criminal-networks-useful-idiots-henchmen-and-organized-criminal-fa/.

13. David Asher, "Attacking Hezbollah's Financial Network: Policy Options," Testimony to House Foreign Affairs Committee, U.S. Congress, Washington, DC, June 8, 2017. http://docs.house.gov/meetings/FA/FA00/20170608/106094/HHRG-115-FA00-Wstate-AsherD-20170608.PDF.

14. Christian Leuprecht, Olivier Walther, David Skillcorn, and Hillary Ryde-Collins, "Hezbollah's Global Tentacles: A Relational Approach to Convergence with Transnational Organised Crime," *Terrorism and Political Violence*, November 23, 2015, 902–921.

15. Matthew Levitt, *Hezbollah's Transnational Organized Crime* (Washington, DC: The Washington Institute for Near East Policy, April 21, 2016). http://www.washingtoninstitute.org/policy-analysis/view/hezbollahs-transnational-organized-crime.

16. Leuprecht, Walther, Skillcorn, and Ryde-Collins, "Hezbollah's Global Tentacles," 903.

17. Jim Weaver, "Paraguayan Man Linked to Hezbollah Faces Drug Charges in Miami," *Miami Herald*, June 26, 2017, http://www.miamiherald.com/news/local/crime/article158334659.html.

18. Alma Keshavarz, "Iran and Hezbollah in the Tri-Border Areas of Latin America: A Look at the 'Old TBA' and the 'New TBA,'" *Small Wars Journal*, November 12, 2015, http://smallwarsjournal.com/jrnl/art/iran-and-hezbollah-in-the-tri-border-areas-of-latin-america-a-look-at-the-%E2%80%9Cold-tba%E2%80%9D-and-the.

19. Dexter Filkins, "Death of a Prosecutor," *New Yorker*, July 20, 2015, https://www.newyorker.com/magazine/2015/07/20/death-of-a-prosecutor.

20. Rex Hudson, *Terrorist and Organized Crime Groups in the Tri-Border Area (TBA) of South America*, Report, Federal Research Division (Washington, DC: Library of Congress, 2010), 5. https://www.loc.gov/rr/frd/pdf-files/TerrOrgCrime_TBA.pdf.

21. Levitt, *Hezbollah's Criminal Networks*, 2016.

22. Hudson, *Terrorist and Organized Crime Groups in the Tri-Border Area (TBA) of South America*, 28.

23. Ibid., 3.

24. Ibid., 25.

25. Ibid., 26.

26. Ibid.

27. Ibid., 28.

28. Ibid., 29–30.

29. Ibid., 30.

30. Keshavarz, "Iran and Hezbollah in the Tri-Border Areas of Latin America."

31. Ibid.

32. Weaver, "Paraguayan Man Linked to Hezbollah Faces Drug Charges in Miami."

33. "Drug Investigations Lead to Treasury 311 Patriot Act Designation against Lebanese Bank Tied to Hizballah," *ProPublica*, February 10, 2011, https://www.propublica.org/documents/item/274487-treasury-department-press-release-on-lebanese.

34. Jo Becker, "Beirut Bank Seen as a Hub of Hezbollah's Financing," *New York Times*, December 13, 2011, http://www.nytimes.com/2011/12/14/world/middleeast/beirut-bank-seen-as-a-hub-of-hezbollahs-financing.html.

35. Ibid.

36. Jo Becker, "US Sues Businesses It Says Helped Hezbollah," *New York Times*, November 15, 2011, http://www.nytimes.com/imagepages/2011/12/13/world/middleeast/joumaa.html#media/joumaa.

37. Matthew Levitt, *The Crackdown on Hezbollah's Financing Network* (Washington, DC: The Washington Institute for Near East Policy, January 27, 2016). http://www.washingtoninstitute.org/policy-analysis/view/the-crackdown-on-hezbollahs-financing-network.

38. "DEA and European Authorities Uncover Massive Hizballah Drug and Money Laundering Schemes," US Drug Enforcement Administration, US Department of Justice, Washington, DC, February 1, 2016. https://www.dea.gov/divisions/hq/2016/hq020116.shtml.

39. Levitt, "Why the CIA Killed Imad Mughniyeh."

40. "DEA and European Authorities Uncover Massive Hizballah Drug and Money Laundering Schemes."

41. Ibid.

42. Ibid.

43. "Hawala and Alternative Remittances," US Department of the Treasury, Resource Center. https://www.treasury.gov/resource-center/terrorist-illicit-finance/Pages/Hawala-and-Alternatives.aspx.

44. "Hezbollah Cell Charged with Laundering Colombian Drug Money in Miami," *Tower*, October 14, 2016, http://www.thetower.org/4037-hezbollah-operatives-laundered-a-half-million-dollars-through-miami-banks/.

45. "Treasury Sanctions Key Hizballah Money Laundering Network," US Department of the Treasury, January 28, 2016, https://www.treasury.gov/press-center/press-releases/Pages/jl0331.aspx; See, Executive Order No. 13224, 3 C.F.R. (2001).

46. See, Executive Order No. 12947, 3 C.F.R. (1995).

47. A.J. Caschetta, "The Terrorist 'Wing' Scam," Middle East Forum, February 2016, http://www.meforum.org/6261/the-terrorist-wing-scam.

48. Nasser Chararah, "No Separation in Hezbollah Political and Military Wings," Al-Monitor, July 26, 2013, http://www.al-monitor.com/pulse/origi nals/2013/07/hezbollah-military-political-nature-eu-decision.html.

49. "Your Guide to Intelligent Giving/Home," Charity Navigator, https://www.charitynavigator.org/.

50. Matthew Levitt, Hezbollah Finances: Funding the Party of God, Washington Institute for Near East Policy, February 2005. http://www.washingtoninstitute .org/policy-analysis/view/hezbollah-finances-funding-the-party-of-god.

51. Levitt, "Hezbollah Finances: Funding the Party of God."

52. Chararah, "No Separation in Hezbollah Political and Military Wings."

53. James Kanter and Jodi Rudoren, "European Union Adds Military Wing of Hezbollah to List of Terrorist Organizations," New York Times, July 22, 2013, http://www.nytimes.com/2013/07/23/world/middleeast/european-union-adds-hezbollah-wing-to-terror-list.html.

54. Peter Margulies, "Terrorist Sanctions: The Clash in US and EU Approaches," Lawfare, February 18, 2016, https://www.lawfareblog.com/terrorist-sanctions-clash-us-and-eu-approaches.

55. Jordan Brunner, "Iran Has Built an Army of Cyber-Proxies," Tower, August 2015, http://www.thetower.org/article/iran-has-built-an-army-of-cyber-proxies.

56. Noah Shachtman, "Hezbollah's Electronic Warriors," Wired, June 5, 2017, https://www.wired.com/2007/07/hezbollahs-elec/.

57. Michael Joseph Gross, "The Changing and Terrifying Nature of the New Cyber-Warfare," Hive, January 29, 2015, https://www.vanityfair.com/news/2013/07/new-cyberwar-victims-american-business.

58. "Hezbollah International Financing Prevention Act," Public Law 114–102, 114th Congress, December 18, 2015.

59. David Schenker and Katherine Bauer, "Targeting Hezbollah's Home-Front Finances," Washington Institute for Near East Policy, Policy Watch 2641, July 5, 2016, http://www.washingtoninstitute.org/policy-analysis/view/targeting-hez bollahs-home-front-finances.

60. Ibid.

CHAPTER 11

Cashing in on Fragility: Al-Qaida in the Islamic Maghreb and Crime in the Sahelo-Saharan Region

Audra Grant

Al-Qaida in the Islamic Maghreb (AQIM)-aided criminal activity in the Sahel and Sahara region (hereafter, Sahelo-Saharan region) has increased significantly since the early 2000s, particularly kidnap for ransom, drug smuggling in cocaine and cannabis, and weapons trafficking. Such activities are enabled by an amalgam of networks of groups, institutions, and individuals that includes a myriad of state actors at multiple levels, who profit from illicit trade. Large swaths of ungoverned territory, state fragility, poor governance, weak military and law enforcement, and lack of socioeconomic opportunity align to nurture the expansion and deepening of terrorism and organized crime in the Sahelo-Saharan region. This chapter discusses the nature and dynamics of the AQIM criminal enterprise in the Sahelo-Saharan region of Africa, defined here as Algeria, Libya, Mali, Mauritania, and Niger. AQIM has proved itself a resistant and rather nimble organization that has taken advantage of the precarious context of the Sahelo-Saharan area.

ORIGINS OF AQIM

AQIM grew out of the conflict and competitive Islamist group dynamics that characterized Algeria's brutal civil war. The conflagration, which began in 1992 and left over 150,000 Algerians dead, was a bitter contest between Islamists and the secular state but was also fraught with fierce competition within and between the Islamist organizations that populated the conflict's tumultuous landscape. Unprecedented reforms in 1989 led to the collapse of Algeria's one-party system, breaking the hegemony of the ruling National Liberation Front (FLN) and paving the way for parliamentary elections in 1992.[1] The watershed election would be the first truly "democratic" election in Algeria in which political parties flourished and openly vied for representation in the new multiparty system. Hopes of an enduring democratic transition were dashed however when Algeria's military-led government nullified the second round of election results that saw a victory for the Islamic Salvation Front (FIS)—a decision that would plunge Algeria into nearly a decade of conflict, known in the memory of many Algerians as the "black decade," and that would also bring Islamist militancy to Africa's Sahelo-Saharan region.

The 1992–1999 civil war was the backdrop for the emergence of a number of militant Islamist organizations that waged jihad against the Algerian apostate regime. The most prolific of those is AQIM. AQIM is an offshoot of Algeria's Armed Islamic Group (GIA), an organization with a salafi-jihadi orientation. AQIM, in its earliest incarnation, was known as the Salafist Group for Preaching and Combat (GSPC), founded in 1998 by Hassan Hatab. The GSPC broke with the GIA over the latter's indiscriminate killings of Algerian civilians they considered hostile to their cause. The GIA embraced an especially hard-line position against those they deemed *takfir*, which included Muslim women, children, and the elderly, as well as foreigners and agents of the state.[2] Unlike the GIA, the GSPC focused its attacks on Algerian law enforcement, rather than civilians, even though the organization also extorted money from residents in the Kabilye region.

In 1999, an Algerian government amnesty brought an end to government-insurgent hostilities, as Islamist fighters were persuaded to turn away from the insurgency. This eroded the cohesion of Algeria's salafi-jihadi movement throwing groups into disarray. Although some armed factions continued their struggle against the state, in March 2006 Hassan Hatab called on members to lay down arms in response to the amnesty. The GSPC, under new leadership, was concerned over the limited opportunities to wage jihad in the Algerian theater and sought to expand its influence globally to boost its capacity in the North Africa region. To accomplish this goal, the group looked to greater cooperation with Al-Qaida Central and its affiliate in Iraq.

GSPC efforts bore fruit. On September 11, 2006, Ayman al-Zawahiri announced a "blessed union" with the GSPC, and in January 2007 the organization officially became known as "Al-Qaida in the Islamic Maghreb." With the advantage of Al-Qaida branding, the nascent AQIM moved into the salafi-jihadi theater with a new name, new funding, and new allies and recruits. With its new moniker, AQIM launched a series of spectacular attacks, an affirmation of the organization's newfound potency. This would serve AQIM ambitions of enhancing its regional Maghrebi base by capitalizing on the collapse of the Libyan Islamic Fighting Group (LIFG) and other North African Islamist militant organizations.[3] AQIM's organizational structure is borrowed from the GIA. It is a loosely based organization comprised of armed cells, led by emirs who function rather autonomously. Senior members of AQIM were Afghan Arabs who fought against the Soviet Union in Afghanistan during the 1980s. The group's central leadership consists of a Council of Notables, a Shura council that presides over Islamic matters,[4] regional commanders, as well heads of political, military, judicial, and media committees. Abdelmalik Droukdel is the leader and sits atop the apex of the organization.[5]

METAMORPHOSIS: DEATH AND REVIVAL

Ongoing aggressive counterterrorism tactics waged by the Algerian government placed AQIM leadership under pressure, threatening the survival of the organization. Cut off from sufficient funding, recruits, and public support amid assaults that also killed civilians, AQIM began to struggle to maintain its capacity to carry out attacks. Thus since 2007, AQIM has turned strategically toward the African Sahel and Sahara. Indeed, the Sahelo-Saharan region, populated by fragile and weak states with ungovernable territories, porous borders, and limited reach of central authority, offers a permissive environment for the expansion of AQIM's terrorist and criminal activities. AQIM's Sahelo-Saharan strategy also reflects efforts to diversify the organization's membership. Although AQIM has managed to maintain an indigenous base of Algerian membership, it has been less successful incorporating Maghrebi members from Tunisia and Morocco into the organization. The disenfranchised populations that reside in countries such as Chad, Mali, Mauritania, and Nigeria provide a more available pool of recruits for radicalization, by contrast. Following AQIM's foray into northern Mali in 2012, the organization gained more Tuaregs. The group is also comprised of Moors from Mauritania, particularly Harratines, who are the descendants of slaves and face political and economic marginalization. These populations are driven to AQIM as a result of declining economic opportunities, ironically exacerbated by the decline in tourism caused by AQIM terrorism.[6]

These socioeconomic and political conditions have ripened opportunities for the establishment of safe havens throughout the African Sahara and Sahel. Mali, for example, which experienced a turbulent transition to democracy after 23 years of military rule, has been on the precipice of collapse, following a prolonged insurgency that has plagued the country since the 1990s. The conflict, where the impoverished Tuareg-dominated north is pitted against the south, escalated in 2012 after the fall of the Libyan regime—an event that flooded the region with loose weapons. AQIM, exploiting the disintegration of rule of law and stability, seized control of north and established Islamic law in the region.[7] AQIM attacks increased in Mali, as the organization expanded its network to include the Tuareg-based Movement for Tawhid and Jihad in West Africa (MUJAO), the National Movement for the Liberation of Azawad (MNLA), and Ansar Ed-dine, led by Iyad Ag Ghali. Although French military intervention in 2013 ran the Islamist militants aground bringing significant strategic losses for the group, AQIM still has a presence in Mali. Niger similarly faces in-surgency in the Tuareg north, amid widespread poverty, illiteracy, and slavery; slavery persists despite being banned in 2003. Mauritania has, likewise, struggled with the vestiges of slavery and long-standing ethnic tensions between its ruling Berber elites and Afro-Mauritanians who have suffered two decades of government-sponsored violence.[8] In Mauritania, most survive on less than $2 a day. According to International Monetary Fund (IMF) indicators from 2016, Mauritania was ranked the 51st poor-est country in the world, while Mali was 27th, and Niger was among the poorest countries at number 5.[9]

As Dalia Ghanem-Yazbeck and others note, since its establishment in 2007, AQIM has conducted well over a thousand attacks in the Sahelo-Sahara, with most launched in Algeria (603), and extending also to Mauri-tania, Niger, and elsewhere in the region.[10] Significantly, the 2015 reunion of Droukdel's AQIM with Mokhtar Belmokhtar, who returned with his newly established Al Mourabitoun organization, marked the resurgence of AQIM. The alliance has fortified AQIM with fresh ranks and capabil-ity, likely contributing to the sharp increase in attacks. AQIM and its net-work conducted at least 257 attacks in Mali and the wider West Africa region in 2016, which is an increase of 150 percent from 2015.[11] AQIM's revitalization has also been aided by the group's ability to expand its interactions with other local communities and its network with other institutions—and criminal enterprises, which is also on the rise.

WHY CRIMINAL ENTERPRISE

AQIM's criminal activities are an extension of GSPC's involvement in various forms of illicit trade that date back to the mid-2000s. Indeed, the Sahelo-Saharan region has become the center of gravity for the growth and expansion of the AQIM criminal enterprise. In the Sahelo-Sahara—and throughout the globe—actors involved in criminal enterprise com-mand substantial political and economic influence, particularly in weaker states where economic opportunities are limited. Thus, the interaction be-tween profitability and expansion of power and influence is a powerful incentive for participation in criminal enterprise. For the Islamist militant organizations, the more immediate lure is profitability, which enables ca-pacity to carry out activities and broader organization goals. State actors, however, are no less an important variable in the equation. Governments are drawn toward organized crime, as criminal activity can be used as an expedient resource that secures political and economic allies that gain from such activities.[12]

In the Sahara and Sahel, trade networks that have survived the ancient trade caravans have been used as key routes for legitimate trade by local communities that rely on trading hubs. In fact, trade in legitimate goods along these routes laid the ground for illicit trade.[13] An analysis by Wolfram Lacher, for example, explains that while contraband trade of Algerian and Libyan goods makes its way to Mali and Niger, based on informal arrangements between officials and traders, legitimate trade also relies on the same networks.[14] Thus, actors involved in the sale of licit goods also might be involved in illicit trade, including members of informal, as well as formal institutions that might include government officials. In addition, these trade routes are critical conduits of communication.

Lacher finds that broader economic and security factors in the Sahelo-Sahara contributed to the growth of trade in contraband in the region. For instance, while economic recession in pivotal Algeria limited opportunities for legitimate trade, sanctions against Libya also led to the proliferation in contraband items. Moreover, conflicts in Algeria, Mali, and Niger throughout the 1990s also led to a flood of weapons into the Sahara, causing a rise in weapons trafficking in the region.[15] Today, AQIM's criminal enterprise includes this and a range of activities. Excluding kidnapping for ransom (KFR), the most profitable for AQIM, the organization reportedly earns $100 million from smuggling in arms, cigarettes, and narcotics.[16]

Cigarette Smuggling

Cigarette trafficking proliferated in the Sahelo-Saharan region during the 1980s and has exploded into a $1 billion business in North Africa.[17] The populations of Algeria, Egypt, Libya, Morocco, and Tunisia smoke 44 percent of cigarettes in Africa, but a significant proportion of this is illicit.[18] According to the UN Office on Drugs and Crime (UNODC), cigarettes are imported through Mauritania to Algeria and Morocco. Cigarettes are also routed through Benin and Togo and through Niger and Burkina Faso to Libya and Algeria. AQIM charges a tax for passage of cigarettes or for assisting with transportation. Legitimate government services are compromised by such trade, however, as customs, security, and trade officials have become a part of this lucrative illicit network. Merchandise is allowed to travel unchecked along roads in Mali and Niger, and in Libya, security officials control the cigarette smuggling market. The Sahrawis, who dwell in the contested Western Sahara, trade cigarettes to Morocco and Algeria as well as humanitarian aid and subsidized Algerian goods to Algeria.[19] These activities are aided by Polisario officials.[20] The cigarette trade comes with low risk and has fomented competition among AQIM partners, complicit government officials, and Tuareg tribes who seek to control the illicit cigarette trade.[21] Amid this expansion and deepening of cigarette smuggling, gangs of traffickers who transport the merchandise into Algeria from Mali, Mauritania, and Niger have increased in number.

Drug Smuggling

Cocaine smuggling in the Sahelo-Saharan region grew during the mid- to late 2000s when cartels from Latin America looked to Europe to re- place saturated U.S. markets. The drugs are first shipped to countries such as Guinea-Bissau and then are moved to Algeria, Libya, and Mo- rocco. AQIM's drug smuggling operation depends on external partners. Throughout the mid-2000s, drug cartels in Colombia and Bolivia served as critical conduits for the dissemination of knowledge, assisting the or- ganization with the acquisition of skills in telecommunications, money laundering, and cash management.[22] AQIM and the remnants of the now-defunct Cali Cartel also allegedly participated in a board meeting in Guinea-Bissau with the aim of coordinating an arrangement. It was pur- portedly agreed that the Cali Cartel would provide cocaine and transat- lantic transportation, while AQIM would provide its critical knowledge of complex trans-Saharan trade routes to move narcotics from Africa to the Mediterranean.[23]

According to *Forbes* magazine, Belmokhtar drew AQIM into the drug- smuggling activities, despite protests from Droukdel, who did not believe drug smuggling was appropriate for AQIM. Belmokhtar, in response, al- legedly created his offshoot organization that would later be known as Al Mourabitoun and diversified into drug smuggling.[24] This aspect of AQ- IM's criminal enterprise functions as a loosely organized firm, like the rest of the organization. AQIM leader Droukdel relies on a decentralized man- agement style, while Belmokhtar serves as a commander who is respon- sible for the day-to-day operations of AQIM, including the smuggling activities. Belmokhtar's role in drug smuggling appears to have added to his infamy. Nicknamed "the Marlboro Man" for his profitable cigarette trafficking enterprise, he is known as "le narco-Islamiste" along Malian and Algerian smuggling routes.[25]

Smuggling, in general, is an accepted social practice in the Sahelo- Saharan region, particularly along the porous border area between Alge- ria and Mali, despite its official closure by Algiers since 2013. Smuggling projects autonomy and control.[26] Basic goods such as oil, wheat, petrol, and other goods are traded on a black market that thrives on commodities smuggled illegally from Algeria to Mali.[27] Drug convoys use old caravan routes, and smugglers' knowledge of those routes' ancient hidden trails makes traffickers difficult to detect.[28] Memorable is the 2009 discovery of a downed Boeing 727 plane in the Malian desert near Gao that allegedly carried up to 10 tons of cocaine from Venezuela.[29] That the aircraft was found in Gao is no accident; Gao is considered a key point of transit for drug convoys that make their way north.[30] Mali is also believed to have become a hub for storage of cocaine.

AQIM also earns revenue reportedly from imposing taxes on drug smugglers in return for safe passage. The group gains profit from cocaine that ultimately is delivered to Britain and elsewhere in Europe. Despite this, Lacher argues that AQIM's forays into drug smuggling are, at most, indirect. He asserts that preoccupation with militant Islamist groups masks the role that state actors play in enabling drug smuggling and other forms of criminal activity. He also suggests that some skepticism is warranted with drawing conclusions based on suspects' claims. Lacher, for example, doubts AQIM links to the Fuerzas Armadas Revolucionarias de Colombia (FARC) and believes that suspects questioned by Western law enforcement agencies falsified information.[31]

Weapons Trafficking

Trafficking in weapons has increased significantly in the Sahelo-Saharan region since the eruption of the 2012 conflict in northern Mali, and particularly since the downfall of Al-Qadhafi. Weapons which were definitively traced in the Sahelo-Saharan region emanate from Libyan and Malian national stockpiles. A preponderance of weapons maintained by AQIM and other terrorist groups operating in and around Mali derive from outflows from Mali and Libya—where there exists little to no government control of armaments—and which are an important source of weapons for AQIM and its affiliates.[32] According to a 2016 UN report, 50 percent of weapons used by terrorist organizations emanate from Libya, 40 percent from Mali, and 10 percent are from other sources.[33] As Malian weapons' stockpiles have become more depleted, Libya has replaced Mali as a key source of weapons for AQIM and other armed groups. Weapons materials from Libya include rockets, grenades, assault rifles, antitank launchers, machine guns, vehicles, and small and medium caliber ammunition.[34]

Interviews among suspects arrested in the region suggest that AQIM, Ansar Eddine, the MNLA, and MUJAO receive support from Libya, either through members of the groups residing in the country or through temporary links and visits by individuals who gather money and arms and arrange logistics for smuggling and violent activity. Libyan materials have been used by AQIM and other armed groups in Mali, as evidenced by the discovery of several caches of weapons traced to Libya.[35]

Weapons have also been found in northern Niger. For example, in November 2014, six vehicles were intercepted transporting three tons of armaments for Mali. According to statements by the occupants, the arms were provided by an Algerian national living in Ubari, Libya, who was a member of the Tareq Ibn Ziyad branch of AQIM. The cache was retrieved in the desert. The arms were for Ansar Eddine leader Iyad Ag Ghali and were intended for distribution between Ansar Eddine and another group linked to AQIM in northern Mali.[36] In February 2015, French and Nigerien authorities intercepted a convoy of six vehicles, which included eight members of the MNLA transporting a large quantity of arms and ammunition, and €539,000 in cash. Sources believe the funds were from a ransom payment. The vehicles were headed for Kidal, Mali.[37]

However, additional reports indicate that AQIM-affiliated Al Mourabitoun may also be using Chinese weapons. The group used AK-pattern Type 56-1 assault rifles in the 2015 Radisson Blu Hotel and Hotel Byblos[38] attacks that may have been manufactured in a Chinese factory. Although these weapons are available in the region, they are not from Mali or Libya and were not documented in the Sahelo-Saharan region prior to the 2015 attacks.[39] More investigation is warranted into this linkage, however.

Human Trafficking

The alarming discovery of modern-day African slave markets in Libya in 2017 points to lack of rule of law and other thriving areas of criminality in the Sahel, including human trafficking. Libyan officials have expressed concern that Belmokhtar, leader of the AQIM-affiliated Al Mourabitoun, may be involved in human trafficking. Intelligence reports suggest that he may have supported groups that smuggled Libyans to Europe from Ajdabiya, a key hot spot in Libya for migrants coming from the Southeast. Officials suspect that Belmokhtar may be enriching his organization through smuggling of migrants to Europe and may have been helping Da'esh establish bases in southern Libya, an area with which he has ties.[40]

KFR

Of all the AQIM-sponsored illicit activities in the Sahelo-Saharan region, KFR remains the most lucrative criminal enterprise for AQIM. From 2003 to 2013, AQIM made $200 million in KFR. From 2003 to 2007, it made $2 million per person annually. From 2007 to 2012, the organization increased its profits, averaging four hostages per year, earning $8 million per hostage. Since 2010, AQIM has reportedly brought in between $75 million and $91.5 million from KFR alone, helping fuel its territorial expansion in northern Mali.[41]

AQIM reinvests KFR funds into Sahelo-Saharan communities, providing services that the region's weak states are unable to. The increase in terrorist attacks has substantially dampened tourism to the region, which has only further eroded already limited economic opportunities. With few prospects for income available, AQIM is the only source of earnings and purpose for populations. Perhaps in a cruel twist of fate, populations turn to the very group—AQIM—that is responsible for the decline of their economic prospects.

AQIM's KFR targets usually are Western citizens from governments or third parties that are known for paying for ransom for release of hostages. In particular, France, Italy, and Spain have been willing to pay ransom for their citizens filling AQIM's coffers. In December 2014, the group released a French and Dutch national who were captured in November. In June 2015, AQIM held a Swedish and South African hostage until the end of that year. In November 2015, the group reportedly was involved in the attack on the Bamako/Radisson Blu Hotel in Bamako, Mali, in which over 170 people were taken hostage, some of whom were American. The attack is believed to have been planned by AQIM partner, Al Mourabitoun.[42] MUJAO has also assisted AQIM in KFR incidents. With more European soldiers heading to Mali from France, Germany, and Sweden, the chance of more kidnappings of Westerners is likely, in the view of some observers.[43]

AQIM fund-raises globally, and it receives assistance from supporters residing in Western Europe. Since 2011, it has also established relations with militant groups elsewhere in the Sahelo-Saharan region, including with Nigeria's Boko Haram, Somalia's al-Shabaab, and Yemen's Al-Qaida in the Arabian Peninsula (AQAP). It has purportedly exchanged funds, arms, and information with these organizations.[44] AQIM's kidnapping and other criminal activity have been able to thrive successfully in the region, in part, as a result of government complicity and the willingness of Western governments to provide ransom.

STATE ACTORS

The links of state actors to criminal enterprise in the Sahelo-Saharan region cannot be underestimated, as they are key enablers of criminal activity there. State actors in each country are involved in varying degrees in what Lacher calls the management of criminal activity. In Mauritania, for instance, links between state officials and tribes involved in weapons smuggling are more or less obviously dependent on who is in power. Under former Mauritanian president Maaouya Ould Sid-Ahem Taya, the links were more apparent.[45] Taya's rule depended on an alliance with the Smacid, Ouled Bou Sba, and Rgeybat tribes, which in turn were involved in weapons smuggling. Furthermore, cocaine arrests and seizures under Taya appear to have been used as tools of competitive struggles for power and retribution. Under current president Mohammed Ould Abdel Aziz, the connections between AQIM's enterprise and state actors are murkier. However, recent arrests of relatives of former leaders Taya and Haidallah in connection with drug smuggling in 2007 suggest potential collusion.[46]

In Niger, the relationship between AQIM's criminal activities and state institutions is clearer by comparison. Authorities essentially ignore criminal activity, and arrests and seizures are rare in the north, where the preponderance of drug and weapons smuggling activity takes place.

Mali is where involvement of criminal activity by state officials is broadest in scope and most pervasive. Malian officials have formed relationships with local community leaders and businesses, which are even more valuable against the backdrop of competition for the dividends of such activity. Collusion includes Malian security officials who have also been complicit in AQIM's KFR activities.

CONCLUSION

Despite vigorous counterterrorism efforts by France and Algeria and a UN peacekeeping force, AQIM remains a potent organization. Still able to operate relatively unencumbered in northern Mali, the group has been able to continue its attacks and maintain its criminal enterprise. Without the cooperation of state actors, however, AQIM's criminal activities would not be sustainable or as profitable. Proceeds from AQIM's illicit enterprises are invested back into communities, which contributes to the group's ability to entrench itself into the region's Sahelo-Saharan communities.[47] An alarming by-product is the erosion of traditional authority in the region, which equates to the destabilization of already fragile countries.[48] Each of these factors contributes to AQIM's resiliency and adaptability, particularly in vulnerable states such as Mali. Yet, as Sergei Boeke points out, it would be premature to conclude that AQIM has transformed into a criminal organization, despite the expansion of its criminal activity.[49] The group appears to still be guided by salafi-jihadi goals and orientation, with criminal activity providing a means to an end. This, of course, does not make AQIM any less lethal. Quite the contrary, the organization poses a security threat to countries in the Sahelo-Saharan theater. A failure to address the fragility may allow it to make inroads beyond the Sahelo-Sahara and further into the larger African region.

RECOMMENDATIONS

- Security forces should be strengthened, and regional approaches to security need to be more robust in order to counter what is at its heart: a transnational problem that does not recognize national borders. Regional counterterrorism efforts also need to be harmonized and strengthened.

- Bolster the national- and local-level institutions of Sahelo-Saharan states. Military security solutions should not be the only approach.[50] As the root causes of state fragility and criminality are found in weak or poor governance, the international community should continue assistance that strengthens governments and that also focuses on improving the livelihoods and lives of local populations.

- Thus, it is critical to create employment and educational opportunities for key population segments, such as youth who comprise at least half the population in Sahelo-Saharan countries.

- There are few sources of income for Sahelo-Saharan populations. Criminal networks must therefore be weakened and replaced with sustainable and viable sources of income. A gradual approach to dismantling networks may be more prudent.

- Governments in the region have not recognized the gravity of drug trafficking and its implications for country stability. Governments, therefore, need to be more proactive with implementing carefully planned, long-term, counter-narcotics programs, rather than responding episodically to international pressure that is itself the product of political crises.

- If countries deem ransom payments appropriate, they should coordinate conditions under which ransom payments are provided and the amounts to be provided.

- Western governments have primarily seen AQIM and similar organizations predominately through the lens of terrorism rather than their criminal activity. More attention needs to focus on the criminal capacities of terrorist organizations. This is not to imply that organizations engaging in criminal activity have transformed into criminal groups. Rather, to the extent that a portion of their operational repertoire includes criminal enterprise, more analysis and attention are warranted for these activities.

- Finally, the role and intricacies of local tribal dynamics and their relationship to trafficking activity are not well understood. As Jourde notes, there exists competition and rivalry between local tribes, which have long shaped trafficking in the Sahelo-Sahara region. Intergroup politics and jockeying for influence among tribes are part and parcel of trade dynamics and efforts to control routes and trade. Often, it is also individuals rather than tribes that drive dynamics more than the other way around. As the influence and power of individuals shift, so do interests.[51]

NOTES

1. Political reforms were introduced following the October riots of 1988 and included a new constitution. See, Michael Willis, *Politics and Power in the Maghreb: Algeria, Tunisia, and Morocco from Independence to Arab Spring* (New York: Columbia University Press, 2012).

2. Sergei Boeke, "Al Qaeda in the Islamic Maghreb: Terrorism, Insurgency, or Organized Crime?" *Small Wars and Insurgencies* 27, no. 5 (2016), 914–936.

3. There were advantages for Al-Qaida as well, however. In 2006, the GSPC/ AQIM was one of the wealthiest organizations in the world, owing its fortunes mostly to kidnapping and other criminal activities. See Christopher Chivvis and Andrew Liepman, *North Africa's Menace: AQIM's Evolution and the U.S. Policy Response* (Washington, DC: RAND Corporation, 2013).

4. See, https://www.counterextremism.com/threat/al-qaeda-islamic-maghreb-aqim.

5. Boeke, "Al Qaeda in the Islamic Maghreb," 914–936.

6. Modia Goita, *West Africa's Growing Terrorist Threat: Confronting AQIM Sahelian Strategy* (Washington, DC: Africa Center for Strategic Studies, 2011).

7. AQIM and its network were able to take over portions of northern Mali, including Gao, Kidal, and Timbuktu.

8. Noel Foster, *Mauritania: The Struggle for Democracy* (Boulder, CO: Lynne Rienner Publishers, 2011).

9. Figures are based on rankings assigned to a total of 189 countries by the IMF World Economic Outlook Database, October 2016.

10. See the Armed Conflict Location and Data Event Project at https://www.acleddata.com/ and Dalia Ghanem-Yazbeck, "Why Is AQIM Still a Regional Threat?" *The New Arab*, March 23, 2016, https://www.alaraby.co.uk/english/comment/2016/3/24/why-aqim-is-still-a-regional-threat?utm_source=twitterfeed&utm_medium=twitter; AQIM has conducted in Mauritania and Tunisia, 32 and 25 attacks, respectively, 17 in Niger, and fewer in Morocco and Libya, 11 and 7, attacks, respectively.

11. The attacks are attributed to AQIM and Al Mourabitoun, Ansar Eddine, and two of Ansar Eddine's affiliates, Katibat Macina and Katibat Khalid bin Walid. These attacks have focused on Mali but have also been conducted in Burkina Faso, Ivory Coast, and Niger. See, for example, Caleb Weiss, "Over 100 al Qaeda-linked Attacks in West Africa So Far in 2017," *FDD Long War Journal*, May 25, 2017, http://www.longwarjournal.org/archives/2017/over-250-al-qaeda-linked-attacks-in-west-africa-in-2016.

12. Wolfram Lacher, *Organized Crime and Conflict in the Sahel-Sahara Region* (Washington, DC: Carnegie Endowment for International Peace, 2012).

13. Ibid., 3.

14. Ibid.

15. Ibid.

16. Abdelmalek Alaoui, "The Secret of Al-Qaeda in the Islamic Maghreb: A Secretive and Highly Resilient Business Model," *Forbes*, December 16, 2013, https://www.forbes.com/sites/kerryadolan/2013/12/16/the-secret-of-al-qaeda-in-islamic-maghreb-inc-a-resilient-and-highly-illegal-business-model/#54cc969d475e.

17. According to the UNODC, Africans smoke 40 billion cigarettes annually. Approximately 60 billion are purchased on the black market. Also, see Jamie Doward, "How Cigarette Smuggling Fuels Africa's Islamist Violence," *Guardian*, January 26, 2013, https://www.theguardian.com/world/2013/jan/27/cigarette-smuggling-mokhtar-belmokhtar-terrorism.

18. See, Doward, "How Cigarette Smuggling Fuels Africa's Islamist Violence."

19. Lacher, *Organized Crime and Conflict in the Sahel-Sahara Region*, 4.

20. The Polisario Front is a political military organization that seeks independence for the Western Sahara from Morocco. The group was established in 1973. It is supported by Algeria, where it is based, and is comprised of indigenous Saharawis. The Polisario has declared the establishment of the Saharawi Arab Democratic Republic and claims to represent Saharawi interests. As such, the Polisario has a level of legitimacy but has been criticized for harsh governance and tactics toward populations in Algerian refugee camps where Saharawis reside.

21. Doward, "How Cigarette Smuggling Fuels Africa's Islamist Violence."

22. Alaoui, "The Secret of Al-Qaeda in the Islamic Maghreb."

23. Ibid.

24. Ibid.

25. Colin Freeman, "Revealed: How Saharan Caravans of Cocaine Helped to Fund al-Qaeda in Terrorists' North Africa Domain," *Telegraph*, January 26, 2013, http://www.telegraph.co.uk/news/worldnews/africaandindianocean/mali/9829099/Revealed-how-Saharan-caravans-of-cocaine-help-to-fund-al-Qaeda-in-terrorists-North-African-domain.html.

26. Cedric Jourde, "Sifting through Layer of Insecurity in the Sahel: The Case of Mauritania," *Africa Security Brief* (Washington, DC: African Center for Strategic Studies, 2011).

27. Lacher, *Organized Crime and Conflict in the Sahel-Sahara Region*; Freeman, "Revealed: How Saharan Caravans of Cocaine Helped to Fund al-Qaeda in Terrorists' North Africa Domain."

28. Freeman, "Revealed: How Saharan Caravans of Cocaine Helped to Fund al-Qaeda in Terrorists' North Africa Domain."

29. Ibid.

30. Ibid.

31. Lacher, *Organized Crime and Conflict in the Sahel-Sahara Region*, 6.

32. *Investigating Cross-Border Weapons Transfers in the Sahel, Conflict Armament Research* (London: Conflict Armament Research Ltd., 2016).

33. The estimates are based on figures from French authorities. See, *United Nations Libya Report Panel of Experts* (New York: United Nations, March 2016), 167.

34. Ibid.

35. *United Nations Libya Report*, Panel of Experts, March 2016, 166.

36. Ibid.

37. Ibid.

38. The Raddison Blu Hotel is located in Bamako, Mali, and the Hotel Byblos is located in Sevare, Mali.

39. *Investigating Cross-Border Weapons Transfers in the Sahel, Conflict Armament Research* (London: Conflict Armament Research Ltd., 2016).

40. Mark Micallef, *The Human Conveyor Belt: Trends in Human Trafficking and Smuggling in Post-Revolution Libya* (Geneva, Switzerland: Global Initiative against Human Trafficking, 2017), 33.

41. David Andrew Weinberg, "Terrorist Financing, Kidnapping, Antiques, Trafficking, and Private Donations," Congressional Testimony, Hearing before the Committee on Foreign Affairs, Subcommittee on Terrorism, Non-Proliferation and Trade, Washington, DC, November 2015.

42. U.S. Department of State, Country Report on Terrorism, 2015, Chapter 6, Al-Qaeda in the Islamic Maghreb, June 2016, https://www.ecoi.net/local_link/324951/451112_en.html.

43. Oliver Guitta, "The Re-emergence of Al-Qaeda in the Islamic Maghreb," *Al Jazeera*, March 20, 2016, http://www.aljazeera.com/indepth/opinion/2016/03/emergence-aqim-africa-160320090928469.html.

44. See, Stanford University, Mapping Militant Organizations at http://web.stanford.edu/group/mappingmilitants/cgi-bin/groups/view/65.

45. See, for example, Lacher, *Organized Crime and Conflict in the Sahel-Sahara Region*.

46. Although state links to AQIM activity are harder to detect in Mauritania under President Ould Abdel Aziz, Lacher notes that arrests have declined and there have been incidents of unexpectedly large amassed fortunes of high-level Mauritanians that have gone uninvestigated. In addition, in 2011, under Aziz a

number of convicted smugglers were released under questionable circumstances, and in a case of an exposed cannabis smuggling network, a former senior-level policeman may have issued permits allowing smugglers to circumvent checkpoints. See, Lacher, *Organized Crime and Conflict in the Sahel-Sahara Region*, 16.

47. Modibo Goïta, "West Africa's Growing Terrorist Threat: Confronting AQ-IM's Sahelian Strategy," *Africa Security Brief*, no. 11 (February 2011). http://africa center.org/wp-content/uploads/2016/06/ASB11EN-West-Africa%E2%80%99s-Growing-Terrorist-Threat-Confronting-AQIM%E2%80%99s-Sahelian-Strategy .pdf.

48. Ibid.

49. Boeke, "Al-Qaeda in the Islamic Maghreb."

50. Indeed, there are risks associated with strategic military approaches, as underscored by the November 2017 deaths of four U.S. soldiers in Niger who were ambushed by insurgents that allegedly had help from local residents.

51. Jourde, "Sifting through Layer of Insecurity in the Sahel: The Case of Mauritania."

CHAPTER 12

The Abu Sayyaf Group: A Destructive Duality

Richard T. Oakley[1]

The Abu Sayyaf Group (ASG) is the quintessential terrorist criminal enterprise. Founded in the Philippines more than a decade before the "Global War on Terrorism," the group was designated a foreign terrorist organization by the United States in 1997. As such, the ASG's early ideological goal was clear: the creation of an autonomous region in the southern Philippine islands.[2] The group undertook many spectacular terrorist operations in its early years, receiving financial support from state and nonstate sponsors, and became one of the first—albeit lesser known—targets of post-9/11 U.S. and international community counterterrorism strategies.[3] The ASG first experienced operational difficulties when financial connections with Al-Qaida frayed. Global counterterrorism efforts to attack terrorist funding in order to disrupt the operational capacity of groups like the ASG added to the dilemma. The ASG lost its remaining external backers as official funders were named and shamed, and unofficial ones were rounded up in financial and security stings. Undeterred, the group's response was to turn increasingly to criminal enterprise to pursue its ideological and political goals.[4] Kidnapping for ransom (KFR) schemes and involvement in the drug trade soon provided an indispensable funding solution for ASG's terrorist activities.

The result of ASG's increased dependence on organized crime was that for at least the past decade it has become more difficult to distinguish its fund-raising for terrorism from its illicit entrepreneurial exploits. The ASG has long been involved in the illicit arms business of the region.[5] It also has expanded its KFR activity to piracy in the surrounding maritime domain, with support networks reaching to Malaysia.[6] Its drug ties are now reportedly international with connections to the notorious Bamboo

Triad of Taiwan and the Hong Kong-based 14K Triad.[7] Yet the ASG has not given up its terrorist roots. Rather, it may have morphed its terrorist identity rather than abandon it, swapping the banner of Al-Qaida for that of Da'esh. This new allegiance was evidenced, inter alia, by the participation of Isnilon Hapilon—the ASG's top leader and Da'esh's emir in Southeast Asia—in the months-long siege of the southern Philippine city of Marawi by Da'esh in 2017.[8] Such destructive duality makes the ASG a resilient threat to security in Southeast Asia, and a prime example of a terrorist criminal enterprise.

ASG IN THE PHILIPPINES: A HISTORICAL, GEOGRAPHIC, AND CULTURAL OVERVIEW

The Bangsamoro—a People and a Place

The southern Philippines is a Muslim majority area consisting of Basilan, Mindanao, the Sulu Archipelago, and Tawi-Tawi. This region is both the historical homeland of the Moros—the original indigenous Muslim people of the Philippines—and the now decades-long base of operations for the ASG. A thriving Muslim resistance has endured for over 400 years. It has survived multiple foreign colonization attempts and invasions, including those by Britain, Japan, Spain, and the United States.[9] Although the Spanish were ultimately successful in spreading Catholicism throughout the Northern Islands (Luzon and the Visayas), the Moros resisted and repelled their attempts.[10] The next major, and somewhat effective, attempt at changing the balance of power in the area was by the Philippine state. Beginning in the early 1930s, the government of the Philippines engaged in a program called "minoritization."[11]

Minoritization, supported by government legislation, facilitated mass migrations by Christians from the Luzon and the Visayas to the south.[12] It provided land grants and subsidies in an attempt to consolidate Manila's influence in that region. It was successful in doing so at least in Mindanao. Unfortunately, this program also effectively spurred the creation of several Muslim separatist groups, including the Moro National Liberation Front (MNLF) and the Moro Islamic Liberation Front (MILF). These organizations undertook peace negotiations with the government to create an autonomous Muslim region. Yet, they also contributed to disaffection and strife, ultimately leading to the formation of the ASG.[13]

The Founding and Rogue Sponsorship

The ASG's orthodox insurgent pedigree is undeniable. Its founder, Abdurajak Abubakar Janjalani, the son of an ulama, was born in Basilan.[14] He traveled extensively in the 1980s, including to study the Islamic faith in Saudi Arabia and Islamic law in Mecca.[15] Abdurajak Janjalani also traveled throughout Afghanistan, Libya, the Middle East, and Pakistan participating in the peak of Mujahedeen fighting against the Soviet Union in Afghanistan.[16] During this time, he was befriended by Osama bin Laden and not only was trained in militant tactics but also was exposed to further radicalization via closer ties with professors of the strict Wahhabi interpretation of Islam.[17]

Abdurajak Janjalani returned to the Philippines between 1988 and 1990 when he began laying the groundwork for the ASG. He had been a member of the MNLF before leaving the Philippines to study and fight abroad. He thus capitalized on the widespread alienation felt by many MNLF members following the announcement of peace talks with the government in 1989.[18] Janjalani's "views and lectures were popularly received," allowing him to rally those who preferred to fight instead of negotiate.[19] He also capitalized on the connections he had made while abroad to gain access to the external sponsorship of Al-Qaida and Libya, with the latter providing an estimated $6 million in funding in 1991.[20] From this foundation, the ASG was formed. The stated goal was the establishment of an independent Muslim state in the southern islands; over time, that goal has remained unchanged—in theory at least.

ASG expert Zachary Abuza aptly refers to the inaugural years of 1991–1995 as the "Anti-Christian/Islamic State Terrorism" period.[21] During this time, ASG conducted 67 attacks including assaulting two American evangelists and an Italian priest; bombing a Christian missionary ship, a housing complex, and a cathedral; kidnapping two Spanish nuns and a priest; and assassinating a Catholic bishop. It also set off a series of bombs in the populous city of Zamboanga and continued on a killing and looting spree in the town of Ipil. The total carnage of this period amounted to 136 dead civilians and hundreds more wounded.[22]

The sponsorship of Al-Qaida during this period undoubtedly aided in the ASG's unmitigated violence. It was provided in the form of both continued training and financial assistance. Although the training was significant in the tactical development of the ASG, it was overshadowed by the strategic impact of the financing. Osama bin Laden's brother-in-law, Jamal Khalifa, was deployed to the Philippines to establish a network of charities—a branch of the Islamic International Relief Organization (IIRO).[23] The IIRO provided money for the ASG's terrorist operations and funded grassroots projects in Muslim communities such as mosques and schools.[24] Both the operations and projects had the effect of increasing popular support among the wider Muslim population and thereby boosted recruitment to the group.

The Turning Point

Several significant events unfolded over the next five to six years that led to ASG's evolution into a terrorist criminal enterprise. The uptick in violence and the appearance of the IIRO drew the attention of the Philippine authorities. Ultimately a foiled bomb plot to destroy several transpacific passenger planes, to be carried out by Al-Qaida operatives but claimed in the name of the ASG, led to the end of IIRO (and Al-Qaida) financing operations.[25] ASG operations declined significantly with the loss of this major source of funding. According to Abuza, by the time the United States designated the ASG a foreign terrorist organization, "the group had all but abandoned terrorism."[26] This lull in terrorist operations revealed early indications of the group's organized criminal proclivities along with the first cases of profit-motivated kidnapping.[27]

Abdurajak Janjalani was killed during a shootout with Philippine authorities in 1998. This, combined with the loss of external sponsorship, crippled the ASG operationally. Despite a crisis of leadership and some organizational fracturing, it maintained a generally cohesive structure. The ASG organized into an even more cellular organization with geographic centers of gravity on the islands of Basilan, Jolo, and Mindanao. Abdurajak's younger brother, Khadaffy Janjalani, also assumed a leadership role. Although he was more ideologically focused than some of the others who assumed leadership in the organization, he was less radicalized and authoritative than his older brother.[28]

The ASG was forced to engage in a wide range of illicit operations for the bulk of its financial support from 2000 onward. The earlier loss of Al-Qaida funding in combination with renewed international pressures on state sponsors of terrorism had limited the financial avenues for the group.[29] In the following years, several more changes in leadership due to combat deaths and law enforcement actions ensued, as well as the post-9/11 deployment of the U.S. counterterrorism mission under Operation Enduring Freedom–Philippines.[30] This included the death of Khadaffy Janjalani and other operational setbacks. Prior to being killed in a firefight with U.S.-backed Philippine forces, the younger Janjalani established a new and enduring connection to the Indonesia-based Jemaah Islamiyah, which increased the ASG's technical expertise in bombing and likely expanded the reach of both groups' illicit criminal networks.[31] However, none of these events are as significant as the overall evolution of Abu Sayyaf from a sponsored terrorist group to a terrorist criminal enterprise.

THE ASG AS A TERRORIST CRIMINAL ENTERPRISE

The activities and behavior of the ASG from 2000 to the present make it an exemplar of Thachuk and Lal's terrorist criminal enterprise model. The group has evolved from its formative years. Between 2001 and 2016, several theoretical models were created to attempt to explain the phenomenon exhibited by the ASG and other organizations involved in both terrorism and activities traditionally considered organized crime. O'Brien and Mullins and Wither suggest that these groups have and will continue to fluctuate, structurally and organizationally, between organized criminal or terrorist groups.[32] This also fits into Dishman's "leaderless nexus" explanation, and Makarenko might suggest that the group is moving across the crime-terror continuum—perhaps on its way to being firmly in one camp eventually.[33] However, a terrorist criminal enterprise is the only model that accounts for ASG's ineluctable duality.

Terrorist Operations and Activities

The ASG undertook some of its most violent terrorist attacks from 2001 through 2016. Although not an exhaustive list, there were at least 11 significant reported incidents of terrorism.[34]

1. Bombing Davao international airport, 22 killed 170 wounded
2. Bombing SuperFerry 14 in Manila Bay, 116 killed
3. Near-simultaneous bombings across three cities, 8 killed
4. Bombing Basilan National High School, ambushing responding security forces, 11 dead, 1 wounded
5. Improvised explosive device (IED) attacks outside schools and on wedding ceremonies, 8 killed
6. Attack on a Mindanao village at the end of Ramadan, 21 killed including 6 children
7. IED attack on a police station, no casualties
8. Bombing a bus in Zamboanga, an 11-year-old child killed, 32 others wounded
9. IED attack on a vice mayor and a passenger bus bombing, 4 killed, 24 wounded
10. Series of attacks on Philippine security forces on the island of Jolo, 15 killed
11. IED attack on a Davao city market, 14 killed, and 71 others injured[35]

Despite the use of terrorist violence, whether the ASG has remained true to its founding ideology and objective to establish an independent state is debatable. Scholars and security professionals argue whether the group's radical ideology is a primary or a secondary concern at any given time. It is also worth noting that in 2015, then ASG leader Isnilon Hapilon pledged the loyalty of the group to Da'esh and its leader Abu Bakr al-Baghdadi.[36] Whether this pledge was ideologically motivated or more for image management, recruitment, and other potential benefits is also the subject of debate. However, it is unquestionable that terrorist operations continue to be a major activity of the ASG.

The presence of Hapilon at the Da'esh-linked seizure of the city of Marawi beginning in May 2017 is an early indication that there was an effort by the ASG to act on its pledge. Hapilon, who had been on the U.S. FBI's Most Wanted Terrorists List since 2001 for hostage-taking that resulted in the death of U.S. citizens, was killed in Marawi by Philippine

Security Forces in October 2017.[37] If past ASG behavior is any predictor, the line between ideologically motivated terror and financially motivated crime will only become blurrier because of Hapilon's death.

Criminal Activity

The ASG's primary revenue streams currently appear to be the criminal activities of KFR and drug trafficking. While kidnapping can be considered a form of terrorist operation when carried out for political concessions, a KFR is profit motivated with any political or ideological benefits being an added bonus.[38] Some incipient ASG kidnappings that focused on westerners and Christian religious figures may fit the former model, but those of the last decade have been decidedly the latter type. The ASG's involvement in drug trafficking ranges from providing protection for drug trade infrastructure to distribution to participation in manufacturing. Additionally, the ASG has benefited, but to a lesser degree from other criminal activities such as extortion and the illicit arms trade.[39]

KFR[40]

It is estimated that the ASG obtains over 90 percent of its funding by conducting KFRs.[41] Following the loss of external support, this became one of the main efforts of the group and has been very lucrative. Conservative estimates range approximately from $65 million to $1.3 billion. The KFR of two German nationals in 2014 allegedly brought in more than $5 million;[42] boastingly, an ASG spokesperson later posted a video on the group's Facebook page of the bundles of cash allegedly received in the payoff.[43] Perhaps a signal that its new members are motivated by the high profits that result from criminal enterprises, there has been a notable uptick in KFRs since the beginning of 2016. The ASG's victims consist of both foreign nationals and Filipino citizens, although foreign nationals are generally considered higher-value targets. According to one consolidated report, there were 45 confirmed high-profile kidnapping incidents between 2011 and 2016; 75 foreign nationals or high-value locals were netted by ASG.[44] Reports indicate that the ASG collected $7 million from KFR proceeds in 2016 alone and still held at least 29 people.[45]

Some ransoms are paid, some victims escape, and some low-value victims, who were likely taken mistakenly, are released. Low-value victims whose executions will not double as an effective political statement are also released. However, if a high-profile target's ransom deadline is not met, he or she will likely be beheaded.[46] A low-profile victim is also likely to be executed if fear-mongering or a political gain can be made; the ASG also may see this as the most economical way to ensure its operational security. This was the case for a Filipino local elected leader, a Malaysian, and two Canadians in a one-year period between 2015 and 2016.[47]

Drug Trafficking

Although detailed information is limited, it is clear the ASG is involved in the transnational drug trade. Some of the first indications that it was engaged in illicit narcotics production and trafficking occurred when it was identified in the 2003 U.S. Department of State International Narcotics Control Strategy Report (INCSR). The group then featured prominently in successive years' reports, especially between 2004 and 2009.[48] ASG's involvement in the drug trade began with the collection of protection money from smugglers and controlling a marijuana production site in Basilan.[49] Likely, this early criminal success led to its subsequent penetration of all aspects of the supply chain of the Philippines' two highest demand drugs: crystal methamphetamine (locally known as "shabu") and cannabis. Such illicit commerce also meant the group was expanding its international underworld connections. Indeed, another U.S. government report confirms ties between the ASG and the Hong Kong-based 14K Triad drug syndicate.[50] Yet, the drug trade was not the group's first association with Chinese organized crime. ASG previously utilized the 14K Triad to launder proceeds from KFRs.[51] Hence, this successful criminal relationship provided a natural entrée into an additional transnational illicit venture.

In 2017, the Philippine government publicized evidence of continued drug trafficking activity, including production facilities and shabu caches throughout the country by three international syndicates: the Taiwan-based Bamboo Triad, the 14K Triad, and China-based Sun Yee On Triad.[52] From 2013 to 2016, it seized over $27.4 million in related illegal drugs and drug paraphernalia.[53] The administration of President Duterte, notorious for his controversial "war on drugs," has made repeated claims that the ASG is connected to the activities of these triads.[54] In particular, it assesses that the Bamboo Triad granted a "franchise" to the ASG.[55] Despite Duterte's dynamic personality, there is evidence from the field that supports the government's assertion of the group's persistent and robust involvement in the transnational aspects of the Philippine drug trade. For instance, a number of counter-drug operations led to the killing or capture of ASG members.[56] Additionally, reports from Philippine Security Forces indicate that drugs are not only a source of funds for the ASG but are also being used to recruit members and embolden them during operations.[57]

POLICY IMPLICATIONS OF A TERRORIST CRIMINAL ENTERPRISE APPROACH TO ABU SAYYAF

The most significant advantage of the terrorist criminal enterprise model over traditional counterterrorism and combatting organized crime approaches is that it avoids a binary conceptualization of the ASG as *either* a terrorist organization *or* an organized criminal group. This is far more than simple semantics. It provides a fundamentally different starting point for designing an effective campaign to defeat the threat. Properly defining the threat is one of the first, most critical steps in that process; it facilitates deep understanding by all stakeholders of the problem that must be solved. Any assessment that starts with a flawed definition of the problem and the threat it poses, such as referring to a terrorist organization being involved in organized criminal activities, or a criminal group that sometimes behaves as a terrorist organization, likely will produce inherently flawed policy solutions.

The ASG's nearly 30-year history consists of a continuous cycle of latent-to-resurgent interconnected terrorist and criminal activities. For almost 15 years, the United States provided intensive counterterrorism assistance to the government of the Philippines during Operation Enduring Freedom–Philippines and brought to bear the most sophisticated technology and intelligence support available, along with the full weight of U.S. diplomatic and development efforts.[58] Although the Philippine security forces are not perfect, they are extremely capable partners. The elite paramilitary police force and military counterterrorism forces are especially well trained and dedicated.[59] However, both the government of the Philippines and the United States were operating under a traditional bifurcated definition of the ASG. By conceptualizing the ASG as a terrorist criminal enterprise instead, the pitfalls of a decidedly law enforcement or counterterrorism approach could be sidestepped in the future.

The U.S. and partner law enforcement, military, and intelligence communities at times face challenges due to the nature of their capabilities, authorities, and unique cultures. This causes them to view and pursue the threat differently, which feeds the false dichotomy discussed above and provides an advantage to the ASG. Additionally, the Philippine government and security forces are hindered by the same "turf wars" fueled by mistrust and poor coordination faced by many other states.[60] There are also legal obstacles to combating the ASG and other terrorist criminal enterprises. In the United States, the military, law enforcement, and intelligence communities all have a part to play in effectively eradicating a terrorist criminal enterprise but are often likely subject to different authorities, requirements, funding streams, regulations, and oversight. In some cases, cooperation can still occur but often does not due to protectionism or other human failures. In other cases, existing legal frameworks create rigid systems, not suited to combat a terrorist criminal enterprise.

Terrorist criminal enterprises are the new normal. Legacy military, law enforcement, and intelligence approaches and authorities do not seem able to operate effectively against them in the current construct. In the short term, the executive branch must seek efficiencies under existing laws to better organize security forces to deal with the ASG as a terrorist criminal enterprise. In the longer term, the legislative branch should review possible changes to existing laws or the creation of new laws to create a more agile security apparatus for addressing the ASG's terrorist criminal enterprise.

CONCLUSION

The ASG's myriad terrorist and organized criminal activities over the past few decades make categorizing it as either a traditional terrorist organization or a traditional organized crime group a handicap for effectively combatting it. The terrorist criminal enterprise model offers a superior way to conceptualize the nature of the threat and organize resources more effectively to counter it. As such, a more effective unified campaign may be designed, which addresses legal and funding gaps that hinder cooperation. Approaching the ASG problem anew and utilizing the terrorist criminal enterprise model must be the next evolution in this struggle.

At the same time, the ASG in the Philippines is only one of a growing number of organizations that represent the destructive duality of terrorist criminal enterprises. The cases of Al-Qaida in the Islamic Maghreb (AQIM), Da'esh, and the Haqqani Network suggest there is cause to apply this analytical model and its policy implications more broadly. Terrorist criminal enterprises represent a better reflection of the new normal and require other countries to explore this model. The United States must also review its bifurcated counterterrorism and combating organized crime approaches and make appropriate adjustments. In doing so, the security challenges presented by the ASG and other terrorist criminal enterprises become more tenable. However, it will require a significant effort by the security community—academicians, policy makers, the military, law enforcement, and intelligence professions—to change the way these groups are approached. As malign actors evolve, so too must the protectors of society. The terrorist criminal enterprise model is not only an approach to analysis, but it is also a framework for making more effective security policy.

NOTES

1. The views expressed in this chapter are those of the author and do not reflect the official policy or position of the Defense Intelligence Agency, Department of Defense, or the U.S. government.

2. Zack Fellman, "Abu Sayyaf Group," in *AQAM Futures Project Case Study Series, Homeland Security and Countering Transnational Threats Project* (Washington, DC: Center for Strategic Studies, 2011), 1.

3. Richard T. Oakley, "Operation Enduring Freedom Philippines: FID Success and the Way Forward," *Special Warfare* 27, no. 1 (January 2014), 46–51.

4. Fellman, "Abu Sayyaf Group," 2.

5. Victor Taylor, *Addressing the Situation of the Abu Sayyaf Group in the Philippines: Part 3* (Toronto, Ontario: Mackenzie Institute, July 7, 2017), http://macken zieinstitute.com/addressing-situation-abu-sayyaf-group-philippines-part-3/.

6. See, for example, Rob Atwell, "Criminals with a Cause: The Crime-Terror Nexus in the Southern Philippines," *The Diplomat*, April 11, 2017, https://thedip lomat.com/2017/04/criminals-with-a-cause-the-crime-terror-nexus-in-the-south ern-philippines/; see also, "Caught, Abu Sayyaf Man Key to Kidnappings in Sabah," *Free Malaysia Today*, May 20, 2017, http://www.freemalaysiatoday.com/category/ nation/2017/05/20/caught-abu-sayyaf-man-key-to-kidnappings-in-sabah/.

7. "Duterte Claims Abu Sayyaf Involved in Bamboo Triad Drugs Operation," *GMA News*, September 30, 2017, http://www.gmanetwork.com/news/news/ nation/627758/duterte-links-bamboo-triad-to-abu-sayyaf/story/.

8. Felipe Villamoor, "Philippines Says It Killed ISIS-Linked Leader in Push to Reclaim City," *New York Times*, October 16, 2017, https://www.nytimes .com/2017/10/16/world/asia/philippines-marawi-isis-isnilon-hapilon.html; Joseph Felter, "ISIS in the Philippines: A Threat to US Interests," *The Caravan*, no. 1715, The Hoover Institute, September 27, 2017, https://www.hoover.org/ research/isis-philippines-threat-us-interests.

9. Bob East, *The Neo Abu Sayyaf: Criminality in the Sulu Archipelago of the Republic of the Philippines* (Newcastle upon Tyne: Cambridge Scholars Publishing, 2016), Kindle, Location 42–60. Colonizing states are listed in chronological order: Spain (1569–1898); Britain (1764–1773), as part of the Seven Years' War; the United States (1898–1942), beginning with the Spanish–American War through the Philippine–American War, until World War II; and Japan (1942–1945) until end of World War II.

10. Ibid.

11. Ibid., Location 177–241.

12. Ibid.

13. McKenzie O'Brien, "Fluctuations between Crime and Terror: The Case of Abu Sayyaf's Kidnapping Activities," *Terrorism and Political Violence* 24, no. 2 (March 14, 2012), 323.

14. Zachary Abuza, *Balik-Terrorism: The Return of the Abu Sayyaf,* Monograph (Carslisle, PA: Strategic Studies Institute, U.S. Army War College, 2005), 2–3. According to the *Oxford English Dictionary*, an "ulama" (also spelled ulema) is a body of Muslim scholars who are recognized as having specialist knowledge of Islamic sacred law and theology, or a member of said body.

15. Ibid.

16. Ibid.

17. Ibid.; Wahhabism, in short, "is an austere form of Islam that insists on a literal interpretation of the Koran. Strict Wahhabis believe that all those who don't practice their form of Islam are heathens and enemies." http://www.pbs.org/ wgbh/pages/frontline/shows/saudi/analyses/wahhabism.html.

18. "Abu Sayyaf Group," Counter Extremism Project, 2017, https://www .counterextremism.com/threat/abu-sayyaf-group-asg.

19. O'Brien, "Fluctuations between Crime and Terror," 323.

20. Wade A. Germann, Eric Hartunian, Richard A. Polen, and Krishnamurti A. Mortela, "Terrorist Financing in the Philippines," in *Financing Terrorism: Case Studies*, ed. Michael Freeman (New York: Routledge, 2016), 150.

21. Abuza, *Balik-Terrorism: The Return of the Abu Sayyaf*, 4.

22. Ibid.

23. Ibid., 5–6.

24. Ibid.

25. O'Brien, "Fluctuations between Crime and Terror," 324.

26. Abuza, *Balik-Terrorism: The Return of the Abu Sayyaf*, 7–8.

27. Steven Rogers, "Beyond Abu Sayyaf: The Lessons of Failure in the Philippines," *Foreign Affairs* 83, no. 1 (February 2004), 15–20.

28. East, *The Neo Abu Sayyaf*, Location 126.

29. Germann, Hartunian, Polen, and Mortela, "Terrorist Financing in the Philippines," 150.

30. Oakley, "Operation Enduring Freedom Philippines," 46.

31. O'Brien, "Fluctuations between Crime and Terror," 325.

32. Ibid.; Sam Mullins and James K. Wither, "Terrorism and Crime," *Connections: The Quarterly Journal* 15, no. 3 (2016), 65–82.

33. Chris Dishman, "The Leaderless Nexus: When Crime and Terror Converge," *Studies in Conflict and Terrorism* 28 (2005), 237–252; Tamara Makarenko, "The Crime-Terror Continuum: Tracing the Interplay between Transnational Organised Crime and Terrorism," *Global Crime* 6, no. 1 (February 2004), 129–145.

34. "Abu Sayyaf Group," Counter Extremism Project. The ASG did not claim responsibility for incident number 9, the authorities attribute the attack to the ASG due to its past activities in the area. Also, the attack is consistent with the ASG's tactics and techniques.

35. Ibid.

36. Ibid.

37. Felipe Villamoor, "Philippines Calls City 'Liberated,' Months after ISIS Allies Seized It," *New York Times*, October 17, 2017, https://www.nytimes.com/2017/10/17/world/asia/philippines-marawi-fighting.html.

38. James A. Piazza and Scott Piazza, "Crime Pays: Terrorist Group Engagement in Crime and Survival," *Terrorism and Political Violence*, November 2017, 8.

39. Soliman M. Santos Jr. and Paz Verdades M. Santos, "Al-Harakatul Al-Islamiyya, aka Abu Sayyaf Group (ASG)," in *Primed and Purposeful: Armed Groups and Human Security Efforts in the Philippines*, ed. Diana Rodriguez (Geneva, Switzerland: Small Arms Survey, 2010), 367–368, 373–374.

40. All monetary values are given in nominal U.S. dollars as of the publication date of each reference.

41. O'Brien, "Fluctuations between Crime and Terror," 325.

42. Taylor, *Addressing the Situation of the Abu Sayyaf Group*.

43. "Abu Sayyaf Shows off P250 Ransom Money," YouTube, NoyPi Stuff, November 5, 2015, https://youtu.be/9AtlcUx2Prc.

44. "Philippines: Overview of the Abu Sayyaf Kidnapping Threat," *Red24 Security Briefing*, June 3, 2016, https://www.red24.com/members/intelligence/newsletters_security_briefings/philippines_overview_abu_sayyaf_kidnapping_03062016.php.

45. Atwell, "Criminals with a Cause."

46. Ibid.

47. "Abu Sayyaf Group," Counter Extremism Project.

48. See, the U.S. Department of State, "Part I: Drug and Chemical Control: Southeast Asia," *International Narcotics Control Strategy Report* (INSCR), 2003–2009. The reports are issued annually for the previous calendar year. For

example, the 2003 INSCR was issued in 2004. https://www.state.gov/j/inl/rls/nrcrpt/index.htm.

49. U.S. Department of State, "Part I: Drug and Chemical Control: Southeast Asia," *International Narcotics Control Strategy Report*, 2003, https://www.state.gov/j/inl/rls/nrcrpt/2003/vol1/html/29837.htm.

50. Nina A. Kollars, "The Abu Sayyaf Group (ASG)," in *A Global Overview of Narcotics-Funded Terrorist and Other Extremist Groups*, ed. Rex A. Hudson (Washington, DC: Library of Congress Federal Research Division, 2002), 104.

51. Ibid.

52. "PDEA Tags Top 3 Drug Triads in PH: Bamboo Gang, Hong Kong-14K, Sun Yee On," *Metro Manila*, October 3, 2017, http://metromanila.politics.com.ph/2017/10/03/pdea-tags-top-3-drug-triads-ph-bamboo-gang-hong-kong-14k-sun-yee/.

53. Ibid.

54. See, for example, "Duterte Claims Abu Sayyaf Involved in Bamboo Triad Drugs Operation," *GMA News*, September 30, 2017, http://www.gmanetwork.com/news/news/nation/627758/duterte-links-bamboo-triad-to-abu-sayyaf/story/.

55. See, for example, Ian Nicolas Cigaral, "Duterte: Bamboo Triad Gave Franchise to Abu Sayyaf," *Philippine Star*, September 29, 2017, http://www.philstar.com/headlines/2017/09/29/1743866/duterte-bamboo-triad-gave-franchise-abu-sayyaf-drugs.

56. See, for example, Roel Pereño, "Abu Sayyaf Being Funded by Drug Money," *Philippine Star*, April 21, 2017, http://www.philstar.com/headlines/2017/04/21/1692376/abu-sayyaf-being-funded-drug-money-military.

57. See, for example, "Philippines: Abu Sayyaf Uses Drugs for Recruits, Funds," *World Bulletin*, September 29, 2016, http://www.worldbulletin.net/haber/177927/philippines-abu-sayyaf-uses-drugs-for-recruits-funds.

58. Oakley, "Operation Enduring Freedom Philippines," 48.

59. Ibid.

60. Christine O. Avendaño, "AFP-PNP Distrust Noted," *Philippine Daily Inquirer*, February 11, 2015, http://newsinfo.inquirer.net/672089/afp-pnp-distrust-noted.

CHAPTER 13

Policy Options: Combating Terrorist Criminal Enterprises

Rollie Lal

Criminal activities often form the lifeline for terrorist groups. Hidden underground, terrorists access weaponry, financing, and personnel most often through the illegal networks of organized crime. In this light, governments need to increase attention to the criminal activities of terrorist groups, rather than view them as singularly terrorist organizations. The international community must also view these groups as terrorist criminal enterprises whose members are as motivated by profit as by ideology. Broadening the net to include criminal activities can enable law enforcement against terror groups in many ways. Just as the antiracketeering acts often intercepted mafia activities by making smaller infractions illegal, antiorganized crime legislation can be leveraged against terror groups today.

The studies in this book indicate that extortion, drug trafficking, money laundering, kidnapping, and other crimes generally attributed to organized crime groups are regularly committed by these terrorist groups. By revealing the connections between organized criminal behavior and terrorist groups, a wide array of policy options become available to governments and policy makers. Viewing the policy options to use against terror groups in the narrow tunnel of military and intelligence tactics will not be effective in dealing with these agile transnational networks. Instead, in this arena of terrorist criminal enterprises, legal avenues, military options, institution building, ideology, employment, education, and financial regulations all have roles to play.

UTILIZE CRIMINAL LAWS INSTEAD OF
COUNTERTERROR LAWS

Governments often find that charging individuals with terrorist activity or intent is either complex or impossible because of the difficulty in providing proof that the person is in fact a terrorist rather than a disgruntled individual. Radicalization in itself is not a basis for legal action in most countries. Proof that an individual is planning to embark upon violent activities for terrorist purposes is required. In most cases, governments do not have that proof until a terrorist act has been committed, which is too late.

However, utilizing the well-established legal norms in place historically against organized crime can be a significant asset in the battle against terror organizations. Many terror groups and individuals heavily lean upon criminal activities to sustain their operations, and these criminal activities can be dealt with in a straightforward manner with existing laws. Strengthening measures that prosecute these groups and individuals for their nonterror offenses, such as extortion, smuggling, immigration violations, or a variety of minor infractions, may be more effective than attempting to prove culpability on terror or intent to commit violence.

An optimal approach would involve coordination between law enforcement and intelligence bureaucracies inside each country. Richard Oakley describes the discord between the Philippine government and its security forces in approaching terrorism and organized crime, a disconnect that provides an advantage to the Abu Sayyaf Group. For a long-term solution, governments will need to reassess and realign their legal and security approaches toward terrorist criminal enterprises.

SECURE LUCRATIVE TERRITORY

Da'esh in Syria and Iraq, Boko Haram and al-Shabaab in Africa, Fuerzas Armadas Revolucionarias de Colombia (FARC), and the Haqqani Network in Afghanistan, all reap tremendous profits from their control of vast tracts of territory. Taxes or extortion of residents, oil assets, agricultural assets, and drug crops are major sources of territory-based funding for these groups. Many groups internationally simply tax the transport of legitimate goods across their land and sea territory, reaping enormous profits from nothing more than control of the transport routes. Kimberley Thachuk's chapter on the Haqqani Network notes the extent to which the group profits from smuggling drugs, minerals, and gems sourced from its territories, among others, and even taxes ordinary travelers to cross their territory.

As a result, losing control of territory has serious implications for the ability to fund their criminal and terrorist activities. Colin P. Clarke and Phil Williams describe how U.S. military action against Da'esh oil operations in Syria and Iraq has been effective in destroying a significant portion of the group's funding. As Da'esh and other groups spread their tentacles in search of new funding sources, the United States and other countries must continue to target these funding avenues. Strengthening governing structures in threatened areas will also go a long way toward securing the area in the long term. Corruption and failing infrastructure often are the access points for terrorist and criminal groups to gain access to vulnerable civilian populations. Training existing law enforcement entities to interdict the taxation and extortion that are occurring is key in expanding regional capabilities against these terrorist criminal enterprises.

PROTECT THE CIVILIAN POPULATION

Protecting the civilian population is critical to isolating terror groups from financing and support networks. While voluntary support of the population is highly desired by the terrorist groups in their area, most terror groups are willing to accept militantly coerced support when volunteers are no longer available. Boko Haram and al-Shabaab fall into this category, according to Omar Mahmood: "Better civilian protection and insulation from the wrath of such groups may help reduce support, especially in cases of duress or intimidation. In this sense, civilian protection should be a key priority." The ability for terror groups to control both people and territory leads to outsized profits. Not only can the groups tax residents, but they can also gain control over lucrative supply chains. As a result, Mahmood emphasizes that control of the rural sector can be key. By protecting the rural areas, governments can deny key economic sectors from militant influence. Current overemphasis on securing urban areas overlooks the opportunities for terrorist criminal enterprises that exist in the rural sphere.

Creating a secure environment for civilians can take many forms. Police and military protection are but one avenue available. Yuliya Zabyelina's work on the Caucasus points out the additional importance of establishing confidential channels for victims and protection for whistleblowers. Establishing secure communication channels for these individuals is key, as are legal frameworks that protect whistleblowers. In many cases civilian victims are the most critical sources of information for criminal and terrorist behavior in their own communities. Information stemming from their experiences must be aggregated and the individuals protected to ensure that others feel safe in coming forward.

BUILD INSTITUTIONS AND TRANSFORM CRIMINAL HUBS

The same policies that may assist in seizing territory from terror groups in Syria, Iraq, and Afghanistan often provide the seeds for a new problem: the growth of criminal hubs. Invasion by Western forces can lead to the defeat of Da'esh or the Taliban but simultaneously destroy the infrastructure and institutions that created a stable society. In the absence of a coordinated effort to rebuild these areas, terrorist and criminal groups have reentered the void in many places and created criminal hubs where even law enforcement dare not go. Policies need to be created to prevent the growth of these hubs and dismantle existing ones.

Investing in national- and local-level institutions in developing countries will create conditions inimical to criminal terrorist enterprises. Weak institutions, including poorly paid and trained security forces, inept judicial systems, and weak political representation for the people are all conditions underpinning corruption. Countries with weak institutions invite terrorists and criminals for many reasons. Foremost, because it is near impossible to catch and prosecute a criminal in a state with weak institutions. Once inside, a terror group may move toward extortion, as a way of "taxing" the residents. The absence of security in these states makes the residents vulnerable to demands for protection money by organized crime and affiliated terror groups. Da'esh in Syria and Iraq, the Haqqani Network in the Afghan-Pakistan region, and Al-Qaida in the Islamic Maghreb (AQIM) in the Sahelo-Saharan states have profited immensely from the absence of security or well-functioning governmental institutions. Corruption is an enabler for terrorist groups to use crime in the pursuit of cash.

In addition to inhibiting criminal hubs, stronger institutions provide broad continuity in operations against terror and criminal enterprises. In the case of Turkey, political tumult resulted in the firing of the entire antiterror police force and decades of institutional memory along with it. Countries must emphasize the creation of policies and institutions that transcend political change so that there can be continuity in fighting crime, terror, and corruption in criminal hubs and the regions beyond.

GAIN THE IDEOLOGICAL UPPER HAND

Drawing the attention of the local public to the criminal activities of the terrorist group operating in their region can be a powerful tool. Populations who support terrorist groups often do so to assist in reaching ideological or religious objectives, or even social goals. They rarely do so to further criminal ideals. Revealing the craven criminal pursuits conducted by these terror organizations would in many cases erode the popular following of terror groups. Most civilians want to believe that their political leadership has high moral standing. According to Kimberley Thachuk, the Haqqani Network is a prime example of this: "By exposing HQN members as criminals, there is an opportunity to dilute local citizen support/passive acceptance for the group, which along with the ability to make money and maintain impunity, is one of the more pernicious enablers of terrorist groups."

Exposing the corruption of these supposedly ideological terror groups is key. Legal action against terror groups involved in criminal pursuits should be highlighted and publicized by the government and media. Rather than the usual statement that the terrorist attacker believed in jihadist/revolutionary ideology, and by the way he was sustaining his life-style and terrorism through the sale of drugs, the communication should be reconsidered. Equal weight should be placed on the criminal activities of these terrorist groups and individuals.

Education programs targeting children and families with this information should also be considered. Children should be informed that these terror groups are not heroes, but in fact criminals/drug traffickers/smugglers/kidnappers. This has the added benefit of deterring children from the draw of terrorist recruiters.

EXPAND EMPLOYMENT AND EDUCATION

Creating employment and education opportunities for youth is also critical to draw possible recruits away from criminal activities as a source of income and livelihood. Youth who are capable and willing to work often have difficulty in procuring employment relevant to their skills and experience. In the Sahelo-Saharan region, poor governance creates the basis for criminality, as the region is bereft of economic opportunity. Audra Grant recommends creating employment and educational opportunities for the youth who comprise half of the population of the region in order to weaken the criminal networks behind AQIM and similar groups.

In many countries, discrimination against class/religion/ethnic groups in education and employment worsens the situation, leading some youth to be disillusioned and resentful toward their country. In that context, criminal and terrorist networks become an attractive employment and leadership opportunity for young men in particular. In addition, Max Manwaring notes that in Colombia and other regions, a new security environment exists where the power to exploit poverty and poor governance is within reach of anyone with a cause. Countering poverty is a key to countering these groups.

Inside Europe, policies must also include further safeguards against the abuse of welfare benefits. As members of Da'esh have clearly stated that raking in welfare benefits in European countries should be done in support of their militant cause, governments must raise the bar for recipients of social welfare. In doing so, the focus should move toward job creation and training.

In many cases, the lack of self-respect and meaning that occurs when unemployed can be a strong factor pushing individuals toward criminal and terrorist violence. A stronger focus on integration into the local economy through training and jobs can move individuals and families into a more positive relationship with their adoptive country. Economic integration into the formal economy has the added benefit of moving these individuals away from the clutches of organized crime, drug trafficking, human trafficking, and so forth as alternative sources of income.

IMPROVE PRISON POLICIES

Data on recruitment and ideological training indicate that prisons are playing a key role in transforming petty criminals into hardened terrorists with criminal interests. Prisons across Europe, Asia, and other regions have provided the environment for small-time criminals to access religious radicalism while expanding their crime and terror networks. Training of both officials and prisoners in prisons needs to be addressed in order to change this dynamic. In addition, overall prison conditions and standards need to be raised for all prisoners, rather than only for those considered at risk for radicalization.[1] Inequities and poor treatment in prison create conditions for prisoners to be more susceptible to recruitment and radicalization.

Governments should expand specialist training of prison officers to include understanding of religious radicalization, how to spot signs of this trend, and where to refer radicalized individuals. Psychological staff and social workers can play a critical role in supporting prisons in dealing with violent extremist prisoners.

Ideally, there should be training programs inside prisons focused upon positive skills that can assist in reintegration into society after release, such as education and employment. Continued support after release through contact with social workers or psychologists can help in preventing individuals from joining terrorist criminal networks upon release.

EXPAND INFORMATION SHARING

Coordination between governments on information sharing is critical. Currently, countries may hold relevant information as classified or for national use only, when in fact important details that connect financial dealings and operatives are being withheld. Sharing this type of information across borders with trusted countries will allow investigators to draw connections between transnational organized crime and terror networks more easily. As the criminals are working seamlessly across national borders, governments must take a similar attitude and be able to see across borders in pursuit.

Lack of coordination creates an insurmountable problem in cases where the terrorist group operates across several countries. For example, Mahmut Cengiz and Süleyman Özeren note that the PKK operates along Turkey's border with Iran, Iraq, and Syria. However, law enforcement cooperation between Turkey and these countries has been minimal or nonexistent, while the information from each country is key to interdicting the PKK's activities in the region.

More coordination also needs to be done among governments regarding how to respond to kidnapping for ransom. If countries determine that paying ransom is appropriate, they need to coordinate on the preconditions and the amounts to be provided. Terrorists and criminals share information on which countries respond positively and for what amounts. If governments are unwilling to share information among themselves, they remain at the disadvantage. Discussions need to be held on how each country is responding, how much is being paid in ransom, and in what situations. While this information need not be made public, intergovernmental discussions on the topic must be held.

DIASPORA ENCLAVES

In the case of members of Da'esh, Al-Qaida, and other groups embedded in large ethnic enclaves established in Europe and the United States, policies addressing the integration of diaspora enclaves can help draw individuals into the mainstream economy rather than the illicit one. While diaspora enclaves provide a social and economic support network for immigrant communities, they also reduce the incentive for immigrants to learn the local language and integrate into local norms. This prevents access to a host of better paying jobs and opportunities that would otherwise be available. The isolation of diaspora enclaves from the general population has the added effect of creating a separate identity from the host nation, and even from the source nation. Residents of diaspora enclaves have stated that they do not feel wholly a part of their new country of residence, and yet also no longer fit into the culture and society of their country of origin.[2]

The isolation, lack of skills, and poor access to local employment opportunities in turn can create disaffection and incentives to join criminal networks and even terrorist groups. Special emphasis must be placed upon language training at schools in diaspora enclaves, as often the schools in these enclaves have fewer resources and children who are communicating daily in the immigrant language. Policies in diaspora enclaves that directly address language training, education, and employment opportunities can help to prevent recruitment into terrorist criminal enterprises.

INTERNATIONAL FINANCIAL CONTROLS

Illicit activities of both the criminal and terrorist type require access to financial support. Continuous reassessment of financial controls is required, as criminal terrorist enterprises adapt rapidly to regulations and controls.

A large portion of financing is sourced from militant-held territory and therefore difficult to intercept. Extortion and taxation of territory under control of these groups provide a steady source of income. However, income flowing across borders with travelers, commodity trade, and financial institutions can be intercepted and tracked by governments. Rhea Siers notes that the Hezbollah International Financing Prevention Act (HIFPA) has restricted sources of funding to the group by applying sanctions to financial institutions that assist Hezbollah and its agents. This type of financial regulation has made money laundering a far more complex and difficult venture for Hezbollah. At the same time, increasing financial controls in the legal economy pressurize terrorist criminal enterprises to move their finances to more illicit modes. The international community and financial institutions must work to track the flow of money through both legal and illegal means into terrorist-held territory, and out of countries that have a historical or political connection with these groups.

MONITOR CYBERSPACE

The Internet enables criminals and terrorists to operate with a semblance of anonymity. As a freely available platform, Kimberley Thachuk notes that it is also a highly effective tool for radicalization, organization, and recruitment for terrorist criminal enterprises. The Dark Web has also been used in equipping terrorists with weaponry. In many cases, the same crimes and money transfers that are taking place in the physical world are simplified and made instantaneous by the use of cyberspace. In particular, cyberspace enables individuals and groups to cross international borders with ease. The advent of cryptocurrencies has created further challenges for law enforcement to track terrorist criminal enterprises that use these tools. Governments need to establish and strengthen capabilities to track the use of cyberspace by terrorist criminal networks. As the technology landscape changes rapidly, cooperation between the private sector and the public sector must be enhanced in order to combat the threat. Some researchers submit that a multinational body must be constructed to counter cyberterrorism, as it is a transnational threat.[3] In any case, international collaboration will be key in detecting the use of cyberspace by terror groups to organize, collect funds, and share information for political or economic profit.

CONCLUSION

Terrorists have long forsaken their ideological ideals in favor of commercialism, as demonstrated by their vast criminal interests. The chapters in this book show repeatedly that terrorist groups from every region are engaged in repeated and long-standing criminal activity for profit, including extortion, drug trafficking, human trafficking, smuggling, money laundering, kidnapping, and a variety of other activities. And while terror groups have invested in these integrated operations over time, governments in most countries continue to view terror groups and criminal organizations as separate and distinct challenges to be addressed by stovepiped bureaucracies. As Christopher A. Kojm notes in the Foreword, our current organizational structures and mental frameworks are inadequate for facing the problem.

As globalization has brought communities across the world together through trade and communication, it has provided opportunities to terrorist criminal enterprises to flourish as well. Groups such as FARC and the Taliban have shown the power of the drug trade in enriching terrorist organizations and corrupting their political mission. Al-Qaida's engagement in smuggling, extortion, and kidnapping for ransom indicates that it is interested in a piece of the pie. And even in diaspora communities across Europe and Asia, it is clear that terrorist criminal enterprise is a venture for both small criminal groups and more extensive networks. Governments must investigate terrorist criminal enterprises as the cohesive threat that they are. Inside each country, an integrated approach must be launched to intercept terrorists engaged in these criminal activities, as criminal acts are far easier to prosecute than extremist behaviors. Across international borders, governments must engage in enhanced cooperation and information sharing in order to close the gaping holes created by these physical borders in the Internet age. Whereas physical pursuit by law enforcement and information-sharing regarding suspects generally end at the physical border, the terrorist criminals themselves are more agile, swapping identities, nationalities, currencies, and professions at will. Their activities erode our political and economic institutions and even have the ability to crumble valuable social structures. These terrorist groups use violent methods to enrich themselves at the expense of our global communities. Our ability to create a coherent and secure world of the future rests on our dedication to addressing this challenge today.

NOTES

1. For an in-depth discussion on the topic of radicalization in prisons and policies for the same, see UNODC, *Handbook on the Management of Violent Extremist Prisoners and the Prevention of Radicalization to Violence in Prisons* (New York: UNODC, 2016). https://www.unodc.org/pdf/criminal_justice/Handbook_on_VEPs.pdf.

2. Author interviews of Muslim residents in Belgium, 2009–2016.

3. Pardis Moslemzadeh Tehrani, Nazura Abdul Manap, and Hossein Taji, "Cyber Terrorism Challenges: The Need for a Global Response to a Multi-Jurisdictional Crime," *Computer Law & Security Review* 29, no. 3 (June 2013), 207–215.

About the Editors
and Contributors

EDITORS

Kimberley L. Thachuk, PhD, is a senior analyst and educator focusing on transnational security issues, including organized crime and terrorism; human, drug, and arms trafficking; corruption; and environmental, health, and energy issues. She served as the National Counterintelligence Officer for Transnational Issues at the Office of the National Counterintelligence Executive, the Office of the Director of National Intelligence, and as a senior analyst and director of research at a number of intelligence community locations.

Prior to this, for over a decade, Dr. Thachuk was a senior research professor and analyst directing policy and projects on transnational threats at the National Defense University, the Department of Defense. She also has been an educator in the postsecondary academic system for 30 years at various universities in both Canada and the United States. In particular, in 2003 as a Visiting Professor of International Relations at the Elliott School of International Affairs, the George Washington University, she stood up the graduate-level Transnational Security Issues Concentration in the Security Policy Studies program whose success was replicated in numerous universities. Since that time, she has continued to teach Transnational Security Issues and Transnational Organized Crime at the Elliott School as well as in the Global Security Studies program at Johns Hopkins University. Finally, Dr. Thachuk consults widely to the intelligence, policy, and academic communities in the United States and internationally on a range of transnational security issues. She has published various scholarly and policy articles in addition to another edited volume entitled, *Transnational Threats: Smuggling and Trafficking in Arms, Drugs, and Human Life* (Praeger, 2007). She may be contacted at kthachuk@yahoo.com.

Rollie Lal, PhD, is a visiting professor of security studies at the Elliott School of International Affairs at the George Washington University where she teaches graduate courses on transnational security and international political economy. Her research focuses on organized crime, religious extremism, energy, China, South Asia, and other areas. Previously Dr. Lal was associate professor at the U.S. Department of Defense's Asia Pacific Center for Security Studies. Dr. Lal also served as assistant professor at the Vlerick Leuven Gent Management School in Gent, Belgium, and St. Petersburg, Russia, where she taught MBA courses on international business management and risk analysis. From 2002 to 2006 Dr. Lal was a political scientist at RAND, where she performed research and analysis on a wide spectrum of economic and security issues.

Dr. Lal is the author of several books, including *Understanding China and India*; *Central Asia and Its Asian Neighbors*; *Iran's Political, Demographic, and Economic Vulnerabilities*; and *The Muslim World after 9/11*. She was a correspondent for the Japanese newspaper the *Yomiuri Shimbun* in the 1990s and has published articles in other newspapers including the *Financial Times* and the *New York Times*. Dr. Lal received her PhD in international relations and her MA in strategic studies and international economics from the Johns Hopkins University School of Advanced International Studies and her BA in economics from the University of Maryland at College Park. She may be contacted at rollielal@yahoo.com.

CONTRIBUTORS

Mahmut Cengiz, PhD, is adjunct faculty at George Mason University (GMU) where he is teaching courses on terrorism. He is also a research scholar at the Terrorism, Transnational Crime and Corruption Center (TraCCC) of GMU. He is a leading expert on transnational crime, corruption, terrorism, money laundering, and terrorist financing as well as human trafficking and smuggling of nuclear materials with a particular focus on the Middle East. He is also a security expert on policies related to crime and terror issues.

Holding two masters and two doctorate degrees in Turkey and the United States, Dr. Cengiz has a broad academic and teaching background on criminal justice, sociology, and public policy. He is the author of five books, a number of articles, and book chapters regarding organized crime, smuggling, terrorist financing, and trafficking issues. He recently conducted research on drug trafficking and its linkages with terrorism in a project with the Brookings Institute. His recent blogs on crime and terrorism have been published by *Vocal Europe* and the Global Initiative against Transnational Organized Crime. He may be contacted at mcengiz@gmu.edu.

Colin P. Clarke, PhD, is a political scientist at the RAND Corporation, where his research focuses on terrorism, insurgency, and criminal networks. At RAND, Dr. Clarke has directed studies on ISIS financing, the future of terrorism and transnational crime, and lessons learned from all insurgencies between the end of World War II and 2009. In addition to his work at RAND, he is an associate fellow at the International Centre for Counter-Terrorism (ICCT)–The Hague, in the Netherlands, and a lecturer at Carnegie Mellon University where he teaches courses on terrorism, insurgency, and the future of warfare.

Dr. Clarke appears frequently in the media, has been quoted in the *New York Times*, the *Washington Post*, and the *Wall Street Journal*, and has published his research in *Foreign Affairs, Foreign Policy, The Atlantic, Politico, Lawfare*, and numerous scholarly journals, including *Small Wars & Insurgencies, Historical Methods*, and *Military Operations Research*. He is the author of *Terrorism, Inc.: The Financing of Terrorism, Insurgency, and Irregular Warfare* (Praeger, 2015) and *Terrorism: The Essential Reference Guide* (ABC-CLIO, 2018). He received his PhD in international security policy from the University of Pittsburgh.

Audra Grant, PhD, has over 20 years of experience conducting analysis and research in fragile states and postconflict societies in transition. Her work has focused on democratization and reform, human trafficking and illicit trade, youth activism, political Islam, and terrorism and insurgency. Her regional areas of emphasis are North Africa and the Sahel, as well as the Middle East. Dr. Grant's publications span the issues to include climate change, migration, and adaptation in the MENA region; the impact of U.S. military drawdown in Iraq on displaced and other vulnerable populations; political activism among Jordanian youth; and "Trafficking in Africa" in *Transnational Threats: Smuggling and Trafficking in Arms, Drugs, and Human Life* (Praeger, 2007). Grant's more recent work includes research and evaluation of youth violence prevention programs in Burundi; the effectiveness of CVE programs in Niger, Mali, and Burkina Faso; and child labor in Cote D'Ivoire and Ghana.

Dr. Grant is currently at the National Opinion Research Center, University of Chicago (NORC). Prior to joining NORC, Grant was a resident program manager in Juba, South Sudan, for the National Democratic Institute and NDI senior program manager for East and South Africa. She is a former senior political scientist at RAND focusing on North Africa and the Western Sahel and a former North Africa analyst with the U.S. Department of State, Office of Opinion Research. A longtime educator and trainer, Grant is also an adjunct professor at NYU–DC and the George Washington University. She may be contacted at grantaudra@gmail.com.

Christopher A. Kojm is a professor at the Elliott School of International Affairs at George Washington University and director of the School's Leadership, Ethics and Practice Initiative. He served as Chairman of the National Intelligence Council from 2009 to 2014 and taught previously at the Elliott School (2007–2009) and Princeton's Woodrow Wilson School (2004–2007).

Earlier in his career he served as a staffer on the House Foreign Affairs Committee (1984–1998) under Rep. Lee H. Hamilton, as a deputy assistant secretary of state in the Bureau of Intelligence and Research (1998–2003), and as Deputy Director of the 9/11 Commission (2003–2004). He was president of the 9/11 Public Discourse Project, the Commission's follow-on public education organization (2004–2005). He also served as a senior advisor to the Iraq Study Group (2006–2007). He can be reached at ckojm@gwu.edu.

Omar S. Mahmood is a researcher at the Institute for Security Studies (ISS), based in Addis Ababa, Ethiopia. His work focuses on political and security dynamics in the Horn of Africa and Lake Chad Basin regions, with a concentration on both Boko Haram and al-Shabaab. Previously, he worked as a senior analyst for a Washington, D.C.-based research firm and also served as a Peace Corps volunteer in Burkina Faso.

Mr. Mahmood's work has been published in outlets such as *African Arguments*, *Fair Observer*, and *Think Africa Press*, among others. He obtained a master's degree in security studies and conflict resolution from the Fletcher School at Tufts University and a bachelor's degree in foreign affairs and economics from the University of Virginia. He has conducted research, lived in, or traveled to over 20 countries across the African continent, spending significant time in Burkina Faso, Benin, South Africa, and Ethiopia. He can be reached at omarsmahmood@gmail.com.

Max G. Manwaring, PhD, is a retired professor of military strategy at the Strategic Studies Institute (SSI) of the U.S. Army War College (USAWC), has held the General Douglas MacArthur Chair of Research at the USAWC, and is a retired U.S. Army Colonel. Over the past 30+ years, he has served in various military and civilian positions. They include the U.S. Southern Command, the Defense Intelligence Agency, Dickinson College, and Memphis University.

Dr. Manwaring is the author and coauthor of several articles, chapters, and books dealing with intranational security affairs, political-military affairs, insurgency, counterinsurgency, and gangs. His most recent book is *The Complexity of Modern Irregular War* (University of Oklahoma Press, 2012). His most recent article is "El lexico de seguridad desde

Westfalia hasta hoy: Un cuento aleccionador" ("The Security Lexicon from Westphalia to Today: A Cautionary Tale"), published in *The Air and Space Power Journal en Espanol* in 2017. Dr. Manwaring remains active in the national security community and may be contacted at maxmanwaring@ gmail.com.

Richard T. Oakley is a policy advisor and educator with extensive practical experience in the national security arena. He is currently an instructor and special operations subject matter expert at the Defense Intelligence Agency's Academy for Defense Intelligence in Washington, D.C. He is also a guest lecturer at the NATO School in Germany. His work focuses on irregular warfare and hybrid threats, including counterterrorism, unconventional warfare, foreign internal defense, counterinsurgency, and stability operations. His policy research areas include illicit networks, threat finance, and state and nonstate cyber activities.

Mr. Oakley served in the U.S. military as a Special Forces officer (Green Beret) and in various command and staff positions at the tactical though strategic levels. He has had operational deployments to Afghanistan and the Asia-Pacific region, including a tour as a senior special operations advisor to the Republic of the Philippines. Since then, he has continued to serve as a civilian consultant in the Defense and Intelligence communities.

Mr. Oakley holds a master's degree in security policy studies from the George Washington University's Elliott School of International Affairs and a bachelor's degree from East Tennessee State University. He also earned a Specialization certificate in Design Thinking and Innovation from the University of Virginia's Darden School Executive Education Program. He may be contacted at richard.t.oakley@gmail.com.

Süleyman Özeren, PhD, is currently a research scholar at the Center for Global Policy at the Schar School of Policy and Government and an adjunct faculty at George Mason University. He formerly served as the President of the Global Policy and Strategy Institute. Dr. Özeren received his MS degree in criminal justice and a PhD degree in information science from the University of North Texas.

His research interests include terrorism and counterterrorism, radicalization, violent extremism, international security, conflict resolution, the Kurdish issue, and Turkish American and Turkey-EU relations. During his research, he examined four terrorist organizations: ISIS, Al-Qaida, Hezbollah, and the PKK (Kurdish Worker's Party). Part of his research included interviewing convicted terrorists and disintegrated and deradicalized individuals. His most recent research project is funded by the U.S. State Department through the U.S. Embassy in Ankara, Turkey, and is entitled "Countering Violent Extremism by Unraveling the Propaganda and Recruitment Techniques of ISIS in Turkey."

Dr. Özeren has numerous publications, and some of the examples include "ISIS in Cyberspace: Findings from Social Media Research," "Countering Terrorism: From Far East to New Continent," "Understanding Terrorism: Analysis of Sociological and Psychological Aspects," "Multi-Faceted Approach to Radicalization in Terrorist Organizations," "Cyberterrorism and Cybercrime: Vulnerabilities and International Cooperation," and "Terrorism Paradox and Turkey." His commentaries and opinion pieces have been published by national and international newspapers and news agencies.

Dr. Özeren has taught numerous graduate and undergraduate courses at different universities on international security, terrorism, radicalization, comparative counterterrorism strategies, and conflict resolution.

Rhea D. Siers, JD, is a veteran of the U.S. Intelligence Community, having served in a variety of operational, legal, and policy capacities, including as Deputy Associate Director for Policy at the National Security Agency (NSA). Her areas of expertise include cybersecurity and cybercrime, terrorism, and national security law. Ms. Siers teaches at the Elliott School of International Affairs, GWU (George Washington University), and the graduate program in Global Security Studies at Johns Hopkins University. Her courses include Non-State Actors, Terrorism and Counterterrorism, Ethics and Privacy in Intelligence Operations, Cyber Threats, Intelligence in the Middle East, and Data Privacy.

Ms. Siers is currently a senior legal and policy fellow at the Institute for Information Infrastructure Protection (I3P), GWU, and previously served as scholar-in-residence at the GWU Center for Cyber and Homeland Security. She also serves as special counsel in the Cybersecurity Practice at Zeichner, Ellman and Kruase and was recognized by the *National Law Journal* as one of its "Trailblazers" in Cybersecurity and Data Privacy. She is a senior expert for the Risk Assistance Network and Exchange (RANE) on cybersecurity issues. She is the coauthor of two recent books: *Cyberwarfare: Understanding the Law, Policy, and Technology* and *The Theory and Practice of Terrorism*. She may be contacted at rdsiers@gwu.edu.

Phil Williams, PhD, holds the Wesley W. Posvar Chair in International Security Studies at the Graduate School of Public and International Affairs at the University of Pittsburgh and is director of the University's Matthew B. Ridgway Center for International Security Studies. Professor Williams has published extensively in the field of international security. During the past 25 years, his research has focused primarily on transnational organized crime, and he has written articles on various aspects of this subject in *Survival, Washington Quarterly, Bulletin on Narcotics, Scientific American, Crime Law and Social Change,* and *International Peacekeeping*.

In addition, Dr. Williams was founding editor of a journal entitled *Transnational Organized Crime* and has edited several volumes on combating organized crime, Russian organized crime, and trafficking in women. In academic years 2007–2008 and 2008–2009, he was visiting research professor at the Strategic Studies Institute (SSI), U.S. Army War College, where he wrote a monograph, *The New Dark Age: The Decline of the State and U.S. Strategy*, and another one, published in August 2009, entitled *Criminals, Militias, and Insurgents: Organized Crime in Iraq*. He has a chapter on Nigerian organized crime in the *Oxford Handbook of Organized Crime*. In addition, he is coeditor of a volume published by SSI, *Cyberspace: Malevolent Actors, Criminal Opportunities, and Strategic Competition* and coauthor of a monograph, *Military Contingencies in Megacities*. He has been researching the crisis of governance in Central America and is currently completing a book on transnational organized crime. He can be reached at ridgway1@ pitt.edu.

Yuliya Zabyelina, PhD, is Assistant Professor at John Jay College of Criminal Justice, City University of New York. She holds a PhD degree in international studies from the University of Trento (Italy). Before moving to the United States in 2014, she held a postdoctoral position at the University of Edinburgh School of Law and lectured at Masaryk University in the Czech Republic. Throughout these appointments, she has taught a diverse curriculum both at the undergraduate and graduate levels and developed interdisciplinary research interests in transnational organized crime and corruption with a regional focus on countries of the former Soviet Union.

Dr. Zabyelina has been recognized with several professional awards, including the Newton Fellowship (2013), SAGE Junior Faculty Teaching Award (2015), Aleksanteri Institute Visiting Scholars Fellowship (2015), and Donald EJ MacNamara Junior Faculty Award (2016). Her scholarly work has appeared in peer-reviewed academic journals, edited volumes, and policy publications.

Index

Note: Page numbers in italics indicate tables.

of, key events in, 103; major
criminal activity, by year, *108*;
policy options, 109–10; Somali
hijackings of vessels, 51; successful
adjustments, 103, 104; sugar trade,
106–7; taxation, 104–5
"Anti-Christian/Islamic State
Terrorism" period, 175
Antiquities trafficking, 34–35
Appropriation, 28, 30–32, 35
Argentina, 148–49
Argentine Israelite Mutual
Association (AMIA), 148, 149,
150
Armed Islamic Group, Algeria (GIA),
17, 160, 161
Artifacts: looted, 34, 35;
trafficking, 50
Assassinations, 68, 81, 83, 85, 150
Assyrian Christians, 32, 34
Attacks, terrorist. *See* Terrorist
attacks
Attention deficit hyperactivity
disorder (ADHD), 53

Babri Masjid, 6
Baghdad, 31, 37
Bamako, 15, 167
Bamboo Triad, 173–74, 179
Bandas Criminals (BACRIM), 82
Bandformirovaniya, 65
Bangsamoro, 174
Bank robbery, 31, *102*, 119
Basilan National High School
bombing, 177
Bastille Day attack in Nice, 49
Bayat/bay'at, 68
Belgium, 16, 18, 48–52, 55, 57–58,
71
Benevolence International Foundation
(BIF), 66
Black decade, 160
Bogotazo, 81
Boko Haram, 5, 95; drug trafficking,
55; early days, 86–87; extortion,
97–98; financial rise and fall of,
95–101; history of, key moments
in, 96; kidnapping for ransom
(KFR), 98–99, *99*; local commodities,

100–101; major criminal activity, by
year, *102*; policy options, 109–10;
robbery and, 97; territorial control,
99–101
Brazil, 148–49
Britain, 33, 165, 174
Brussels, 18, 49, 50, 51, 57
Brussels attacks, 49–50, 57
Business Affairs Component
(BAC), 150

Cameroon, 55, 95, 98, *99*, 100
Cannabis, 51–53
Captagon, 37, 53, 146
Catholicism, 174
Cattle rustling, 100, *102*
Caucasus Emirate (CE): decline of,
71–73; financing, 67–68; foreign
financial injections and, 71;
jammaat-based OCGs and, 68–70;
overview of, 5, 63–64
Central Asia, 4, 17, 48
Chad, 55, 95, 98, 161
Charcoal, 106–7, *108*
Charlie Hebdo attack, 18, 49, 50
Chechen Republic of Ichkeria (ChRI),
65
Chechnya/Chechens, 63–74;
Al-Qaida (AQ) as part of resistance
movement, 65; concluding
assessment, 73–74; crime and
terrorist ideology, 65–67; decline
of Caucasus Emirate (CE), 71–73;
fininacing of Caucasus Emirate
(CE), 67–68; foreign financial
injections, 71; introduction,
63–64; *jamaat*-based OCGs, 68–70;
organized crime groups (OCGs),
64–65; policy options, 73–74;
resistance movement, 65; Russo-
Chechen wars, 63–65, 67, 68
China, 119, 123, 124, 179
Christians, 32, 34, 174
Citizen support, diminished, 13
Civilian population, protecting, 187
Cocaine, 54–56
Cocainebougou, 14
Colombia: AQIM's drug smuggling
operation and, 164–65; *Bandas*